OLD JULES COUNTRY

Books by Mari Sandoz published by the UNP

The Battle of the Little Bighorn (BB677)
The Beaver Men: Spearheads of Empire (BB 658)
The Buffalo Hunters: The Story of the Hide Men (BB 659)
Capital City (Cloth and BB 787)
The Cattlemen: From the Rio Grande across the Far Marias (BB 660)
The Christmas of the Phonograph Records: A Recollection (Cloth only)
Crazy Horse, the Strange Man of the Oglalas: A Biography (BB 110)
Hostiles and Friendlies: Selected Short Writings of Mari Sandoz
    (Cloth only)
Love Song to the Plains (BB 349)
Miss Morissa: Doctor of the Gold Trail (BB 739)
Old Jules (BB 100)
Old Jules Country (BB 829)
Sandhill Sundays and Other Recollections (Cloth only)
Slogum House (Cloth and BB 756)
Son of the Gamblin' Man: The Youth of an Artist (Cloth and BB 626)

OLD JULES
COUNTRY

By Mari Sandoz

A SELECTION FROM *OLD JULES*

AND THIRTY YEARS OF WRITING

SINCE THE BOOK WAS PUBLISHED

University of Nebraska Press

Lincoln and London

Manufactured in the United States of America

First Bison Book Printing: February 1982

Most recent printing indicated by the first digit below:
1   2   3   4   5   6   7   8   9   10

Library of Congress Cataloging in Publication Data

Sandoz, Mari, 1896–1966.
   Old Jules country.

   Bibliography: p.
   1. West (U.S.)—Literary collections. I. Title.
PS3537.A667Z6 1983   978   82–16041
ISBN 0–8032–9136–1 (pbk.)

Published by arrangement with Hastings House, Publishers

CONTENTS

from THE BEAVER MEN

Bearded Men and Summer Fairs

"Gone" Rendezvous and Foppish Silk

BEARDED MEN AND
SUMMER FAIRS

THE EVENING SUN lay warm and brooding on the upper Missouri valley and on the little creek that flowed from the eastern coteau, coming quietly through the yellowing timber of the canyon and a little more noisily over several beaver dams, one after the other. The last pond was very smooth, with only an occasional browning leaf to settle to the shadowed surface under the timber of the bank. Farther out three beaver houses stood solid and gray, the largest wide as a little knoll of roots and mud, with two half-grown beavers on the top, idling and combing their shining brownish fur.

Out on the bottoms young Indians, stripped to breechclout and moccasins, knocked a wool-filled ball flying this way and that with clubs, everybody racing after it, perhaps striking it out from between the feet of an opponent with whoops of triumph. Not until the ball came soaring into the water did either of the young beavers look up, or move, and now only to slide down off the house toward the water, waiting there, looking back over their flat tails as the youths plunged into the pond and wrestled for the floating ball, splashing the water high.

On the benchland overlooking the river twists of smoke

9

rose from domed earth houses just visible above the palisade of
tree trunks set into the ground. Women in short buckskin
dresses worked on the worn space outside of the moated wall.
Others, bending low under their burdens, came from the fields
along the bottoms where clouds of ducks, geese and sandhill
cranes were kept flying by boys and girls shouting and swinging
branches with strips of painted hide to flap and pop. Women
and old men and children bore in the last of the plums and
grapes from the canyons while the herb gatherers trailed in
from the browning prairie. At a scout's wolf howl, the youths
near the beaver pond stopped their game, picked up their robes
and bows and scattered to night guard far out on the coteau
and in the other directions.

A signal from off west of the Missouri brought men hurrying down to the cluster of round bullboats lying upside down
on the bank. Flipping them up and into the water, they paddled across to pick up the hunting party, ten or twelve of the
men carrying antelope across their shoulders. As they came up
the rise, maidens ran out to welcome them, to sing the antelope
song, while in front of the village the smoke of the cooking fires
began to spread.

By now the moon had come to stand a moment on the
eastern ridge, meeting the sun's reflected path over the ponds
where the beavers had ignored all the man-noises. The encroaching shadows of the timber crept out upon the water and
a whiskered nose came gently through the surface, followed by
a bit of glossy back as the animal moved before a spreading
lance of ripples toward the darkest, brushiest bank. Several
other beavers broke the water and headed out to cut wood for
the winter food—young willow and cottonwood to be sunk below the deepest ice of the frozen time. The heavy animals
crawled out upon the bank, darker forms in the dusk. Snuffling,
they set to work at bush and tree, with soft sounds of shaking
where they gnawed that stopped as they drew back from the
slow, noisy fall and then moved to the work again. One of the
old beavers started to drag a sapling across the shadowed grass
toward the water, tugging and pulling. Suddenly he stopped,

his head lifted and turned back toward the creek. An exploding burst of light broke from the blackness there and knocked the beaver forward, the roar of the blast followed by loud plungings all along the ponds, the echo of the shot lost in the cries of alarm and warning up at the village, and in the shouted orders, the running moccasins.

Down at the pond everything was still except the lap of the disturbed water and a soft kicking from the lone beaver left on the bank. Once he lurched forward, slid halfway into the shallow edge of water, and then lay still.

Silent as the darkness about him, a man moved out of the timber to the shadowy bank, listening, looking off toward the village, still in reflected sun-glow. Then he pulled the beaver out upon the grass by the tail as the figure of another hunter came to stand behind him, peering carefully all around under his palm to shut out the brightness left in the sky, and off toward the village. Breechclouted Indians with bows and spears were racing through streaks of light and shade toward the pond, separating as they came, some to one side, some on the other, in a sort of surround. When the stink of the powder smoke struck them, they stopped, shouting their surprise, their alarm, at this unknown scent, and moved more cautiously, the leader motioning the most impetuous back, beside him. As they neared, one of the hunters stepped out into the fading light, stroking his long beard to show his difference from their smoothness, then holding up his left hand, palm forward, in the sign of friendship, his companion, also bearded, but smaller, close behind him.

Seeing these were only men, of man's stature, not some strange, gigantic, thundering relatives of the civet and the skunk, the warriors whooped and leapt forward, spears poised, arrows set to the bow. Calmly the short stranger pointed a long thin pole out before him. There was another of the fiery roaring blasts and the top of the nearest beaver lodge exploded into the air, sticks and dried mud flying over the pale gleam of water, scattering and falling.

The Indians had jumped back, crying out in awe and fear, but the leader shouted his scorn upon them. "Do you not see that they are the thunder-stick men of whom we have all been told?—those with the hairy faces?" he demanded. "It is known that these men can also bleed from the pale skin, and die!"

The taller of the strangers nodded to what the Indians seemed to be saying, and coming farther from the shadows, he pushed his ragged sleeve up to show the whiteness underneath.

"Ah-h-h!" the leader exclaimed in triumph, and, motioning the warriors back, he pointed toward the village, making the beckoning sign of welcome.

There were growls of protest to this, but plainly guests, and strange ones, had to be thus welcomed, even enemies, no matter how dangerous. The bearded men were taken up through the late evening light, walking between the leaders and the warriors, the two in ragged and mud-caked cloth, unlike anything those around them had ever seen. But they walked like Indians, the tall one ahead, saying something quietly over his shoulder to his companion, both certainly aware of the covetous eyes on the guns, but ready to thrust the barrels quickly toward anyone approaching too close.

The Indian directly behind the white men was carrying the dead beaver by the tail, holding him away, dark blood still dripping a little off the whiskered nose. He was measuring the big hole in the plump flank, a hole bigger than the fist he held against it, and made without arrow or spear, just the hole and the bleeding and torn flesh. Repeatedly he exclaimed at the wonder of it to those behind him, and to those running out to see and then racing back to send alarm spreading through the village, alarm that such mysterious and powerful weapons were to come into the midst of their families. The flat ground outside of the high palisades darkened with Indians standing to look, the women and children out too, but back, and ready to run for the gates.

Yet there must be no show of fear, and so the guests were taken to the council fire and motioned to sit before the headmen gathered in a solemn and formal half circle. The strangers squatted like the Indians, cross-legged, but still holding the guns, standing tall in the crooks of their arms, the powder horns and ball pockets turned forward so no sly, quick fingers could cut them away, nor were the small bundles on the backs of the men laid aside.

When the long-stemmed pipe of red stone had been filled and passed around the scar-breasted men in silence, the bearded ones took the slow pull at it with more ease than some stranger Indians. Afterward the oldest of the chiefs made a welcoming speech, the words no more intelligible than the wind to the guests but the tone mellow on the cheek. It was answered by the taller stranger, already called Long Beard by the Indians for the wonderful face hair that fell far down his breast, the name by which he would be remembered hundreds of years. Everybody pushed forward to hear the alien words. They had seen the beaver stretched out at a fire off behind the council circle, where men and women too, came to examine the mysterious hole in the fat flank, and then looked toward their guests in alarm and horror.

After a while Long Beard tried some sign talk, awkwardly, and a little strange but the old chief seemed to understand some of it and answered slowly, for understanding, through a young sign talker from an eastern people. Yes, the chief said, it was truly as they had been told by visitors returning from the far southwest, for here among them were two of those pale skins with the thunder sticks, except that they did not have the hard shells like the turtle as the southwest men had, shells that must be chopped away to make a good killing. Nor did these men have big dogs to sit upon as part of themselves. They must be of those described to the village sons who made their youth journeys eastward to the People of the Seven Fires and on past the great sweet-water seas with a war party. They were told of bearded men, with no hard shirts or the big-dogs—men with garments that seemed soft to the eye but were perhaps not to be penetrated either, for all the bearded ones seem to have powerful magic.

When the orations to the strangers were done, the two men made some gifts more wonderful than seemed possible to the head chiefs, one kind that the men called *mireor**—bright, round image-catchers which held the face for the observer as

* Old French for *miroir*.

still water does, but much clearer. The round objects could also catch the firelight and send it far, even to the shadowed bluffs across the river. A scout was called over to test the mirrors against the flake of mica he carried on a rawhide string and exclaimed in dismay at the poor light his sliver of stone cast compared to the work of the others. There were also gifts for the young wives of the chiefs, strings of blue beads, and small cakes of vermilion for the face, a red such as the Indians had never seen except in the evening sky and the fall leaves of the sugar trees or the creeper vines. And for these things there were solid walls of admiring faces shining in the firelight, small children held up high to see, to remember, so the story could still be told in their years of age and feebleness.

Afterward the young women brought the food to the headmen and their guests, wooden bowls of bean soup, and big chunks of fresh roasted antelope set on slabs of cottonwood. The bearded guests drew out weapons three times as long as the stone knives of the Indians, gleaming in the firelight and so sharp that the men cut off large mouthfuls with single thrusts and, spearing the pieces, lifted them to be savored on the tongue. The Indians looked up from their meat, the serving women stopped with their gourd dippers in the air in astonishment, wanting to feel the edges of these weapons, murmuring among themselves, and embarrassed at their unseemly conduct before strangers.

"*Le couteau,*" it seems Long Beard tried to explain in French, tapping the cutting tool, and then spoke some Indian words for *knife,* probably Huron or Ottawa that he had picked up on his way west.

The headmen sat unresponsive, understanding one language no better than the others, none as well as the use of the tool. It was a little more difficult, with the awkward signs, to make the Indians understand that these things—the knife, the beads, the vermilion and much more—could be obtained for the skins of the castor, the beaver, like the one with the hole in the flank. Long Beard did not include the guns in his gestures. It was some time, the old stories tell, before the Indians discovered that even those without special medicine could own a thunder stick—that it could be obtained with hides of their beavers—and that there were other dangerous things to be bought with their animal neighbors.

Soon after dawn a runner came in to say that the meat makers, out a full moon's time, were approaching, hurrying because there were signs of a large war party not far away. Even those watching outside of the chief's house where the palefaces slept went out to look, but only for a moment. A hunter appeared on the river bluffs, a dark figure against the eastern sky. He started down the worn trail and others came close behind him, warriors with bows and shields, those in the lead singing the song of a good hunt, followed by a string of women bowed under bundles of dried meat, some leading big dogs carrying packs or drawing their burdens on stickdrags behind them. The hunters were loaded too, proof of a very good buffalo surround. Finally the rear guard of warriors appeared, bows and spears in their hands, always unencumbered by bundles, always ready for instant defense. Off to the sides, some far out, strode the flankers with their large shields, large enough to protect a lone defender for a little while.

Plainly the hunting party was returning in triumphant pride, unaware of the happenings at their village, unaware that in one boom of a gun at a beaver pond the tribe had been thrust into a new age.

A welcoming escort went out the village gate in the old way but it was very small, the faces looking back, afraid something of the bearded ones might be missed. Only the crippled old man in a mountain-lion skin, an honored old hunter wearing the hide of the animal that had wounded him, led out properly, limping fast. His going shamed more of the young men and women, even a few girls and boys, into joining to sing the meat makers home, rejoicing that no one had been injured by stampede or wounded buffalo, no one reached by enemy arrow, or captured. The young people lifted the burdens from those who had carried them a far distance, even through the uneasy night, and bore them home in erect pride and gratitude.

Somehow even the old women who usually worked to teach

the girls the care of the meat and the thanking ceremonials were half-hearted in these tasks now, busy telling the hunting party of all that had happened yesterday and to come today. There had been two visitors here from the village down the river when the bearded men arrived. They had hurried out to send home messages of the strangers with the powerful and magical things. After the village had quieted for the late sleep, runners brought news of a planned visit; everybody of the neighboring people not watching for men with thunder sticks too, or standing off possible raiders, was coming up for the evening fires.

The headmen had been awakened and called together. There must be a feast for these neighbors coming, one proudly made for the great honor of the strangers here among them. It was not good to use up winter meat for this, and not a proper feast, so there must be a beaver hunt. But not among the playmates of their children, the friends of anyone wishing to sit at the ponds in communion with these examples of diligence and orderliness. The beaver neighbors were only to be thinned a little now and then, one or two taken for the surprise visit of some far chieftain, and then all done quietly and decently, with a proper thanking ceremony for their little brothers of the water. The big hunts, which damaged the beaver villages and frightened all those left behind, must be made on ponds far from any people, friend or enemy.

The special hunting scouts sent out immediately in the night were now signaling that there were no enemies among the ponds up along White Earth River, nobody around at all. By the time the sun was two fingers high a man with the beaver skin and toothed mask of his hunting power led a party up the trail along the river bluffs, the pale-skinned visitors behind the hunters, behind the beaver-dog men and those who carried bundles of stakes and large stone hammers hafted to stout ash handles. They turned up the side stream, so rich in the castor that the Frenchmen had stopped at the rim of the valley in astonishment, pushing their old muskrat caps back at the sight of the ponds, like a string of mica disks on a thong trailing down from the north to the Missouri.

The Indians had stopped back out of sight of the stream while the man with the beaver mask made his medicine pleas to the beavers for enough of their brothers to show a proper honoring of their guests, and promised a good thanking ceremony after the feast. Then the hunters started at the lowest pond. The hammer men drove stakes across the spillway of the dam, so close together that only a very young mink could snake through, and then left several Indians with spears and clubs to kill any animal that might try to climb over the dam. Next several young men swam out to the beaver houses and chopped them open with their stone axes, starting dull sounds of diving deep down, and dark shadows fleeing through the water toward the washes, the escape tunnels that ended far under the bank. By then the dogs were barking, wild with excitement. Released, they ran around the pond, whining, smelling out the washes. Where they stopped to sniff and scratch, the Indians stamped on the sod to follow the direction of the tunnel to the entrance at the water's edge. There they drove more stakes, to close the opening and prevent the beaver's escape into the pond while the hunter kicked the growling dogs aside and tore a hole into the tunnel, usually as large around as the circle of two arms, and half-filled with roily water. A gentle rise and fall of the surface showed the beaver's presence by the breathing. Sometimes the Indian plunged his arm into the hole, dragged the fighting animal out by the tail and gave him a swift blow on the spine back of the head to kill him instantly, before the sharp incisors cut into an arm or a leg. Sometimes the hunter drove a stake with one mighty blow of the stone hammer where the dogs pointed and then dug out the impaled beaver to be dispatched swiftly and thrown on the pile with the rest.

Long Beard, seeing this easy killing, ran in excitement from one dead animal to the next, rubbing his hand over the soft, dense fur that would have been winter-prime very soon, reluctantly letting them be taken to the river, to be rafted down to the women waiting at the roasting fires.

By the time the three ponds had been worked and the beaver dogs weary and full of rewarding meat, fifty-two of the fat beavers were dead, surely enough for the feast. Long Beard became talkative with words and hands, making signs as well as he could. The traders down the St. Lawrence, down the great stream of the sweet-water seas, would pay with knives, hatchets and beads and red paint for the skins of these beavers.

"Even give the thunder sticks—" he added, patting the gun across his forearm, trying to make the Indians understand, but this thing of the gun they could not believe. Surely such power must lie in the magic of a man's own dreaming, perhaps carried in the medicine bundle, perhaps in the strange horns these men guarded so carefully.

The dark faces around Long Beard were grave and intent to understand, but watchful too. Some must have thought of overpowering the two strangers, away from the protection of the chiefs, but there was the sacredness of the guest over them. Besides, even the hot-headed warriors must have realized that one had to learn the use of these thunder sticks and perhaps have the dreamer's gift for the magic.

On the way back the hunters saw a cow elk and her half-grown bull calf coming out of a patch of brush, to stand, heads raised. No one was eager for the long sneak to get down wind from them for a bow shot, but the Little Beard stopped, took aim by steadying his gun against a tree and fired. The young elk jumped up in front, as though startled, turned to run and began to fall, going down to his knees and over, some Indians running to cut the tawny throat, while others stood in astonishment, the blast of the gun still in their ears.

"It seems far," they made Little Beard understand. He grinned, his lips turned back red in the black tangle of his hairy face. It really was no farther than a good arrow's flight with the iron point they would soon have instead of the heavy stone, but the effect of the great noise and stink of the gun pleased the fox-faced little Frenchman.

When the hunters reached the village there was a rising heat shimmer in the fall air over the roasting fires. Some women hurried to butcher the young elk, to be cooked for those whose dreaming forbade the meat of the beaver.

Toward evening several buffalo bulls plodded down to

Old Crossing along the same trail that had brought the bearded men to the village on the rise. The bulls stopped to drink and then climbed out on the other side, ignored by a party of far hunters with winter meat approaching the river from the west, to camp there for the night at the place that was sacred to all travelers, man and animal, as free and open to them as to the moving sun. Here all creatures could find a wide, shallow and solid-bottomed way to the other side of the Missouri and the country beyond, east or west.

Up at the village the hunters rested and slept a little, to be awakened by the drumming and the song of the visitors coming up around the river bend, the young from the village going out to welcome them to the feasting, to hear of the medicine sticks, perhaps to see one make a great hole in game without the touching, and then let them think of such things pointed against people, the women and children.

At the row of fires the beavers were roasting in their skins, the tails, livers and other choice bits to be offered to the guests and the headmen and war leaders. The sun settled beyond the river during the orations and the quiet eyeing of the strangers and their possessions, the men seated in the place of honor at the chief's fire. During the feast all the beaver bones were carefully gathered into willow baskets and later taken out through the moonlight by a procession following the beaver medicine man and two bearers of flaming pitchpine torches. At the nearest pond the bones were dropped into the depths just above the dam, where no dogs or wolves or magpies could dishonor them. Then there was dancing around big fires outside of the village wall, and some sly offers of great advantage to the bearded men if they would come to dwell in the lower village, with good earth lodges of their own and power in the tribe through the relatives of handsome young wives.

Long Beard pushed his cap back to look straight into the eyes of the offering chieftains, one after the other, and shook his head, but there were some who said that the smaller man, the one with the fox face in the short bearding, already cast eyes at one of the maidens from down the river.

The stories vary or are silent about the Village of the Bearded Men the next few years. It seems that many beaver pelts were properly cured for market that first winter and carried eastward by a special party of young Indians early in the spring, early enough to catch those in the upper lakes country going to trade with a tribe far east, the Hurons perhaps. The bearded men told the Indians how it was to be done, and warned the leader of something called firewater, the brandy of the French. This was not to be tasted until after they had obtained the knives, hatchets, needles and awls, and the thin iron for lighter, sharper arrow and spear heads. If they bargained well there might be furs enough for some small luxuries and trinkets too, and a little powder and ball for the two thunder sticks here, if this was possible, although the whites seldom traded these things to the Indians.

When the beaver was thickening his fur again the party returned. They came without signals of joy, and with empty hands. Robbers, perhaps the Iroquois, had waylaid them, as happened to many. The next spring another party went out, not openly but as through enemy country. They traded with the Hurons but were cheated, Long Beard complained. The third return was apparently a triumphant one and when the news of it spread along the Missouri the two Beards, in buckskin now like any Indian of the village, had to help stand off the raiders lured by the stories of wonderful new things. These raiders were surely the first in the region preferring to steal the white-man goods to preparing the beaver hides and making the long journey to market, but they were not the last.

If the Indians are right in dating the coming of the bearded men, the coming of powder and iron, to the upper Missouri during the late 1630's or the earliest 1640's, the first fur fair reached by anyone from the Village of the Bearded Men must have been at Montreal. The fair at the mouth of the Richelieu in 1623 is surely too early, although there were men with reason enough to flee to the wilderness in New France long before that, either from such authority as existed (enforceable by flogging, legal for generations after this, even for women) or from vengeance, white or red. There were Indians on the Missouri who had been to Montreal long before the news of the massacre of the Hurons and the missionaries in 1649 sifted westward, men shocked by what had been done in what was plainly dangerous country.

The fur fairs of the St. Lawrence region grew out of the marketing carnival of small-town France, a time of noisy trade and robust entertainment that was enlarged and exaggerated in the transplanting to America. Even the environment contributed to this, although in midsummer, the usual fair time, the roar of the saults, the rapids, of the St. Lawrence above Montreal usually quieted a little as the sun leveled off toward noon. The depths of the water darkened under the white leap and break upon the rocks, and under the boiling flow past the stony, tree-tufted islands. Afterward the foam-streaked river smoothed out a little as it rounded the bend to the fur-trade town and rolled past the Atlantic-worn vessels, their salt-stained canvas furled, the anchors down.

The town lay between the rises toward Mount Royal and the river. Along the bottoms, below the buildings, a commons had been set aside for pasturage and trade, which was fur trade. Here every summer for two weeks or more the dust or the mud was stirred by the soft tread of thousands of moccasins on red man's feet and white. There were wide-spaced rows of temporary booths, log and rough board, and always the last-minute goods borne up by strings of men bent under their burdens from some newly arrived vessel. They came along the muddy paths, past hammerings of the tardy and delayed hurrying to set out their goods as merchants had been doing in the annual fairs around the world for thousands of years.

But here there was a difference. Here the earliest parties were brown-skinned men with long black braids of hair, painted faces and silent feet wandering around, looking, while their few women remained at the camps at the water front, looking up to the commons, perhaps wondering about the new goods this summer, and the feasts and entertainment and dancing to come. After a while one of the Indians among the booths lifted his head, then others around him stopped too in the In-

dian concentration of listening, catching sounds too far to hear,
their brown lips parted to trap the faintest quiver of air. More
and more of them turned to look off northwest, up the noisy St.
Lawrence toward the mouth of the tamer Ottawa. Seeing
these listening Indians told even the rawest immigrant what was
coming, led him to join in the shouting that went up all over
the commons, echoing up the slope and over the farthest palisade that protected the merchant houses and the scattered
dwellings of the town.

"They come!" was the shout carried on the light wind.
"They come!"

Yes, of a certainty the furs from the Great Lakes and beyond—some of the finest beaver of all—were coming, and before long the head canoe would appear. In the meantime rafts
loaded with baled peltry were pushing out from the southern
shore of the river, from the small village of tame, missionary
Iroquois, and poled past the scattered islands toward Montreal.
There were canoes from the other side too, and long slender
ones from down river, the lines of men at each side digging
their paddles deep, the whole party like a string of millipedes
struggling against the power of even the lowish summer current
and then turning in toward the Montreal shore where bits of
foam from the rapids above still ran in thin lacy threads.

Finally a loud whoop swept over the commons and along
the river as the wind brought bits of a far rising song that told
the listeners the portage around the wildest saults of the St.
Lawrence had been completed and that the crafts were once
more afloat, the men fighting the lesser rapids. In a short time
the first of these stout, heavily loaded western canoes shot
around the bend, a brown figure squatting in the painted prow,
the man painted too, with beads swinging on his shiny, gnarled
breast, bright brass bands around the upper arms and rings on
the fingers that held the feathered lance erect before his pad-
dlers, gaudy too, but struggling hard against the river's thrust.
Behind this first canoe came more, as painted and gay, strings
of them reaching back out of sight, each as long and loaded as
the first, so loaded that it seemed they must all slip under the
rolling current. The voyageurs, lean-armed from perhaps a

thousand miles of water and portage worked frantically with
their paddles, tipping, thrusting, backing, the force of the
stream driving them on, the drops from the paddles glistening
as the canoes slid between the outcroppings of rock and spray-
ing foam, guided with skill and noisy, joyous concentration.

Other parties followed, Indian or coureur de bois. Shouting, singing, quarreling for space, the canoes turned in at the
landing just outside of town until they looked like rows of insect eggs in the neatness of some of nature's creatures. The men
poured out upon the muddy bank, tipis of bark and skin went
up, and fires began to twist their smoke into the air. Perhaps a
great, wide-hulled vessel, belated somewhere, drew in from the
far sea, the sails bleached and billowing as they faltered and
came down. Eager merchants at the landing strode back and
forth, peering under their wide-brimmed beaver hats, arms
folded behind them, silver-buckled shoes clumping on the rocky
pier, now and then one shouting across the narrowing strip of
water to the boats coming in.

Even after the local merchants and those from as far as
Quebec and France were ready, and most of the fur men there,
no word of business could be spoken until after the proper cere-
monies—an official welcome extended to all from the upper
stretch of the commons. Finally the little parade of dignitaries
came marching down the slope, eight or ten soldiers and two
priests escorting the governor in plumed hat and satin coat and
breeches in the lead. The governor settled himself in the
gilded armchair, his gold-hilted sword across his knees, with the
rest of the welcoming company in formal array behind him.
Then the Indian chiefs came up, one behind the other according to rank, and seated themselves on the ground, the headmen
in the center, the others to one side or the other in a large arc
wide as a drawn bow. Now there was the invocation from one
of the priests, the lighted pipe went around the Indian chieftains, and the welcoming speech of the governor was translated
into Iroquois and Algonquin as he spoke, with perhaps none to
explain it all to those of Siouan stock, like those from the Village of the Bearded Men.

In reply one chief after another rose, wrapped the robe or

blanket of his high position about him, over one shoulder and under the opposite arm, and spoke with the soft murmurings of the Algonquin, the emphasis of the Iroquois or the Athapascan or perhaps in the gutturals of the Sioux, all orators among people where oration was the power that moved men.

While the bales of furs down at the landings were examined and perhaps evaluated, with credit sticks issued by most buyers, the trading started on the commons. The first requests were always for guns, powder and lead and, as usual, denied. There was some smuggling of those items, but certainly not the opening day of the fair, very public, with gentlemen escorting plumed and bewigged ladies among the picturesque groups, and priests and sometimes gray nuns there too, curious and pleased with the scene. On display at the booths were all the items of the Indian trade, including knives, axes, awls, hoop and sheet iron for arrow and spear points, netting for fish and for beaver, cooking kettles, good red cloth, paint, vermilion, beads and other finery, brass wire for rings, ribbons and gilded trinkets, mirrors by the thousand, and many other offerings.

One item was always in demand—French brandy, particularly by the eastern tribes, many long trapped by alcohol as no beaver was ever ensnared by net or trap or stake-closed wash. Whole tribes like the Montagnais from down around Quebec were sharply reduced, almost destroyed. During this first day of the fair brandy barter would be less open than later, but it was there because alcohol not only brought a high price in beaver for itself but made the purchaser, Indian or mixed-blood, reckless and foolish in all his other trades, sometimes the white man too.

At first the Indians, mostly men but including some women even from the far western tribes, weighed the values carefully, standing in dignity and deliberation, perhaps to savor the pleasure. By evening there was less reserve around the great fires kindled along the avenues of the booths, with feasting on roasted venison, fowl and fish, vegetables too, and ending with the sweets the Indians liked, dark sugars perhaps and *la melasse*. Afterward there was dancing, and the drums too, and singing, and the music of fiddles and flutes, far toward morning.

Now and then a voice was lifted in anger or hilarity above the usual Indian tone; perhaps the boisterous one was a Frenchman, one of the coureurs de bois—the bush lopers—or of the many mixed-bloods, with the ambiguity of two cultures and the discipline of neither.

By the second trading day there was plain sign of brandy and high wines, some fermented in the St. Lawrence country from the great yields of wild grapes and other fruits and berries. By the second afternoon the people of Montreal usually took to their homes up along the rise, locked the palisade gates where these had been erected, at least barred the doors and shuttered the windows close, particularly at the large houses belonging to traders dealing in brandy. Yet some of the Indians had come a thousand miles for this heat that raced through the body, for the visions and dreamings it brought while awake, surely something sacred. But in the laughter of the alcohol or its anger and fighting violence before the sickness and the stupor, many ran through the avenues of the commons and up among the houses, brandishing war clubs and knives, singing, shouting, whooping, perhaps stripping off their last garment, the breechclout, in most tribes not to be removed publicly except in deliberate and deadly insult and scorn. Any nuns around covered their shocked faces, and the priests tried to rescue their Christianized charges, to quiet them in spite of insult and worse.

It was grieving too that some Frenchmen, particularly the bush lopers, were as wild in their drinking and fighting, and as ready to strip off their clothing in the heat of the alcohol as any brown-skinned heathen from beyond the lakes. The missionaries, Sulpicians and Jesuits, tried to control at least their countrymen during these wild days when their years of work with the Indians seemed a hopeless waste. They protested the sale of alcohol but the income by which the missions were maintained came from the profits of the fur trade augmented by the foolishness that the liquor brought, even though the town usually fell into chaos all the fair time and for days later.

By the time the fur rendezvous of Montreal had become well established, there were always young men from the far western tribes with some of the more experienced trading groups, as those from the Village of the Bearded Men had come. Usually such young men had been to the lake country in their journey years, that time after the budding warrior had honored his family with a bold exploit or two and before he settled down to larger war duties and a family. It was considered very important that any man rising in the tribe should know something of other places, other peoples. Even so the paddling around the tops of the lakes seemed very long and strange to the youths from the walking country, youths like those Long Beard sent with beaver to Montreal. They could scarcely believe that the world could be so large, and contain all the wonderful things that the whites below the rapids possessed. Usually the newcomers had never seen drunkenness, never tasted firewater, and when they asked why no warrior or policing society kept order, controlled the unseemly conduct, they were told that it would interfere with trade.

Ah-h-h, the trade, they said, not understanding. The great summer trading fairs of the Indians, from the valley of the Annapolis westward, north and south, were carefully managed.

But then there was no comprehending these pale-faced men here, although some were as smooth-cheeked as any Indian, with not even the down of the skin on chin or jaw, and with curling hair falling over the shoulders, many dressed to gleam and glitter like sun on the rapids, the colors like the drawn bow in the sky after rain. There were women too, among these pale-skinned people, and the stories of these told at the home villages seemed less strange. With their smooth faces and their soft voices, soft as an Indian woman's in the lodge, they seemed less alien, more akin than any of their men.

But perhaps strangest of all to the far Indians were the great winged ships, and the vast mounds of beaver pelts on the piers, great bales and mountains, surely so many that most of the beaver in the world must be dead.

"GONE" RENDEZVOUS
AND FOPPISH SILK

By the end of 1832 Hudson's Bay officials considered the region between the mouth of the Snake and the Rockies a fur desert. Their harvest proved it, dropping from 2,099 large beaver or the equivalent in 1826 to 788 in 1832 and going down to 220 in 1835. Not that much of the whole Oregon country had ever been rich in fur, even before it was scurried over by Americans following a varied number of French and British—Bay, Montreal or North West—searching like hungry ants, smelling out the least cut or canyon for live water.

"We're goners, gone beavers—" some of the Americans said, men who had grown old in ten, twenty years, plodding over the country from the Kootenai to the Gila with little but broken dams now where water flowed at all.

With or without George Simpson, the end had been inevitable long before the turning of those first wheels up the Platte in 1824, even though only on a cannon. In 1830 Smith, Jackson and Sublette took ten heavily loaded wagons with five mules each to within fifty miles of the waters that flowed to the Pacific. Two years later Bonneville's wagons crossed South Pass to the Green. But the first settlers headed toward Oregon were not beaver men who suddenly found the steel jaws of their traps empty or traders with no furs but a party of greenhorn home-seekers escorted by Nathaniel Wyeth. Inspired by Hall J. Kelley, who had dreamed of an American Oregon since 1815 with all the intensity of the 17th-century searcher for the route to the

27

western sea, Wyeth sent a ship around the Horn in 1832 and led
his twenty-four hale young men overland westward. He planned
to raise funds by some hunting and trapping on the way, to
provide a cargo of furs for the vessel's return. At St. Louis he
was surprised to discover the vast operations already carried on
west of the mountains, operations growing all the twenty-two
years since Henry planted his little post at the fork of the Snake.

Undaunted, Wyeth attached his tenderfeet to the Rocky
Mountain Fur caravan carrying goods to the annual trader
rendezvous. By the time they reached Pierre's Hole and had
gone through a Blackfeet attack near there, the majority of his
men were discouraged by the dangers still ahead and, turning
back, lost seven, killed. With a handful of followers Wyeth went
on to the Pacific, to find that his vessel had been wrecked on a
reef, his cargo lost, and was graciously taken in by the Hudson's
Bay men.

By 1834 Wyeth was back in Boston with big plans for fur
posts, a salmon fishery and a solid colony. He started another
vessel to Oregon and with a contract from Milton Sublette and
Thomas Fitzpatrick to carry their goods of the Rocky Mountain outfit to the annual rendezvous, he returned to St. Louis.
With him were two naturalists, Thomas Nuttall, who had been
over much of the wilderness, and John K. Townsend, a newcomer, who, on Wyeth's advice, bought several pairs of buckskin pants, an enormous green blanket overcoat and a hard-
crowned, wide-brimmed white wool hat to protect the skull and
shade the eyes. Together the naturalists started out some days
ahead of the party, to walk the first hundred miles or so, enjoy-
ing the river valley, pleased with flocks of the handsome green
and red parrots (paroquets), going perhaps as far as the tower
in the forest that, according to the Iowa legend, was formed by
the dung of an ancient and gigantic race of buffaloes.

Wyeth's party also included the missionaries for the Nez
Perces and Flatheads, the Indians hoping, with the white man's
magic, to produce the guns, powder and other good things that
the Iroquois hunters of the North West Company said were
made by the power that came from the rituals in the white
man's Book. But the magic of Jason and Daniel Lee and their

helpers could not make the cows they drove walk fast, and Milton Sublette was in a hurry to get his goods to the rendezvous. There would be at least four other large caravans in the politically open region of Ham's Fork, in dually controlled Oregon: another for the Rocky Mountain Fur Company under Milton's brother Bill, and surely the American Fur, Hudson's Bay, Bonneville and who could tell what others, besides perhaps one from Santa Fe.

April 28 Wyeth and Sublette headed out on the trail, the seventy men, including twenty old-timers, in double file behind them, each rider leading two horses that carried two eighty-pound packs apiece, the missionaries with their cattle driving the flanks. The camp was divided into messes of eight men each, with a tent and a daily ration of flour, and other essentials in addition to pork until fresh meat came in. Evenings the packs were arranged in a sort of fortification—a large hollow square, the horses picketed inside to graze, with a walking guard of six or eight men outside.

Unfortunately Milton Sublette's diseased* leg grew worse from the saddle and he had to return to St. Louis, but urging speed on Wyeth to keep ahead of Bill with the other Rocky Mountain goods. The missionary cows set the pace and so late one evening Wyeth was passed, with only a fresh trail in the morning to show that Bill Sublette was now in the lead. The delay, aggravated by the thought of generally officious preachers, angered the brigaders but Jason Lee, large-bodied and calm-faced driver of cows, managed to avoid open clashes with the rough, and rough-tongued, fur men except when he protested against Sunday travel. The two Lees were the first emigrants to stop at the post Bill Sublette's men were building as a trading house on a fork of the North Platte, to become Fort Laramie, the great center on the busy emigrant path to Oregon.

There must have been many things that the naturalist, Townsend, had never seen before: the dry-land whirlwinds, zig-zagging here and there, tossing up dead leaves and grass; heat

---

* From an old injury. After an amputation or two Milton Sublette accompanied the 1836 caravan west in a cart drawn by two mules, and died in pain at Fort Laramie in December.

dances; mirages of snowy mountains that rose beyond shimmering lakes where there were only dusty plains; thunderheads in magnificent mushrooms of white to deepest black climbing toward the zenith, flickering in pinkish lightning or breaking into blinding bolts that shook the earth, the thunder crashing and rolling. And between there would be the burning sun and stinging dust, black sometimes, or gray-white in blistering alkali, the clouds of buffalo gnats, fine as dust, itching and swelling the eyes. Townsend found much to record on the trip, everything from swallows and sagehens, which were remarkably tame, but bitter roasted, to antelope, elk, buffalo and bear, and rattlesnakes, but there seems to have been little sign of beaver on all that long river route most of the way to Ham's Fork in 1834. It was an ominous portent.

The first sight of the rendezvous was the usual shadowing of horse herds on the ridges on both sides of the hidden river valley and off toward the hazed and barren mountains beyond. Strings of meat hunters were coming in off the plains and on the left another trader caravan drew near, jackasses braying, while half a dozen small parties gathered, trappers with pack-horses, the men perhaps afoot, an occasional glint of sun on a gun ready across the arm. Thin layerings of smoke clung to the brush and timber along the bluffs, rising from clusters of tents and tipis out along the grassy bottoms and among the scattered brush and cottonwoods. These were groups of traders and trappers, company and freemen, and the various and often more orderly Indian camps. Horsebackers tore this way and that along the river, guns boomed with the slow flowering of powder smoke in the still afternoon air, punctuating the faint sound of whoops and yells. Plainly alcohol had already arrived.

It was not a happy arrival for Nathaniel Wyeth. The loss of Milton Sublette had seemed sad enough. Now, without him for protection, Bill Sublette had managed to pressure or bribe Fitzpatrick into repudiating the contract for the goods Wyeth brought, leaving him not only with an unpaid freight bill but with a whole trading stock on his hands and no connections, trapper or Indians, but having to compete with all the powerful organizations left in the western fur business.

One of Milton's experienced hands had selected a camp ground. Here the packs were dropped, the horses turned loose to roll ease into their sore and sweaty backs, and then start off to water, the herders following. And while tents and tipis went up in a row and the bales were piled for counters and sitting space, Wyeth and some of his men rode out along the other camps, the leader probably trying to get a reconsideration from Bill Sublette, who was moving over from the Green River, or to make a deal elsewhere.

The rendezvous gathered swiftly now: Fitzpatrick in, but evasive with Wyeth; Cerré bringing Bonneville's goods; the Hudson's Bay outfit; and the American Fur too, but with a surprisingly small stock, drawing guarded looks from some, knowing and uneasy looks. There were Indians everywhere, fifteen hundred, Anderson, a tenderfoot with Bill Sublette, wrote later, but perhaps his enchanted eyes and the constant shifting, the coming and going, led him into exaggeration. Large parties of Bannocks, Shoshonis, Nez Perces and Flatheads were there, and Crows, Sioux and smaller groups from other tribes, even several Hidatsas from the Missouri with products to trade to far Indians, but mostly to lure some back there for the corn, and the feasts of squash and melons now that they no longer came to the big fair with beaver and horses to trade for whiteman goods. It was a disturbing time for the Hidatsas, and back home a medicine man was fasting on a hill overlooking the Old Crossing of the Missouri, a place still sacred to them.

The trappers and mountain men were a tangle-bearded lot —some Americans, more French-Canadians and breeds, with a scattering of Kanakas, all in soiled and greasy buckskin pants, most of them looking like any Indian except that an Indian would be smooth-faced, his hair usually neat. Certainly many were more earth-footed than their constant associates in one tribe or another, perhaps through the curious accommodations demanded of the outsider by wilderness life. Some even carried medicine bags for their mystical powers as they carried the little bags of castoreum for its power over the beaver.

After more than two hundred years the fur fair, the rendezvous, was little changed from that of the Richelieu or Montreal.

There was no gray of Recollets or black of Jesuits here, the two Lees dressed much like any trader's followers, and certainly nobody in the satin small clothes or silver buckles of the governors. The nearest to this was Capt. William Drummond Stewart, Scotsman like many others here, but no canny trader. He was a romantic sightseer at his second rendezvous and to become Sir William some day. Otherwise there was little change since 1623 beyond better guns, perhaps, and less fur.

The Indians went from camp to camp for the welcoming treat, not a drinking match, *une boisson,* but a burning cup. Slow-paced, dignified old chiefs with their blankets about them had come first, followed by their powerful war leaders and painted braves. But as they moved on and on, the dignity melted, moccasins began to stumble, the wearers to whoop and fight and finally fall in sickness and stupor. There were still a few more responsible leaders, refusing all alcohol, and many women with small ones on their backs out to see what else was offered. Youths ran here and there, but some of the pretty young girls still kept modestly to the moccasin heels of the old women as they went from booth to tent to tipi. Excited, they spoke softly among themselves, considering the goods offered: powder, lead and bales of tobacco; boxes of hatchets, knives and awls; bolts of calico, red and yellow and black; strouding, flannel and silks in reds and blues; all displayed to the brilliant sunlight of day or the evening candles of buffalo tallow often stuck into bull horns hung point down from tent and tipi poles. There were boxes of paint and vermilion too, and hanks of beads, great clumps of necklaces of every color; clusters of bracelets, brass arm-bands and hawkbells; bolts of ribbon and even some lace, not much, but a little for the special favorite of some mountain man who still carried the memory of a woman in laces, far away.

There were foods too, coffee, with tea for those from the British trade regions; hard brown lumps of sugar and perhaps raisins dried on the stem.

But always there was the whisky, frontier whisky made from alcohol and water, first usually a gift round to make good will and rekindle the craving, particularly at Sublette's camp, and more for the chiefs in conferences. Later, when paid for by the Indians, there was often tallow in the bottom of the cup, to make it less, and more and more water from Ham's Fork. Sold in quantity it was often $3 a pint and more. Tobacco, very rough and inferior, brought $2 a pound, these and all other things usually to be paid for by the counters the Indians received for furs and robes still in the old unit of made-beaver.

The missionaries and some of the visitors in fringed buckskin were astonished and horrified by what Jason Lee called the sins that kill, the infidelity and gambling, drunkenness and fornication, with none to protect or to police the region. He had the urge to preach a sermon to the hundreds of white men but knew that none would listen. Once, for a few moments, he was pleased to hear the Indians sing what sounded faintly like a hymn, but then they built a fire and began a war dance, in which white men joined. He was probably mistaken; all Indian dances seem war dances to the tenderfoot, the greenhorn in Indian country. He might have caught sight of a scalp dance for some Indian killed on the way to the Fork, or there, but what he saw was probably one of the dozens of show-offs and social dances of the tribes. There was, however, a great deal of trade in women and maidens for goods, particularly whisky. Townsend was at least impressed by the "available loveliness of the Nez Perce maidens," and so was Anderson, but he seems to have been more startled to see them sit their horses astride. This was not side-saddle country, or a side-saddle time.

There was horse racing, with high bets, as usual, and other gambling, particularly the hand game among the Indians, and buffalo chases over the sun-burnt prairie, horse trading, and pasture changing, as well as formal camp moves. One day a grizzly bear charged through the rendezvous, probably as alarmed as all the people who fled until a Flathead ran out and killed him. Another time a Nez Perce brought a buffalo bull charging through Bill Sublette's camp. He had promised to entertain Bill's guests and this was his attempt—whooping, everybody running out to see, and help fill the bull full of arrows and lead, the body left to wash down the river.

There was much drunkenness among the white men and

breeds, and as much fighting and other violence by them as by all the Indians together. The more sober might be cursing the Blackfeet, who had attacked parties around the rendezvous of 1832 up at Pierre's Hole, in what they considered the fringes of their country. Men were killed there and since, good men, who knew the west. Even Bill Sublette had stopped an arrow with his shoulder, and others had dropped their bones in quiet, remote places since, to bleach among the weathered remains of the beaver. The weary and experienced Jedediah Smith was gone too, caught stooping to drink from a hole dug in the bed of the dry Cimarron. Comanche arrows succeeded where a hundred others had failed.

Although the skies were clear and high over Ham's Fork, with noise and boisterousness up and down the stream, there was caution among the traders. Some of their lesser men, particularly the mixed-bloods, were sent out to visit with the trappers and Indians at their fires, acting lonesome for companions, looking, estimating, coming back, perhaps shaking their heads, particularly those from the Indian camps. The bales of furs seemed small, very small.

As the trappers and Indians traded out their harvest, the competition grew, not only for beaver and otter, marten and mink, but lesser hides. Even robes became desirable, bulky as they were to move the far distance overland to St. Louis, and deer and elk—anything, practically. Gradually even the newcomers suspected that the rendezvous was not to be as great as they had expected. Plainly Bill Sublette had pushed Fitzpatrick to refuse the goods he had ordered through Wyeth because they were not needed, would be surplus. Yes, the high, prosperous days of 1832 and 1833 were done, the fabulous ones of the 1820's only a legend—those days when Ashley's men, without a rival at the gatherings, roared and swaggered across beaver land.

Outside rumors thickened the gloom. Some had heard of the elegant French duke, who, it was said, had lost his beaver hat in China and, unable to have it replaced, had a similar one made of silk. The first sight of the hat on his return to Paris sent the fops into cries of envy. Immediately they began to discard their beavers and ordered hats of silk. The usual great train of little imitators, the sheep of fashion, followed. The fad reached London, Montreal, New York and Canton. No more beavers.

To this the rendezvous added another rumor, one proved truer, at least in source. Ever since the difficulties of the American Fur Company with the government over Leclerc, and then McKenzie's still, bolstered by the decrease in beaver, both supply and demand, Astor was moving to unload, to sell out. The name, American Fur Company, went with the Western Department to Pratte, Chouteau and Company, the Great Lakes region to Ramsay Crooks and associates. From now on John Jacob Astor, as banker for the new owners, would take a safe profit, free from blame or loss.

But not all the disasters reached the rendezvous from far off. The campaign begun by Astor's McKenzie and Chouteau against the Opposition, the Rocky Mountain Fur Company, ended here. The price-cutting, ruthless trade practices, incitement of Indians, subsidization of upstart rivals, bribery, piracy and general corruption, as well as suspicion of murder, most of which the Rocky Mountain outfit also attempted, but with limited resources and experience, had succeeded against them. The company went under there around Ham's Fork, only a real whooping distance from Ashley's great rendezvous nine years ago on the Green. True, Fitzpatrick and Bridger, counting Milton Sublette in, made an attempt to carry on as a company because there was nothing else for them. Somehow most of the money they would make would flow to Bill Sublette and his partner, Robert Campbell, both finally rich men. Wyeth, not without bitterness, wrote Milton Sublette: "You will be kept as you have been, a mere slave to catch beaver for others."

The new company lasted only a short time and then Fitzpatrick and Bridger, better men than any that Astor or Chouteau ever developed, finally became company hired hands.

But there at Ham's Fork Wyeth had had the satisfaction of seeing some of the men who cut his throat bleed as deeply. When the rendezvous began to break up, he headed for the west coast, taking the goods left on his hands over toward the Snake where he started Fort Hall as a trading post to dispose of them. Townsend wrote of the going, of Stewart's departure westward, to the "lower country from which he may probably take passage to England by sea," and of the missionaries in the same party. Jason Lee, who had come to bring the white man's Book to the Nez Perces and Flatheads, didn't even visit the camp of the tribes at the rendezvous. Instead the Lees became colonizers in the Willamette valley. There, more interested in agricultural development than in missions, they helped start the Oregon fever.

As the dust settled on Ham's Fork, the wolves and magpies picked the last bones of the camp grounds and finally the grass thrust exploratory spears through the worn earth. Some memories of things done there were less easily healed. A few people had died, of violence and sickness and age, as happens. The Flatheads, instead of obtaining a missionary with a new vision for the new times, lost their oldest man there, a man said to be almost a hundred years of age. Bissonette, one of the Pratte and Cabanné young men sent to feel out the amount of fur in the Indian camps, had evidently sat with him a while. Too ancient to ride a saddle, he had been dragged there in the skin travois of the crippled and the feeble. But he could still move his long bony fingers in sign talk.

"When I was a boy it was a good time," the old Flathead said. "Then the white man came like no wild creature comes—straight into the village, to eat the beaver, all the game, with his iron teeth. Now my grandchildren and their grandchildren are hungry."

The man stopped a long time, his hands down, his eyes closed in the gray and wrinkled face, like an old piece of stained and weathered rawhide lost among the rocks. Then his arms lifted, and he began to talk again. "If the lion or the grizzly come so into the village, he go down under arrow and spear—"

Now the old man was dead, as so many other things died there at the rendezvous. The creature most desperately involved in the developments of that year knew nothing of them, knew nothing of the curious and far distant luck that was to save him from extinction. True, the beaver would still be pursued, still have to flee the steel trap in his waters, the gun among the breaking ice of spring, but never again from men with the hunger of gold seekers burning within them. Now he was no longer the prey, and the pay, of the beaver men and their empire-hungry rulers as he had been for 225 years, from the mouth of the St. Lawrence, from Hudson's River and Bay, westward to the Pacific and back to the remote pockets of the mountain country.

Not that the spread of empire was done. It moved on over the path the beaver men had already worn up the Platte River and along the west-flowing streams, aimed, like a spear, into the flank of the Oregon country. Thousands, tens and many hundreds of thousands would follow its direction, driven less by an appetite for gold, glittering or soft, than a hunger—the ancient and universal hunger for a home.

from CRAZY HORSE

THE COMING OF THE
WAGON GUNS

(Note: *"Curly"* was the childhood name of the brown-haired, light-skinned Oglala Sioux who later became the great war chief, Crazy Horse. Curly's father, an Oglala holy man, was also named Crazy Horse.)

The morning sun came up over the breaks of the Platte into a sky that was red as the coals of the council fire. It touched the ridge above the Oglala camp, brightened the smoky tops of the lodges, and moved swiftly down their painted sides. Here and there a dog stretched, or an impatient horse pulled at its rope, nickering towards the herds on the far hills. Blackbirds awoke in the rushes of the river, and from the prairie the sky singers rose straight up into the sun, scattering their song as they sloped back to their earth. It was morning, but no Indian stirred into the dew that would soften the soles of his moccasins.

When the sunlight had spread itself well over the worn camp ground, the old women came out to light the cooking fires, the smoke rising straight up and then flattening into a haze that clung along the breaks. Clubbing the dogs from the emptying parfleches of meat, they called the girls to help bring wood and water, the boys to relieve the night watchers of the pony herds. Then the younger women came out of the lodges in their wing-sleeved deer-skin dresses, their dark hair smoothly combed, their cheeks vermilioned, to put up the spears and the shield cases or other regalia of their warriors beside the lodges.

Now the day had begun. But the cloud-streaked sky was still red, with the long, late red that speaks of a troubled day. Many of the men looked off towards the west as they lifted the lodge flaps and came out. Crazy Horse, the father of Curly, and several others who treasured the deeds of their people went to sit with Bad Heart Bull, the Oglala historian, one of those who paint the stories of the people on skins, the big things of the winter counts and the little too, for the singing and retelling when important visitors come, or the people are together. There was a bad thing to be done at the Brule camp today and now came this red morning, deeper in foreboding than the one before Bull Bear was killed, making a long fighting in the village, splitting the Oglalas and shaming them before the people. There had been a red sky that morning, a red sky that brought a day from which to count time.

Although it was still early several horses stomped flies beside the lodge of Man Afraid. He was the head of a great family known for their strength in battle, their wisdom in the councils, their fatherhood of the people clear back to the days remembered only in the hero stories, long before the Lakotas had horses, back when they lived beside the great water and fought battles against enemies whose names were now forgotten. Man Afraid was six foot four as the whites named this tallness, and known as one with a straight tongue, one not looking for power or for ponies. So last night the council had chosen him to go to the fort, to see what such a man could do about soldiers coming with guns where the helpless women and children were. He took three or four of the younger headmen with him, riding close together, for there was much that needed talking.

When they were gone, Curly, young He Dog, and the son of Man Afraid followed along the other side of the river, racing their ponies, whooping, wishing for something to happen. They got past the Gratiot stone houses where their government annuities waited for the agent and well into sight of the white walls of Laramie before Man Afraid signaled the boys back, so they turned off into the breaks north of the river, passing and repassing each other as they whipped their ponies, pretending they were winding them for battle. But as soon as they were out of sight they sneaked back to the brush along the bottoms and loafed the hot summer hours away, watching for signals, waiting.

When the sun was past the middle the Indians and several white visitors from the fort started down the trail. There were soldiers with them, an officer on horseback and a wagon full of walking soldiers with more riding on the two wagon guns, the wheels lifting the thick dust from the earth of the Holy Road. The boys rode for their camp with the news. But it was already known to those at the council lodge. Scouts had reported that the big-talking young Grattan and thirty soldiers were coming, with Lucien, the trader's son called Wyuse by the Indians, along as interpreter. Again he was not right from the white man's whisky and got more of the burning cup at the stone trading houses where the soldiers loaded their guns ready for shooting.

Most of the Indians of the great encampment were out to see the soldiers come over the ridge to the west and stop a little there to look down on this broad valley with its three great lodge circles and probably twelve hundred warriors. Then the dust started again and the women, knowing about the cannons and the long knives, ran to call their children together, take in the spears and shields, and loosen the lodge stakes for swift striking.

When the soldiers reached the Oglala circle, Man Afraid and the others had dropped back to show that they were not in this thing. By now the camp was as sleeping; almost everybody out of sight. Leaving the soldiers in a little bunch at the trail, the officer rode up to the spreading poles of the council lodge and jerking his lathered horse to a stop, called out: "Hey, you! You infernal red devils, come out here!"

But there was no movement in the circle of blanketed backs that he could see under the partly lifted lodge skins, no sign at all, so he called for Wyuse.

"Tell the damn Indians they better stay close to their tipis or I'll crack into them," he ordered and spurred on, leaving the drunken interpreter to repeat the warning in bad Lakota as he clung to the saddle horn with one hand and shook the other in a white-man fist at the empty camp circle. But off to the north the pony herds were coming in fast from the breaks, their manes and tails flying, the herd boys whooping hard behind them as they splashed through the river and thundered over the bottom towards the camp. The soldiers in the wagon pointed to them, shouting something to one another, but the wheels carried them along after the little soldier chief, hungry to take an Indian today.

At the Bordeaux stockade, just above the camp of Conquering Bear, Grattan stopped to get old Jim to help him. But the stocky little Frenchman would not go, although he knew that the officer could make him much trouble, perhaps even have him and his traders driven out of the Indian country. So he talked in slow confusion, making it seem he did not understand, making it take time.

What was this talk of wanting him to go to the Brule camp with soldiers carrying guns? Something about a cow? Whose cow? Oh, the cow! Yes, yes, the Mormon cow. But the owner had been offered good pay for her, much more than the old carcass was worth. It could not be that they were foolishly taking cannons into the Indian camp for this? Somebody would get hurt. There was much mourning in the Brule camp for old Chief Bull Tail, who had died last night; the women and some of the men wild and excited, their arms cut and bleeding, their hair full of dirt. It was not a good time to go to the camp, not even for visiting. No, positively he, Jim Bordeaux, would not go there.

So the whites who came down from the fort stayed at the stockade but the soldiers pushed on, the Indians about the trading houses watching them go. It was a bad thing they were doing, and their friend Jim could smell trouble as far as a horse the coming storm. Always he was a man of peace when it came to shooting-fights, even if he had to hide in the robes of his wife's bed, as he once did. And nothing she could do got him out. So today the soldiers had to go on without him although Man Afraid, who was very anxious to save trouble, talked strong to his trader friend. This day they needed a good man for the interpreting and they had only the drunken Iowa.

It was true that Wyuse was already doing a bad thing, running his horse up and down the road past the Brule camp to give him second wind, as the warriors did before a fight. And as he whipped and spurred, the interpreter slapped his mouth in the war whoop and called out insulting words to the Indians as though they were chunks of green buffalo chips he was throwing at them. So they would laugh at him, these enemy Sioux, set themselves above him as on a snow mountain? He would bring them down, cut their hearts out and eat them! He would give them new ears so they could understand the words he carried in his mouth!

While a few of the Brules stood at their lodge doors watching, the last of the women and children slipped away to the willows of the river. Many of the warriors were going too. Their hands full of the things of war, they came dropping over the bank behind the lodge circle, to the brush where the camp horses were often tied in the shade. Some were already stripped to the breechcloth, others tying their hair in knots on their foreheads, painting themselves in their sacred way. There were not only Brules and Minneconjous but Oglalas, too, who had come down along the bottoms. More of them rode openly on the Holy Road: Red Cloud, Black Twin and his brother No Water, and many others past the first heat of warrior youth, coming slowly, in little talking bunches, as though for a visiting.

Conquering Bear had gone out to meet the soldiers at his camp. His broad, concerned face was free of paint today, his hair loose without fur or feather, a faded old blanket of mourning held around his body with a steady arm. He urged the officer to keep the soldiers out of the camp, as Man Afraid and Big Partisan had done, and the thickset Little Thunder of the Brules. They would sit and smoke as friends with him, settle the trouble like good men.

But the officer would not have the thing done so. Loudly he ordered the soldiers into the center space of the camp circle and down towards the place of the Minneconjous, near the chief's own lodge. There he lined them up, running around to load and aim the wagon guns himself.

While a few of the chiefs and headmen stayed near the officers, standing straight and silent in their blankets, making no

answer to his loud threats, more and more of their warriors
slipped away over the bank. Even boys came now, and were
sent away, all but Lone Bear and young Curly, who was known
as the follower of Hump and the blood nephew of Spotted Tail.
By keeping quiet, they got to stay, to hear what the watchers
told of the things done up in the camp, of Conquering Bear and
Man Afraid going back and forth between Straight Foretop and
the soldiers, trying to get the Minneconjou to surrender, or the
soldier chief to go away until their father, the agent, came and
said what must be done. But it was plain that the one called
Grattan had come for a fight, although the Bear offered a good
mule from his own herd for the cow and sent the camp crier
around to collect some horses. When the old man came back he
had five marked sticks, meaning a horse each from the herds of
five good men. These he laid down on the ground before the
soldier chief, saying there were others who would have given
but they said it was enough and too much for a poor cow, slow
with many far miles and the load of years.

But the officer did not want mules or horses. He would
have the young Minneconjou standing there in the door of his
lodge, leaning on his gun, a bow and arrow in one hand, his
bare breast scarred from the sundance. And Straight Foretop
would not go with the whites. Last year the soldiers had killed
three of his people over the trouble about a boat on the Shell
River and this year, while some of them were sitting beside the
white man's road, an emigrant had shot at them and hit a child
in the head. The little one recovered, but it was a long sickness
and made the heart dark. He would die where he stood rather
than go with the people who did these things. Yet he did not
wish to make trouble, so he asked that the chiefs take the people
away and leave him to the soldiers.

"I am alone now," he said. "Last fall the whites killed my
two brothers. This spring my uncle, my only relative, died. Today my hands are full of weapons, my arms strong. I will not go
alive."

These were brave words, sent straight as from a good bow,
the Indians saw, but the interpreter was not making them right
for the soldier chief, or those of Conquering Bear and Man

Afraid either. Instead he said something the Indians did not understand but many thought meant that the Bear had refused to give up the Minneconjou. Those were crooked, lying words, but the soldier chief got even redder and roared out that it was enough. The Indian must be brought to him immediately. Against the advice of all the others, Conquering Bear said he would try, but as a Lakota he had no right to do this thing and so must go to the man as an enemy. For that he must get his gun from his lodge.

There was no telling what words Wyuse made of this either, for as the chief turned, the officer gave an angry order. His men jumped up, leveled their guns. A shot was fired and the brother of Conquering Bear fell, his mouth gushing blood. The other chiefs scattered but the Bear stayed, jumping around so he would be hard to hit, calling to the Indians to keep cool, not to charge the soldiers. The whites would probably be satisfied now that they had hurt a good man.

But the one called Grattan was not done. Aiming the wagon guns himself, he ordered his row of soldiers to fire. This time Conquering Bear went down, and then the cannons boomed, the blasts tearing through the tops of the lodges and away across the river.

Now Straight Foretop lifted his gun and shot through the stinking black smoke. Grattan fell, and almost before he was down the Indians were upon him, cutting and hacking him to pieces as, with a whooping, Spotted Tail led the hidden warriors up over the bank, pouring a wall of arrows into the soldiers at the wagon guns as they came. With spears and war clubs they trampled the white men to the earth, grabbing their guns and swinging them like clubs upon the rest. A few of the soldiers managed to get on the cannon carriages and the wagon and whipped the mules towards the emigrant road, firing back until they, too, went down in the charge of warriors. A few who were cut off made a stand, for one breath a brave little island of whites facing the Indians. Then they were gone too.

At the first shot Wyuse and Grattan's horse-holder spurred away up the road, mounted Brules hard after them, the Oglalas from the upper camp cutting them off. As the soldier was struck from the saddle, the horse of the Iowa fell, and kicking loose from the stirrups, he fled into the death lodge of Bull Tail. But the Indians went into that sacred place after him and pulled him out, bawling like a cow-calf. His own brother-in-law struck him down with his war club, tore off his clothes, cut a long gash up each leg from the ankle to the waist, and left him there outside of the death lodge. So it was done to the man who would give the Lakotas new ears to hear with, cut their hearts out to eat. A dozen struck him with their bows or their knives but none would take his scalp.

As soon as the warriors were gone, Lone Bear and young Curly sneaked up. Feeling strange and a little sick under their belts, the two boys stood over the naked, mutilated man, the blood already clotted in the darkening gashes of his legs, the face twisted and afraid, the eyes sticking out like stones. This man, mostly Indian himself, and accepted into the Lakotas as one of them when they gave him a wife, had brought only trouble upon them—many smaller troubles before, and today this big thing.

As the young Curly looked down upon this enemy of his people, his Indian blood rose like a war drum in his ears, swelling hot. For a moment it seemed he must kill, kill whites, many of them to make his heart good after what this man and the soldier chief had done in the Brule camp today. Then suddenly he was big and powerful, so powerful there was only contempt for a miserable thing like this Wyuse, and with a quick motion he jerked his breechcloth away and stood bare before the staring eyes of the dead man, offering him the ultimate insult of the Lakota.

For a moment the boy was dizzy with the boldness of this act of chiefs in the council lodge. Then he was once more just young Curly, the slender twelve-year-old son of Crazy Horse, a holy man, counselor and father to all who came to him. So the boy covered himself before anyone could notice and, running for his pony, headed towards the Oglala camp. There would be trouble from all this killing, perhaps a great war, and he must be with his people to help. Faster and faster he hurried his pony until the little pinto was laying his hairy belly low to the ground.

Behind him came the forgotten Lone Bear, trying hard to catch up with his friend, for already there was nothing else he could do.

As Conquering Bear fell, Man Afraid and Big Partisan and others ran in to lift him, to carry him down over the bank out of the way of the charging warriors. They saw he had many wounds, three bad ones: a shattered arm, a bullet through one knee and another deep through the soft middle parts that would bring down even a buffalo bull. They laid him out straight on his mourning blanket and stood about the Great Father's peace chief who was brought to the ground by the guns of the soldiers, who fell as a great man falls, shielding the people of his village.

In the meantime the warriors who had followed the fleeing soldiers up the trail stopped at Bordeaux on the way back to the camp, demanding the whites who had watched the fight from the flat tops of the houses and were now suddenly gone.

"Where are the rabbits hiding today? Shake the brush, scare them out!" the young Brules cried, going through one house after another, their lean, brown bodies shining in sweat and streaking paint, their faces fierce. Some were blood-spattered; some had fresh, short-haired white-man scalps hanging from their belts or their bow-tops. And beside them ran the little Jim Bordeaux rubbing his hands, pleading. They had done nothing, these whites that they were hunting, only ridden along with the soldiers from the fort as people going the same way on the road often do. They were blameless.

"They are of the enemy!" the nephew of Conquering Bear roared out, plunging his new soldier sword into the bed rolls, one after another. By now Curly and He Dog had slipped back down to follow Hump. They heard Swift Bear and two more Brule brothers-in-law of old Jim talk for him and the other whites, haranguing the wild young men. The warriors were an-

gry at this but they listened because Swift Bear was still a strong
man among them, if too much for peace. He was one of the best
catchers of the wild horses that lived in the sandhills of the
Running Water country, and so they let him say that they were
like the foolish white soldiers, coming to kill people who had
done them no harm. Let those who would be men go help the
fleeing people, Swift Bear said, or had the years of peace they
so despised really softened the young Lakotas, made such weak-
lings and fools of them that they could not see the people were
truly in great danger today and needed men to help them, not
bush-shaking boys playing at war?

So the wild young warriors went away like dogs caught at
the meat racks, some still looking back. But when they turned
their eyes ahead they saw that Swift Bear had spoken true.
The Lakotas were fleeing as these so young men had never seen
them go. The whole river bottom was one great herd of milling
people, women, children, and old ones, horses and travois and
dogs, all mixed together, with many men among them, trying
hard to get everybody to the river, where Little Thunder was
splashing his horse through the water marking a path across
the quicksands of the Shell with standing poles of willow.

And at the Brule camp it was as though a great wind had
come that way, leaving only one lodge standing, that of Conquering Bear, guarded by members of his *akicita,* his warrior
society, and a few of those strong in the councils of the Lakotas,
like Man Afraid and Big Partisan. And before the door were
scattered the naked bodies of the soldiers. These the young warriors charged again, Curly along, jumping them with their
horses, driving spears into them and more arrows. They threw
their ropes over the wagon guns and dragged them around the
camp, upside down, tearing up the worn sod. One they took
down into the river and cut it loose in the deepest current, to
be lost. Then they piled brush around the gun carriages and the
wagons and, firing them, circled the blaze, whooping and riding
wilder and wilder as they heard the women along the river
make the trilling cry for them.

And when the fire was done they swung around the moving
camp of their people and on up the river to meet some of the

warriors returning from a talk with the Oglalas, making the call for charging the enemy, the whites.

"Hoppo!" they cried. "Let us go!"

Now Little Thunder came riding fast to the Bordeaux houses, his heavy face lined with the things of this day. It seemed the warriors were planning to burn the soldier fort on the Laramie.

"Stop them, *sacré*, stop them!" the little Frenchman shouted, sputtering like wet buffalo fat thrown on the fire. "If they do no more damage the Great Father may forgive it. They have some reason for fighting the soldiers who come and kill their chief before their eyes, but if they burn his fort he will send a hundred wagon guns; the soldiers will come thick as the grasshoppers in summer to fight them, to butcher the women and children."

"Hou!" Little Thunder said, making it a sorrowful agreement. He saw that the things their trader brother said were true. They must do what they could. Getting some of the head warriors together, he made a long talk to hold them while Jim and his Brule wife sent tobacco and hard bread and a barrel of black molasses out to the rest, still angry as bumblebees stirred up with a stick. They were all mounted now and new painted, riding in circles, whipping their ponies with the war ropes, sliding down behind them as in attack, whooping. But Little Thunder held their leaders through their respect for a man of years and honor. Besides, it was getting towards the time of the evening meat, the sun near to setting. It would be long dark before they could reach the soldier town, and war at night was not good, as every Lakota knew. Tomorrow they would go.

Ahh-h, tomorrow! And now it was time to eat, so getting off their horses they pushed up to the things the trader had set out. Holding up the long tails of their breechcloths like white-woman aprons, they filled them with tobacco and hard bread; dipping their hunting knives, sticks, or even their fingers into the barrel of molasses, they licked the sweet drippings. Tomorrow was time enough for fighting.

But the trouble was not yet done, not for Little Thunder or for Bordeaux. As soon as it was dark the whites hidden at the trading houses wanted to ride for Laramie, and get killed on the way. And when Swift Bear and another Indian found a wounded soldier hidden in the brush holding his arrow-split belly together with his hands, they brought him to the stockade too. But Jim and Little Thunder ordered him taken away at once, Bordeaux's wife slipping out to help him in her Lakota way, wrapping his belly tight in wet buckskin and giving him a little whisky and a robe and covering him with brush.

Almost before all these whites were hidden again, more warriors, hundreds of them now, were whooping outside, slapping their mouths with their palms, sliding their voices into high, thin cries like the panther in the darkness. They pushed into the candle-lit trading house until it was tight full, many milling around outside, demanding, threatening. To prove that their chief was not dead and so not yet to be avenged, some of their leaders, like Spotted Tail and High Back Bone had been taken into his lodge, lit only by a few coals and the smoldering grass wick in the bowl of the medicine man. Besides, the chief was covered, so they could not see the slow-oozing, yellow-brown blood, almost as yellow as that of the gut-shot buffalo that the hunter need only follow a little way. But the man's eyes had dropped back so deep into his head that they knew how it was, and so once more the ten white men at the trader stockade cowered under the robes of the warehouses while Little Thunder rode back and forth from the people huddled north of the river in their fear of more soldiers and wagon guns to the lodge of the wounded chief and then on to the Bordeaux houses.

"Wait," he kept saying to the warriors everywhere. "Wait —nothing can be done until it is seen what will happen. Making war against the whites is a big thing and not to be decided fast as a lead ball flies from the gun. There must be counciling. Wait!"

Ahh-h wait, wait! That was all the chiefs had been saying for two moons, some of the warriors cried out against him. Their supplies had been used up waiting for their father, the agent, and he had not come. Now they would not get their annuity goods at all, and their children would starve.

"Nobody will starve! We will kill the whites and take the goods for the people!" one among them promised, the others answering him with their loud "Hoye!" pushing closer upon Little Thunder and the French trader, their faces wild in the candlelight, their paint-ringed eyes fierce. The Brule chief saw how it was and moving his eagle-wing fan wearily, advised Bordeaux to give them more goods, anything they wanted, for they were only trying to pick a fight to start the killing.

So Jim Bordeaux gave out tobacco, the sweet lumps, coffee and hard bread, raisins and bacon and beans until these were gone. Then he pulled calico and blue cloth and blankets from the shelves, brought powder and ball from the back room, even gave away his cattle and his horses. Tears running down his dark, hairy cheeks, he gave out all his goods, and when everything was gone and he stood behind an empty counter with only Little Thunder and Swift Bear beside him and the mass of dark-faced warriors pushing against them, he began to talk. One white man, unarmed and alone, he began to talk to the fight-hungry warriors, flattering here, blaming there, bringing up old angers and spites and hatreds among them, dividing them with his smooth trader's tongue, talking long and hard for his life and for the life of all the whites of the upper Platte River country.

Most of the night Curly was with the pony herd, the boys taking turns to slip away to the Bordeaux houses, where there was surely much going on. But it was not easy, with the *akicita* watching the herders very close, for the horses must not be lost this night. After the excitement of the day they were restless and easy to stampede by soldiers or by Indians from up at the woman's camp at the fort, or even from among their own people here.

Curly managed to get away once, sneaking down a gully black under the late moon. He stopped at the back of the Conquering Bear lodge, away from the guard. A faint redness glowed through the skins between the dark shadows of the men with the chief, but everything was so still he could hear the ar-

row hawks falling upon the mosquitoes over the river bottoms.
There was an owl hoot too, a signal to returning hunters who
did not know of this day. And behind all this was the rumbling
of the warriors over at the trading houses.

As the boy listened he noticed a dark figure huddled at the
lodge of the chief, a woman, probably the old wife of Conquering Bear, with her blanket drawn over her head, sorrowing
for the wounded one. It was bad for a woman to see her man
dying so, not from battle or even sickness, but by the hand of
those who called him friend.

⫴ ⫴ ⫴

THE SONG OF
A GOOD NAME

UP IN THE NORTH COUNTRY there was a strange thing—several
white buffaloes had been shot this fall, more than were sometimes seen in all the days of a man's life. Nobody understood
this and so the robes were painted and given back to the earth,
as was good with such sacred things. Then, the evening of a
thawing winter day, Curly saw one. He was coming in alone
from the mountains, his horse loaded with fresh elk. The buffalo stood on a south slope, almost as white as the snow patches
about him. Curly was near enough for a good shot but before
he raised his gun the animal threw up his fine, curly head,
sniffed the wind, and was gone over the ridge, his hoofs throwing snow and pounding on the dark, freezing earth. The boy
whipped his loaded horse after the buffalo but he found noth-

ing except tracks leading through a dusk-filled little valley. In a bare place they ended, as when the long-eared rabbit doubles back on his trail and then jumps to the side to sleep with his eyes open and watching. But the buffalo is not small and helpless and has no need for such tricks. It must have been a holy animal, so instead of searching for more tracks, the young Oglala hobbled his horse, made a wickiup of cedar branches where the trail ended, and spent the night there, hoping to dream. He slept well, awakened only once or twice by the howling of wolves drawn to his fire by the smell of the fresh meat. In the morning it was snowing, soft, warm, with the promise of a spring sun to break through and free the bowing cedars of their load. All the tracks were gone, everything covered, and he had dreamed nothing he could remember. So he started home.

The day he got back to the big Oglala village a crier went around calling everyone to the woman feast for the niece of Red Cloud, Black Buffalo Woman as she was now called. Young Curly looked out to make certain he had heard right, and then hurried to dress himself for the feast. It was lucky he had not tried to hunt for the white buffalo or he would have missed this great time in the life of the pretty Oglala girl. He had not seen her very often the last few years, with all his visiting among the Brules and the Cheyennes. But she was always in his heart, as surely in a certain place as a warrior's weapons are, so even while sleeping he can grasp them at any strange thing in the night.

Curly had been a small boy when Black Buffalo Woman was born. He remembered it because the one he called mother had stayed back with a woman one day when her people were moving with them. Later the two came into camp with one who hadn't been with them before, a new little daughter for the brother of Red Cloud. Young Curly looked upon this small thing as somehow belonging to his own lodge, and when she got bigger he often stopped his playing to chase flies from her face as she swung in her cradleboard from a branch or leaned against the lodge while her mother scraped the hides. With the long spear of grass he used for playing he tickled the corners of her sober little mouth until she awoke and laughed, learning to look around for him with her round black eyes before she could make words. She had been one of the little girls in the ceremony when he was given the name of His Horse Looking, which no one used, although it was done with the parading through the village, the feasting, and the horses given away. Then there was the time he threw plums at the girl, his sister and brother teasing him about this, making him so warm and happy in his blanket. Since then he had been much away from the Oglalas, and often when he was home the Bad Face village of her people was not camped near. But the last year the girl had grown tall and was much alone. When the people were close together Curly sometimes loafed along the water path to walk a little with her, but the old woman of her lodge always chased him with such loud shouting and abuse that he ran, laughing much and pretending to be afraid. But sometimes it seemed the soft eyes of the girl sought him out, even in the daylight circle, where many were ready to see.

Now the old camp crier was running through the village announcing that the niece of Red Cloud had become a woman and that all the people were invited to visit her father's lodge. There was much excitement, much dressing up by the young men, much noisy moving down towards the lodge, for there would be feasting and ponies given away and a fine first woman-dress to see.

When Curly worked up through the crowd of men, women, and children, he found that the whole front of the lodge had been thrown open and behind the coals of ash wood, on a pile of robes, was Black Buffalo Woman. She was sitting in the woman's way, her feet to one side, and her hair smooth and shining, the part vermilioned, her slender young face too. Her dress was of white buckskin with a deep beaded yoke of blue, the wing sleeves and the bottom fringed, the leggings beaded too, and the moccasins. On her breast hung many strings of beads, blue, red, and yellow, and on her arms were bracelets of copper and silver. Beside the girl stood an old man of the village, shouting advice in a voice loud enough for all to hear, earning the good pony he would receive for his work. He spoke first of her duty to her father and her brothers, to honor them by bringing a strong man into their family and giving them good sons, to hear them in all things.

"A Bad Face is speaking," some of the women of the other bands whispered, laughing a little among themselves, remembering the troubles of the son of Smoke. But the old man had words for the other things, too, the old, old things that make a good Lakota woman—diligence, modesty, virtue, and the mother heart for the people.

"Follow Mother Earth in all things," he counseled. "See how she feeds her children, clothes and shelters them, comforts them with her good silence when their hearts have fallen down. Be like Mother Earth in all things and so be a good woman of the Lakota!"

Hou! the people agreed, while the girl sat with lowered eyes. Once she looked up and, seeing young Curly so near, her cheeks turned ruddy under the vermilion as she dropped her head.

When the talk was done and the people crowded around her to see the fine new clothes, the young men passing before her in their best regalia, Curly pushed his way out, not waiting for the feasting. At the lodge he threw himself upon his bed, buried his face in the wolfskin that was his pillow, and thought of things that filled his breast hard with strength and greatness.

The next day Curly and Crazy Horse rode off into the hills for a smoke. There he told his father of the white buffalo and the way that it was lost. A long time the holy man of the Oglalas sat silent.

"It seems there are many sacred things happening to you, my son," the father said. "It is hard to tell what they will bring, but it seems they will be good things if you work alone like the buffalo you saw and do not try to carry anything back for yourself."

The next day Hump led a party out to raid a small tribe of Indians said to be relatives of the Snakes, but speaking a changed tongue. The Oglalas knew little of them, for they had seldom camped as far west as the Wind River country but the scouts said they lived in grass houses, so they would not be a

fighting people like lodge Indians, and they had some very good
horses. The warriors were hot to try their hearts against these
strangers.

But the people of the unknown tongue evidently had
scouts out and long before the Lakota party reached their
houses their warriors started shooting from the top of a hill. It
was a good fighting place they had selected, high up, covered
with big rocks, and there seemed to be many guns among them.
Hump and his warriors circled the place several times, whooping, shooting under the necks of their horses, but it seemed
these people had seen such fighting before and did not waste
much powder on running horses so far away. Then Hump led
his warriors in a crawling up the hillside, but there was little to
hide behind and some good men might be lost before they got
into bow range, so they gave that up too, and tried charging a
few times and more circling, still hoping to waste all the enemy
powder.

It was a hard two-hour fight, the Lakotas losing some of
their horses and getting a man hurt. They killed one or two
men but couldn't drive the others from the rocks. Finally
Curly's horse went down, and as he jumped from it, he remembered his vision and, catching a loose one of the enemy, he got
on and was waiting for another circling when somebody behind
him fired a shot. The horse was young and wild and it charged
straight ahead, up the hill into the enemy. As in his vision he
rode light and safe through the arrows and bullets that flew all
around him making a wind past his bare breast, hitting stones
and spurting up gravel. Flat against his horse he managed to
draw his bow and drive an arrow into a warrior rising with a
gun from a gully before him. The man fell back, the horse
jumped him, and shying sideways from another one, swung off
down the hill. There was a great whooping over this strong
medicine from the Oglalas. Hump rode out to meet the boy,
but before the warrior reached him, Curly had turned the horse
and charged up the hill into the wall of shooting again. Once
more he got a man, this time with the revolver from his belt,
dropping him lower down in the gully, and as the whoop of

approval went up from the Lakotas, Curly's heart swelled. Forgetting all his vision, he slipped off to take the scalp, and the other man's too, in full sight of the enemy. Just as he ripped up the second lock he was hit in the leg, the wild horse jerked loose, and so he had to flee down the hill afoot, jumping this way and that, the ground and the bushes on both sides cut by the flying lead. The Oglala warriors were in a half circle watching this thing—those with guns firing at the enemies who looked from behind their rocks at the boy getting away through all their shooting.

Only when the boy was back among the others did he remember about the hair he held in his hand. He should not have taken it, and because he did he was wounded. So he threw it away and sat down behind a rock to stop the bleeding. Hump looped the scalps under his belt, cut the iron arrow from the boy's leg, and tied it tightly with a fresh piece of skin from a dead horse. It was enough for today, the warriors said, and leaving the enemies in the rocks they started home.

Outside of the village the party stopped and sent a man ahead to announce their return. Then they came in, the two shield men leading, their spears bright in the sun. Behind them came the warriors in rows four abreast, their weapons in their hands, the war-bonnet men in their feathers. And in the back was the boy the village knew as Curly, without paint or feathers, only a red-backed hawk in his hair and the small brown stone half hidden behind his ear.

That night there was a big victory dance, for they had killed four, counted eight first coups, got some good horses, and lost no man at all. One after another the deeds were told, the people cheering each man for what he had done. Only Curly would not tell of his exploits. Twice he was pushed forward into the circle and each time he backed out. So they went on to dance the scalps, the mother of Curly, the only woman with two on her staff, leading them. Many eyes were on the boy, seventeen now but still small among the warriors, many eyes that were friendly—Hump's and his father's proud, his brother's excited and adoring, and those of Black Buffalo Woman soft and no longer so shy. But there were some eyes that were envious of this light-haired one and these, too, young Curly could not forget.

That night the boy did not sleep. His leg pained very little in its wet bandage of herbs that his father had cooked in a stone bowl in the old way, touching no iron or other metal, but there were so many things to think about, particularly his forgetting about the scalps. What good was a strong vision to a man if he forgot it in the first fight?

The next morning he still felt bad and so he lay still on his side of the lodge, so still that even his brother thought him sleeping. As his people got up they went out quietly, and finally young Curly slept. When the sun stood almost straight up, he awoke and was given a horn spoon of soup. Then Crazy Horse came in and took his ceremonial blanket from its case, the one with the beaded band across the middle showing all the sacred things of his holy vision. With this blanket about him, his braids long and fur-wrapped on his breast, the father walked slowly through the village, making a song as he went, singing it so all might hear:

> My son has been against the people of unknown tongue.
> He has done a brave thing;
> For this I give him a new name, the name of his father,
> and of many fathers before him—
> I give him a great name
> I call him Crazy Horse.

And behind the father came all those of the village who wished to honor the young man among them who had done a brave deed. By the time they came to the lodge where the boy sat, there was a mighty double line of the people until it seemed that everybody was walking in it: young men, old men, great men, wise ones, and all the women and the children too, all singing and laughing.

Then there was feasting and dancing all that day and late into the night, for among the Oglalas there was a new warrior, a warrior to be known by the great name of Crazy Horse.

SITTING ON THE
WHITE MAN'S ISLAND

Crazy Horse's puberty dreaming told him he should always be plain and modest, not wearing paint or warbonnet, not dancing or singing or lifting his voice in council. He took a vow of selfless dedication to the people: their good must always come first. Once he broke this vow, when he ran away with another man's wife; but he gave the woman back and after that he kept the people first. Crazy Horse became a great war leader, first in fights with other Indian tribes and later in battles against the white soldiers, reaching a high point in the defeat of Custer and the Seventh Cavalry at the Little Big Horn. But a few months later his warriors lost to the troops under General Miles in the Wolf Mountain fight. When he decided that further resistance was hopeless, Crazy Horse led his people to Fort Robinson in search of peace with honor, General Crook having promised them an agency in their own country. . . .

MAY, the Moon of Shedding Ponies, lay spring-warm over the plains of the upper White Earth River and the bluffs that rose here and there like walls against the wind. On a bank above the timbered little path of the stream was the stockade of Red Cloud agency, where the father of the Oglalas lived and kept their goods locked inside the high walls that nobody could climb. A mile westward was the soldier town called Fort Robinson; to the east, rising alone beyond the greening slopes of the broad river valley, stood Crow Butte; and across the north stretched a row of the whitish bluffs with a straggling of pines along the top, the Indian horsemen among them dark and motionless as the trees. Scattered over the rolling ground about the agency and the fort were more Indians, thousands of them, sitting together in little bunches like chewing buffaloes or slouching on their horses, waiting, watching the bluffs for the circling signal of many people coming.

When the sun had passed over the head awhile there was a movement on the bluffs, and a stirring among the people below, not much, for the Indian police in the blue soldier coats were among them, to hold them back. Then, far up where the lodge trail dipped into the valley, riders came into sight against the sky. As they wound down towards the fort, the watching ones saw that the little soldier chief, Clark, called White Hat, was in front. With him were Red Cloud and his headmen and some horse soldiers too. Then there was a long empty place with only dust in it, and behind that came the one the Oglalas called their Strange Man, and to see him the people pushed forward.

When he came closer those who had not known him made surprised words to one another. He was a small man for a fighter, less than six of the white man's feet, and slim as a young warrior. But they knew it was Crazy Horse, for he wore no paint and nothing to show his greatness. One feather stood alone at the back of his head, and his brown, fur-wrapped braids hung long over a plain buckskin shirt, his Winchester in a scabbard at his knee. Beside him, making a straight row, in paint, war bonnets, and fringed buckskin, rode his headmen, Little Hawk, Big Road, He Dog, and Little Big Man strong among them. Behind these came the warriors and then the people, reaching clear back to the bluffs and out upon the highland, men and women and children, with travois and bundles and horses and the dogs of the agency Indians.

At the little army post everybody was out to see this wild war leader who had scared the whites so many years, who whipped two of their big soldier chiefs, Crook and Custer, in eight days—to see him give up his gun and his horse and become a coffee-cooler like the rest. But there was one among the watching soldier chiefs who was not pleased with what the farseeing glasses he held to his face told him. "By God!" he said to those around him. "This is a triumphal march, not a surrender!"

And as the warriors neared the little fort, with all its bluecoated soldiers out, they began to sing, the women and children behind them taking it up, carrying it back through the line, until all the broad valley of the White Earth and the bluffs that stood against the northern sky were filled with the chanting of the peace song of the Lakotas.

Slowly the Indians moved down past the fort, the painted warriors with their weapons, the women with the beaded saddle hangings, the travois baskets of children, the lodge drags, and the horse herds. So the people followed their man past the fort, around the agency, and out upon a wide, flat place that had been kept clear of watchers, all the Indian scouts who had gone north to see the hostiles in standing rows on their horses along the side, as if waiting. Here White Hat stopped, and while many of the friendlies pushed up close, No Water and Woman's Dress and his brothers in the front, the bad thing began to happen, the horses and arms were taken.

First it was the horses. They were counted, seventeen hundred of them, and turned over to the waiting Indian scouts, and now Crazy Horse and all his people saw why they had so many good friends on the agency willing to come north through the snows of the winter to bring them in. Even men like Young Man Afraid and Sword led away the war horses of their friends and the pack mares of the women when the soldiers gave them.

And while this was done those watching Red Cloud saw that his face was motionless, his eyes looking straight before him, but they knew he must be remembering the day only a few months ago when he, a long time agency chief, was so dismounted, his chieftainship taken from him, and his heart made dark for a long, long time.

When the horses were gone the lodges were pitched in the usual circle camp, round as all the sacred things are round, with the opening towards the rising sun. Then there was the counting of the people, one hundred and forty-five lodges, two hundred and seventeen grown men, eight hundred and eighty-nine

people all together, not counting those with stronger ponies
who had come in ahead, or those who had preferred to live under Spotted Tail, as did Touch the Clouds and even Worm, the
father of Crazy Horse.

When the counting was finished, White Hat made a little
talking through Billy Garnett and the Grabber, saying he would
now take the arms, all the arms. First he went to Crazy Horse
and his uncle Little Hawk. When the others saw this done so
quietly, they laid their guns down too. A few of the men did
try to hold something back, but the friendlies who were with
them from the headwaters of the Powder had been watching
and spoke out. So one hundred and seventeen pieces were
taken, revolvers, muzzle-loaders, rifles, cavalry carbines, and a
few Winchesters. Some laid sticks on the ground, saying:
"Friend, this is my gun and this short one my pistol. Send to
my lodge to get them."

It was hard, but the people let it be done with good face,
the two interpreters making the words, and when they didn't
please White Hat, who understood a little Lakota, he made it
good with the sign-talking he knew.

As soon as he could get away, Crazy Horse went to his
lodge. While the women bent over the cooking fires in the
warm evening outside and visited with their relatives who came
with presents for the kettle, the bowl, and the pan, he sat alone
in his place, the little pipe cold in his palm. Now it was done
he had to look back as a man who is still wet from crossing a
dangerous river looks back to his own country left behind forever for a new one that seems cold and bare and strange.

*Months passed and Crazy Horse grew restive, with no progress
being made in getting the agency promised his people. The white
officers who became acquainted with him learned to like and
respect the light-skinned chief, but there was grumbling among
some of the Indians at the rumor the whites planned to make
Crazy Horse a big chief over everybody, Brules as well as Oglalas.
Clark, the officer the Indians called White Hat, arranged for the*

pretty young daughter of a half-breed trader to go into Crazy Horse's lodge, thinking this would take the Oglala's mind off his grievances.

Crazy Horse lived as far as he could from the whites, the whole three miles from the agency, with the other northern Oglalas around him and some from the other camps, too. As the moon began to fatten towards sundance time, almost everybody else, including the breeds and whites, moved down with their tents and covered wagons to watch this ceremonial done in the old-time way by the northern people.

Crazy Horse knew why they came but he made them welcome, the *akicita* showing the people where to camp for water, wood, and grass. When the time came all the Indian lodges were moved into a great circle, set very close together, and yet making a camp over two miles long. In the center stood the holy pole with its smooth dance place and the sun shelter of new-cut pines all around the outside. White Hat was there to see everything, watching the pole selected and carried in, and the warriors from all the camp charge the man-monument that was made as nearly like a man as could be in all its parts, the one striking it first to be the strongest against the enemy all the year. They made a great running for it, even though there was no enemy left that they might fight.

Next there was the play battle, this time the fight on the Little Big Horn, with the Crazy Horse warriors taking the part of the Indians, the friendlies and some of the traders' sons being Long Hair's soldiers. But when the fighting started the blood of the warriors ran too hot and instead of using the bows just for touching, they cried "Hoka hey!" and struck hard or even grabbed up the war clubs from their belts. So the scouts and traders' sons fired with their revolvers and drove the unarmed Indians from the dancing camp. But they got some guns and came charging back, and now there was real shooting, the women crying out as the sides pushed together. If one man was hit to fall, it would be a bloody fight. White Hat saw this and galloped in to stop his scouts, but the fighting was done before

he got there. Crazy Horse had ridden into the place of smoke
and bullets between the two sides and, holding his hand up in
the peace sign, cried: "Friends! You are shooting your own
people!"

Everything stopped, the air still as before lightning, the
people not seeming to breathe, afraid a bullet might find the
man of the Oglalas, for there were surely some who would
shoot if they thought no one could say who it was, afraid only
that the Crazy Horse people would tear them to pieces as the
angry grizzly does the rabbit that gets in his way.

The rest of the dance went on as always, some making the
sun-gazing, some dancing with the tongs from the top of the
holy pole tied through the bloody breast, others dragging the
buffalo skulls from rawhide ropes fastened through the back
muscles until they tore loose. The whites watched these things,
their faces excited or pale according to their nature, but seeing
everything, White Hat speaking often of the following the warriors gave Crazy Horse and his power not only over the hostiles,
but over the young men of the friendlies when they were war-
heated. It beat anything the soldier chief had ever seen, he said,
some noticing that his mouth was sour as from green plums as
he spoke, for it seemed he would like to call the young men his
own.

Crazy Horse never was much to watch the dancing, besides, there was a new woman in his lodge, the eighteen-year-old
daughter of Joe Larrabee. She was pretty, one of the prettiest of
the traders' daughters, and Long Joe had hoped to make a better marriage for her, not just a few ponies.

"Wait, if things come out right, you will be well paid,"
White Hat had promised him.

And as soon as Long Joe had the ponies, Crazy Horse carried the girl off on his pinto. It was said the wives of the soldier
chiefs liked this way very much, and came riding towards the
northern camps more than ever, hoping to see the great war
chief and his young second wife.

It caused much talking over the beadwork and the plum-pit
games, or in the line waiting for the weekly issue of rations—

wherever the women gathered. Some of the northern Oglalas thought Crazy Horse should have taken a wife from his own people, at least an Indian. But the friendlies said not many of the flower-pattern women, the traders' daughters, married full bloods until they were old and thrown away. They thought Crazy Horse had been honored.

"Hoh!" the northern women cried in astonishment at this foolish talking. There were many traders' daughters, but only one Crazy Horse on all the earth.

Some of the Indians looked at this thing done as the bait of a dead-fall swallowed, thinking there must be something secret to this, with the agents and other whites always talking against the second wives, wanting them thrown away, a thing the older people had found hard to understand. And now a soldier chief himself planned it for Crazy Horse to take another wife into his lodge. It was the girl who told these things. She liked to visit and talk. Long Joe, too, had the busy and complaining tongue.

"Another woman to take his heart from the people, when they are needing him—" Little Hawk said to Worm in the lodge carefully darkened so none could know that he had left Red Cloud agency without permission.

"Ahh-h, it is a little thing, and if it gives him even a short time of joy—there may not be much more for the Strange One," the father said, speaking slowly. And Little Hawk, remembering the holy medicine of his brother, made no more words of his uneasiness.

But nothing of this seemed to touch the lodge of Crazy Horse. With more resting for Black Shawl, no meat to make here, no skins and robes to tan, no lodges to strike for fleeing over the snow, and with the good white man's medicine, her face, bent over the beadwork with her friends, was rounding once more, as a Lakota woman's should be. Under the pine-branch shelter beside the lodge Crazy Horse listened to his new wife talk of the white-man things she knew and the news she brought back from her visits with her people, from the trading store or the dances, for as a Lakota wife she was free to go where she liked.

Sometimes she brought back the white-man newspapers,

with stories of the iron road, the railroad, wanting to give the people running it less pay-money, and when they would not have this done, the soldiers shooting the strikers. Truly the whites were hungry for killing to be making war on their own people all the time, Crazy Horse thought.

A RED BLANKET

OF HIS OWN

General Crook pleased Crazy Horse's people with an announcement that they would be allowed to go north on a forty-day buffalo hunt but the plan was abandoned after Red Cloud and other friendlies insisted that the hunters never would return. Words mistranslated by an interpreter in council alarmed the army officers, making it appear that Crazy Horse was talking war against the whites. A false report convinced Crook that the Oglala planned an uprising, and he ordered that Crazy Horse be taken into custody. Crazy Horse fled to the Spotted Tail agency, asking that his people be allowed to stay there pending the establishment of an agency of their own. Major Lee, convinced of the Oglala's good faith, persuaded Crazy Horse to return to Fort Robinson, promising that he would intercede with the officers there on the Oglala's behalf.

As THEY REACHED the fort, He Dog came loping up, bareback, his war bonnet slapped hastily on his head. He pulled up beside Crazy Horse, shook hands with him and saw that he did not look right today, not as in those days of war when his medicine was very strong, but they rode with their horses together once more, their leggings touching, and Crazy Horse knew the anger between them was gone.

At the fort Little Big Man came walking important as the Indian police and, jerking Crazy Horse by the arm, said: "Come along, you man of no-fight. You are a coward!" The Oglala let it be said and went into an office with those from the ambulance. By now the open spaces between the buildings of the fort were filled with Indians, on one side the few who were still Crazy Horse warriors, on the other the agency scouts, with Red Cloud and American Horse at their heads, while all around them, clear back over the plain, were more Indians and horses and wagons hurrying in, making a rising noise like blood-smelling buffalo. But nowhere around was Woman's Dress, or the Grabber or White Hat or any of the others who had said so hard that Crazy Horse must be captured, nor was Spotted Tail there, although hundreds of Brules had come the long road.

While Crazy Horse and the others waited, Lee went to General Bradley. He told the officer of the wrong he believed had been done to the man of the Oglalas, and the promise he and Burke, the agent, had made that Crazy Horse should be heard, but Bradley said nothing could be done any more.

Nothing? Then it was really very bad?

Yes, the general agreed, very bad. Not even Crook could change the orders they had received. Not a hair of the chief's head would be harmed, but he must now be turned over to the officer of the day. "Say to him it is too late to have a talk."

So Major Lee put on a good face and came to Crazy Horse, telling him that night was almost here and General Bradley said it was too late for talking, but he should go with the little soldier chief and he would not be harmed.

"Hou!" the Indians said, and arose, Crazy Horse the last among them. But he shook friendly hands with the officer and went away with him, Little Big Man on the other side, two soldiers behind, some of the agency Indians hurrying ahead, seeming to know where to go. As they crossed to another building the warriors and the scouts pushing in on both sides raised a noise that became a roaring, and under it sounded the click of guns made ready to shoot.

Quietly, his blanket folded over his arm as though he were going to his lodge between two friends, Crazy Horse let himself be taken past a soldier walking up and down with a bayoneted gun on his shoulder and in through a door. Only then did he see the barred windows, the men with chains on their legs, and realize it was the iron house. Like a grizzly feeling the deadfall on his neck, the Indian jumped back, drawing the hidden gift knife to strike out around him, but Little Big Man grabbed his arms from behind. Trying to wrench free, Crazy Horse struggled into the open, dragging the stocky Indian through the door, his warriors crying out the warning: "He is holding the arms, the arms!" while on the other side the scouts raised their guns, Red Cloud and American Horse ordering: "Shoot in the middle; shoot to kill!" the officer of the day knocking the scout guns down with his sword as fast as they came up.

And between them the Indian, like a trapped animal, was heaving, plunging to get free, growling: "Let me go! Let me go!" as the angry bear growls, the knife flashing in the late sun. Then with a mighty jerk he threw himself sideways and Little Big Man had to drop one hand, blood running from a slash across his arm. But Swift Bear and other old Brule friendlies already had Crazy Horse, held him while the officer of the day tried to use his sword against him, yelling: "Stab him! Kill the son of a bitch!"

The guard came running up, lunged with his bayonet and, hitting the door, jerked the weapon free and lunged twice more. At the redness of the steel a noise of alarm, of warning rose from the watching Indians. Crazy Horse pulled at his old captors once more. "Let me go, my friends," he panted. "You have got me hurt enough."

And at these soft words all the Indians suddenly dropped their hands from him as though very much afraid. Released, Crazy Horse staggered backward, turned half around, and sank to the ground, his shirt and leggings already wet and blood-darkened.

So the people sat around their darkened lodges, wandering in their minds like buffalo who have lost their leader. Of them

all only He Dog had seen the man since he sank down into the
dust before the guardhouse, with his warriors on one side,
armed mostly with war clubs, and across from them the many
agency scouts holding their soldier rifles, loaded with the ammunition issued today for the attack. And no one was running
in to carry away the wounded man between them, not one of
the dozen there who had been helped from the battlefield by
him.

Before this, and before the shame of his own weakness, He
Dog stood bowed a long time, his head down in sorrow, and
when he could look again, he saw that all the Indians had fallen
back and many, many soldiers had come up all around him,
guns in their hands, their eyes in anger upon him. With his red
agency blanket around him, the man waited, motionless, for
whatever was to come.

Finally White Hat ran up from somewhere, saying he
might go to Crazy Horse, and so He Dog went to the wounded
man with the knife lying in the dust beside him and the dark
patch of his blood that reflected the sacred sky. Stooping to
speak, he saw that the Oglala was bad hurt and so he laid his
red blanket over him and with arms folded stood at the feet of
his friend.

Then Touch the Clouds came wading through the soldiers,
parting them before him like grass with the barrel of his gun.
He, too, saw how it was and waited beside He Dog for the army
medicine man. And when the doctor was there, pulling the
blood-soaked shirt from the wounds, one deep through the kid-
ney, he looked to the two friends and made no word. So Touch
the Clouds went to ask that the chief might be taken to a lodge
of his people to die, but this, too, Bradley refused, not believing
the doctor's word that the hurt was a bad one, but saying he
could be put into the adjutant's office instead of the guardhouse.
And when Touch the Clouds asked permission to stay with his
cousin-friend, he was told he must give up his gun.

Quietly the tall Minneconjou looked down upon the white-
man soldier. "You are many and I am only one, but I will trust
you," he said.

Then they carried the wounded man to the place where he

now lay, in the kerosene-lighted room under the red blanket on
the floor, with only Touch the Clouds permitted to sit with
him. Several times the white medicine man came with the sleeping water that quieted his moving and the low growling to the
enemies Crazy Horse thought were about him. But none of
them were there, and none of those who came to his lodge all
the summer, talking this way and that, turning his face in as
many directions as a *heyoka* dancer. The agent had not come to
him, or White Hat or Bradley and Randall, or Three Stars,
who was far away, getting ready to set up new forts in that
north country and to make a hunt for himself, a hunt for buffalo and elk and big-horn sheep.

As the night lengthened, the stars turned towards midnight,
and there was still no good sign to the watchers, no sign at all,
many of the northern people lost their ears for the stories of
hope and sat silent and dark in their blankets. Some of the
women began to keen a little to themselves, afraid, for it was
well known that their Strange Man could never be hurt by an
enemy except when his arms were held, as the time that No
Water shot him, and today—the arms always held by Little Big
Man.

In the soldier house Touch the Clouds still sat beside the
wounded man on the floor, with Worm there too now, his
wrinkled old face half-covered with his blanket. When the father first came for permission to go to his son, the soldier chiefs
asked for his bow and his knife. He knew why it was done but
he gave them up without protest, for they would indeed be poor
weapons to meet the sorrows of this day. Never could there be
a gun strong enough or whites enough to kill if Crazy Horse
died, never enough whites on all the earth to kill to make the
heart of a father good for such a son gone.

And when Worm was brought to the bare, dusky room
where Touch the Clouds was watching, he stooped over the
wounded man, saying, "Son, I am here—"

But there was only the slow, heavy breathing of the medicine sleep and the feet of the soldier guard outside, walking up
and down on the gravel, turning his face away from the shadow
huddled against the wall, a shadow such as young Curly had

once seen when another Lakota woman, the wife of Conquering Bear, watched the place of her wounded man.

So the night grew old and the fading moon arose, bringing a coldness into the soldier house. Gradually the breathing of the sleeping man changed. Once or twice he stirred a little and each time Worm stooped over him, but there was nothing. Then, slowly the eyes of the wounded warrior opened, moved guardedly over the strange room of his enemies.

"I am here," Worm said.

Now the son saw him. "Ahh-h, my father," he whispered. "I am bad hurt. Tell the people it is no use to depend on me any more now—"

For a while it seemed he would say more, then slowly his head seemed to settle back, the eyes opened wide, and one long brown braid slid to the floor. Gently Touch the Clouds replaced it, holding it on the breast of his friend with his strong hand. And in the yellow light of the lamp the two men wept, the tears like rain washing over live rocks, rocks in that old north country of the Powder and the Yellowstone, for the Strange Man of the Oglalas was dead.

from CHEYENNE AUTUMN

Gone Before

The Ordeal Begins

This Remnant

In the Aftertime

GONE BEFORE

EARLY IN THE SPRING of 1877 nearly a thousand hungry and half-naked Northern Cheyennes came in from the Yellowstone country to Red Cloud Agency in northwest Nebraska. They surrendered to the promise of food and shelter and an agency in their hunting region. But almost before the children were warmed on both sides, they were told they must go to Indian Territory,* the far south country many already knew and hated. The two Old Man Chiefs, as the tribal heads were called, listened to this command in silent refusal, but some lesser men shouted the *"Hou!"* of agreement almost before the white men got their mouths open. These Indians were given horses and fine blue blankets, and the meat and coffee and tobacco for a big feast that would build their power and following in the tribe.

"It is a trick of the spider," the chiefs protested. "The *veho*† has long spun his web for the feet of those who have wings but are too foolish to fly. . . ."

Yet even after the feasting there were barely as many as one has fingers who wanted to go south, so the Indian agent an-

* Now the state of Oklahoma.
† Cheyenne word for spider, and after the white man's coming, for him also.

77

nounced that he would issue no more rations to the Cheyennes here. While the Sioux women moved in their long line, holding their blankets out to receive their goods, the Cheyennes were kept off on a little knoll, their ragged blankets flapping empty in the wind, the children silent and big-eyed, watching.

Then Little Wolf and Dull Knife were told by the coaxing interpreters that the officials had said, "Just go down to see. If you don't like it you can come back. . . ." Finally they agreed, for meat for the kettles, and so, with blue-coated troopers riding ahead and behind, they pointed their moccasins down through Nebraska and Kansas toward their southern relatives who were already hungry.

The chiefs rode ahead, old Dull Knife on his yellow and white spotted horse, Little Wolf beside him on a strong, shaggy black with patches white as winter snow. At the ridge south of the agency the Indians stopped, in spite of all the urging against it, looking back toward the country that had fed and sheltered them long before one white man's track shadowed the buffalo grass. The women keened as for death, and water ran down the dark, stony faces of old Dull Knife and the rest.

It wasn't that these Cheyennes had not seen years ago that their hunting life must pass as certainly as summer died. Back in 1846, Little Wolf heard his cousin Yellow Wolf say that the buffalo was angered by the chasing with gun and bullet and by his carcasses left to rot on the prairie, and so was turning back to the place of his coming, leaving the Indian to die. Yellow Wolf spoke of this before an army officer at Bent's Fort, earnestly offering to hire a man to build the Indians a fort too, and teach them to plow the earth and grow cattle to eat. The soldier chief listened, but the wind of laughter from Bent and many of the Indians blew the words away, and when Yellow Wolf, the prophet and man of peace, was shot down at Sand Creek almost twenty years later, nothing had been done.

Through Little Wolf's boyhood the Cheyennes had been very friendly to all the whites except those of the whisky wagons that carried the brown water of violence and death. In those days these Indians ranged as far southwest as the Staked Plains of Texas, but mostly they still returned to the traders of the Platte River and up toward the Black Hills. Then, by 1832, William Bent established a trading post on the upper Arkansas River and married a Cheyenne woman. After that her relatives and their adherents no longer made the long journey by pony drag to the northern traders.

All this time more and more blue-coated troopers came riding, and the emigrants began to run on the trails like dark strings of ants hurrying before the winter, bringing strange sicknesses, eating up the grass of the pony herds, killing the buffalo until the wind stank and the bleaching bones lay white as morning frost on the valleys of the Platte and the Arkansas.

The leaders of those who still traded around the Overland Trail, like Dull Knife, had held the angry young men from attack, but the pockmarked face of Little Wolf grew dark as any in the hooding blanket of the warriors as they watched the white man come. The Cheyennes were famous for their reckless war charges, their pony herds like clouds over the hills, their painted villages, and their regalia and trappings that were as handsome as their country under the October sun. They had been a rather small tribe even before the new diseases scattered their dead over the prairie, but while no one owned the earth and the buffalo herds, any people who fought well and worked to keep the parfleches full of meat could live.

As more hungry Indians were pushed westward and the encroaching whites grabbed the earth in their hands, the Cheyennes of the north began to move closer to the powerful Sioux. With bold warriors and handsome straight-walking women among both peoples, there was considerable intermarriage. Warrior societies like the Dog Soldiers set up lodges in both tribes and often fought their red enemies together. Then, in 1851, the whites called a great conference at Fort Laramie to bring peace forever to the land west of the Missouri, with wagon trains of goods to pay for the emigrant trails and for giving up the glories of the warpath. More goods would keep coming, and government agencies would be established, with an agent, a Little Father, perhaps to live there much of the year to

enforce the treaty on the Indians and to distribute the annuities. The agency for the Southern Cheyennes, as the whites
called them now, was at Bent's fort, but the Northern Cheyennes had to go to the Sioux agency far up the Platte.

The first big break in the peace came three years later from
the whites themselves. A few whisky-smelling soldiers under
Grattan killed the leading chief of the Sioux with a cannon. It
was after this that the Cheyenne chiefs showed their first real
anger in the government council. They wanted no more
drunken soldiers shooting into peaceful camps, or emigrants
scaring their buffalo. It was then that one spoke of something
new, so quietly that his soft Cheyenne was barely to be heard.
"We want a thousand white women as wives," he said, "to teach
us and our children the new life that must be lived when the
buffalo is gone. . . ."

The chiefs saw the bearded dignity of the white men break
into anger at this. Plainly they did not understand that the children of Cheyennes belong to the mother's people and that this
was a desperate measure to assure the food and the survival of
their descendants, although in a few generations there might be
not one left to be called Cheyenne anywhere under the blue kettle of the sky.

The white women did not come, and the Indians received
little or nothing of the treaty goods for the lands and privileges
they had sold. In 1856, some restless young men went to beg a
little tobacco at the Oregon trail and got bullets instead. They
fired arrows back, hit a man in the arm, and troops came shooting. For months General Sumner chased them around their
south country. Angry that they got away, he went to Bent's fort,
where Yellow Wolf was waiting peacefully for his treaty goods
stored in the fort. Sumner took what he wanted for his troops
and gave the rest to the Arapahos while the Wolf's young men
had to look on, their empty fingers creeping toward the trigger.
But their women and children were surrounded by troops like
those who had killed Little Thunder's peaceful Sioux on the
Platte last summer, so the chiefs fled with their people up beyond the North Platte, where their relatives lived in peace.

Little Wolf had watched them come, and a spark of anger to smolder a lifetime was lit in his breast. He had never heard of Cheyennes running from anybody, but he lived to see it again, for this was only the first of many times.

Perhaps because the tribe seemed too few to make much trouble, they got very little of their treaty goods, and never an agency of their own. The chiefs had even been to Washington, where Little Wolf smelled the hated whisky on the general who was the Great Father, and yet they had to beg him to pity their hungry children. But his promises were like the others—no more than the shimmering mirage lakes on the summer horizon.

For most of the twenty years since that first flight north, the Cheyennes had tried to keep peaceful, but repeatedly starvation drove them out to the shrinking buffalo herds, up north to the roving Sioux, in the south to the Kiowas and the Comanches. Everywhere their strong warriors were welcomed. Yet when the Army was sent to punish Indians for making trouble, there seemed always a camp of peaceful Cheyennes near, where some agent had told them was a safe place to go. So Chivington had found them at Sand Creek in 1864, Custer on the Washita in 1868, and who could say how many times more?

By 1876, Little Wolf, long a peace man, and Dull Knife, who had worked for peace half his life, were starved off the hungry Sioux agency of Red Cloud once more. They slipped away north for their treaty-given summer hunt. Most of them were too late for the Custer battle but not for the soldiers who came chasing the Crazy Horse Sioux afterward, driving the Indians indiscriminately over their snow-covered treaty grounds with cavalry and cannon. In one of the fights Dull Knife lost three warriors from his family and Little Wolf got six wounds. Constantly fleeing, they could not hunt the few buffaloes left, and so to save their people, they surrendered while some of the strong young men still lived, and the fine young women like the daughters of Dull Knife and the Pretty Walker of Little Wolf. They came in on the good promise of friendship and peace, of plenty of food, warm clothing, and a reservation in their own country, with wagons and plows, and the cattle they had wanted so long.

But instead they were dismounted and disarmed, except for a few guns they managed to hide, and now, with blankets drawn in sorrow to the eyes, they had to start far south, the 980 Indians going quietly, morosely, mostly afoot. Seventy days later 937 arrived at the Cheyenne and Arapahoe Agency in the Territory, and no one mentioned the missing who had slipped back northward along the road, some perhaps left dead by the pursuing soldiers.

There had been a little trouble on the way. It was after they saw that the buffalo trails through their old hunting grounds were edged with sunflowers. Bleaching bones lay all around, the ribs standing naked as the wagon bows of the settlers who drove their shining plows where the great dark herds had grazed even two years ago. Then one day a leader among the women was found hanging from a cottonwood, a noose made of her long braids.

Lieutenant Lawton came to see about the women keening as for a warrior dead. "Our sister had three husbands, all famous chiefs," the wife of Little Wolf told him. "One after the other was lost to the soldiers, the last in the Custer fighting. Now the same bluecoats are riding around us here, and just ahead is the place where many of her relatives died from their guns."

When the long string of Indians reached the Sappa Creek where the Cheyennes were killed under a white flag of surrender two years ago, the warriors stopped, their faces covered with the blankets of sorrow and anger. Men who were crippled here or compelled to leave their dead harangued for a fight, and when the lieutenant galloped back to see, he was surrounded by stripped and painted warriors, singing, ready to die empty-handed. They jerked away his pistol and were knocking him off his horse when the angry Little Wolf charged in, striking to both sides with his fork-tailed pony whip.

"Will you have all the helpless people here killed?" he roared out. "Your hearts are as empty as your hands. This is not the time!"

The warriors broke before the chief's fury, the officer escaped, and the ringleaders were put into irons and thrown on the supply wagons. But their followers slipped away in the night.

On the North Fork of the Canadian the chiefs were led to the wide agency bottoms, the earth already worn bare by too many Indians. The soldiers set up their tents close by to watch. That night the Southern Cheyennes made the customary feast for the newcomers, with a small circle for the headmen, and for others farther out—such a thin feast as Little Wolf had never seen before. Plainly the people here were very poor with no horses or guns allowed them.

"Ahh-h, game is very scarce for the bow," the agency chief Little Robe said meaningfully. "But hungry men have good eyes and the fast moccasin, is it not true, my friends?"

Dull Knife and Little Wolf and the rest looked down into the water soup of their bowls, as their warrior sons and wives did in other circles. It was an embarrassment to eat from the kettles of the hungry, and hard to pretend the great appetite that was good manners. But the northerners would not stay to divide the little of this poor country. They would go back immediately, where there was game, good water, tolerable heat, and clean air. They said this over their moving eagle-wing fans, sitting in grass smoke that burned the eyes but kept some of the swarming mosquitoes away.

Later Little Robe carried these words to the agency, and a light bloomed in a window there until morning. Then Standing Elk was sent for, the Elk who had said *"Hou!"* to coming south. As Little Wolf watched him go, he pressed his arm against the sacred bundle of chieftainship under his shirt, the bundle that made him keeper of the people. Trouble had already begun, and so with Dull Knife he went to tell the agent that they did not like anything here and were starting home right away, before the snows fell on the Yellowstone.

But the Quaker agent said they could not go. He was a man of peace, but if the Indians left, the soldiers would whip them back.

Soon a cold wind blew up between the younger Indians too.

The newcomers were full of stories of the fighting up north only a few moons ago, some from the killing of Custer, the man who had left the southern chiefs dead down here on the Washita in 1868. They showed a few Custer trophies, even a carbine that had been hidden under a woman's skirts all the way through the disarming and the road here.

The southern chiefs moved their turkey-wing fans. Killing the Long Hair Custer was a strong thing, they said, even though he was a relative to some here, the man who took their Monah-setah as wife and became the father of her son, the Yellow Swallow.

Many listening ones drew in their breath and wished to ask more about this Custer son, but the southern faces seemed turned away, and soon the tauntings against them as agency sitters came out bold as spring snakes when the rocks grow warm. So Little Wolf and the others tried to talk of the old-time victories against Pawnee and Kiowa and Comanche, where no southerner need look bad-faced. But his younger men talked of the soldier victories over these tame southern relatives, victories which ended with the survivors always running north for refuge. Finally an agency sitter matched their rudeness. Was it not, he asked, the wise and wily old Dull Knife himself who let his village be destroyed last winter?

"Ahh-h, yes, but the soldiers were led by Cheyenne scouts, our own relatives," one of the northern warriors defended.

"Relatives of the Sioux led soldiers against them the same way, but Crazy Horse was never caught!"

So it went, Dull Knife sitting, a silent gray rock in his blanket, the angry words washing over him as he remembered all those left with their faces turned up to the cold winter light that morning on the fork of the Powder.* It was Old Bear and the blunt, outspoken Hog who finally answered the southerners. Everybody knew soldiers were close that time. The horses were saddled for flight, the lodges coming down fast under the direction of Little Wolf's Elks. But some Fox soldiers brought in two Crow scalps and demanded that a dance be made. Last Bull, their warrior society little chief, had the cinches of the

* Mackenzie attack on Dull Knife village, November 25, 1876.

saddles cut, the goods scattered—a small, stubborn man feeling big that he could do this because none must shed Cheyenne blood, even to stop him. So Last Bull held the people for a late dancing, and at dawn the soldiers struck. That could not have happened when the Cheyennes were a larger people. "But now we must make the war leader too big a man, bigger than our oath-bound Old Man Chiefs or our wise and holy men. And still they have not saved us. Today we are only a crumbling sand bar in the spring Platte, with the flood waters rising all around. . . ."

In two months the newcomers were even fewer. Seventy had died of the measles and of the starvation that was everywhere except in the lodges of the agency yes-sayers like Standing Elk, whose women walked proud and plump in their new dresses. General Pope wrote to Washington, asking that the Cheyenne issues be increased to cover the new people from the north. It was important, "both in view of the safety of this new frontier and in the interest of humanity and fair dealing that all these Indians be far better fed than they are now or have been."

Nothing was done except that the agent complained against rising beef prices, cuts in appropriations, and grafting contractors. The winter was the worst Little Wolf had ever seen, with the coughing sickness in the hungry lodges and nothing for the idle hands. So the Cheyennes took on the white man's quarreling ways. Some even whipped their women and children, a shocking, paleface thing to do. Families were broken, men threw away the mothers of their children, wives slipped out the side of the lodge at night, daughters hung up their chastity ropes and became the pay women of the soldiers, a thing never seen before among these people, whose women General Crook called the most chaste he had known. And always the soldier guns were there, long shadows across the moccasin toe. Yet many young southerners were drawn to the camp of the visitors.

Then Little Wolf heard that Crazy Horse was killed up at Fort Robinson. He carried the news like gall in the mouth to Dull Knife's lodge. Their friend had led the roaming Sioux of the Powder and Yellowstone country since Red Cloud moved to the agency eight years ago. A fiercely brave man with the simple ways of his fathers, who were holy men, many Cheyennes had gladly fought beside him. Later some joined him against the whites too, the time Fetterman was destroyed, in 1866, and when he whipped General Crook on the Rosebud and the next week cut off the retreat of Custer on the Little Big Horn. But with the buffalo going he came to the agency under the same promise given the Cheyennes: food, safety, and an agency for his people. Now he was dead, killed by a soldier in an attempt to take him away to a Florida prison because some agency Indians were jealous and lied about him.

Dull Knife sat bleak-faced. Here, too, the agency chief was jealous because his young warriors strayed, and men like Standing Elk were hot to be Old Man Chiefs. But for that Little Wolf and the Knife would have to be sent away or, like Crazy Horse, die.

So the chiefs went to the agent. "You are a good man," the Wolf said. "You can see that in this small hungry place we must stand on the moccasins of our brothers. Let us go before something bad happens."

First the agent tried to content the Wolf with a pretty southern girl for his bed. The chief refused, but the girl was sent anyway, and turned out to be his fifteen-year-old granddaughter through the wife of his youth who had died of cholera. Next the agent tried making policemen of some Southern Cheyennes just back from prison for causing trouble in 1874. Fifteen of them were given soldier coats and guns and set to walk the angry village. But no Cheyenne could take the life of a fellow tribesman, even in self-defense, so the agent gave the jobs to the Arapahos, old-time allies of the Cheyennes, who, like the whites, could kill anybody.

Summer brought Indian trouble all through the West. The Northern Cheyennes were shaking with malaria, and there was none of the bitter white powder the agent had promised. There was dysentery too, and very little food, but they were not allowed to go on their authorized summer hunt. They must remain quiet, foment no trouble, husband the issues carefully, and till the earth, the Quaker man told them.

"Make the issues last, when there was too little even before we were brought here? Till the earth with plows that never come—make no trouble, while our people die?" Dull Knife demanded, with the warriors so noisy and threatening against the whites that Little Wolf had to rise in his shaking chill to roar out his anger against them. It was too late for anything now, the Wolf said. The people were too sick, with someone carried to the burial rocks every day. They longed for their mountain and pine country, where there was no sickness and few died. If the agent would not let them go, he could telegraph the Great Father or let a few see him again.

Now the agent roared too. He wanted the young men who had already started north. Little Wolf said he knew of no one gone except to hunt stolen horses or try to get a deer or some rabbits for the sick. But still the agent demanded ten young men as hostages until everybody was back.

Hostages—for prison, for the irons on hands and feet—this was something the chiefs could not decide. They must go ask the people.

Anger broke out that night against Standing Elk, riding in with a fine new blanket and another new horse. Yes, he had talked for coming down here and was now talking strong for staying. Otherwise they would all be killed. Any man who advocated leaving now should be broken, even if it was the bundle-bearing chief, Little Wolf. For his bad counsel the Wolf should be thrown from his high place.

Ahh-h, now it was out—Standing Elk wanting to be head chief! There was a roaring as of battle, red shots cut through the air, and the women ran toward the dark hills with the children. But the peace pipe was hurried in and before it the silence came back. Then Standing Elk folded his new blanket and moved from the camp, his followers along, never to return.

Afterward Little Wolf went across the night to the north ridge, to sit alone as in other times of hard decision. As the chief began to sing his old-time medicine song, there were moccasin steps in the dry darkness. He did not stop the song or move, for if his place was to be emptied by death, that too he must accept by his oath.

It was the Keeper of the Sacred Buffalo Hat, old, and sick too. Little Wolf must not think of giving himself up as hostage for the young men. Several chiefs had done that here and had been killed. "You cannot let yourself be turned from what seems right, not by gun or knife or the wounded pride and weakness of doubt. We made you the bearer of our Medicine Bundle, our leader."

"But if I have lost the vision of the good way?"

"No Cheyenne can be compelled to do anything, nobody except our Selected Man. You must lead even if not one man follows, not even a village dog—if any had escaped the hungry pot," the Keeper added ruefully.

Afterward they went back down to the camp, silent, with no drumming, no singing from the young people. The hot, still air was thick with mosquitoes and the stink of a village too long unmoved, one full of the running sickness. And now there was the stench of dissension too.

In the morning they went a day's pony drag up the river for wood and grass and air. The agent called for soldiers. Two companies of cavalry with a howitzer took up the trail, and troops were readied northward to the Yellowstone, the telegraph wires humming with the demand for extermination. Then the Indians were discovered just above the fort inside a little horseshoe of reservation hills, the men trying to snare rabbits and gophers, the women digging roots. Still the howitzer was set to look down into the camp, and the red-faced captain galloped into the lodge circle, his double line of troopers close behind, their guns shining. The women and children fled but were ordered back, to hear the officer announce that, until they all returned to the agency and sent the children to school, there would be no rations—not just a little as before, but nothing, not even the moldy flour.

The women trembled in their rags as they shielded the sick and the young, remembering the guns that had killed so many helpless ones before. The soldiers stayed and the howitzer too. Finally, on the eighth of September the agency doctor came. With the chiefs silent beside him he walked among the lodges, past all the sick ones, the women turning the kettles upside down in the symbol of emptiness as he came, or holding out bowls of roots and grass for his eyes.

"This is a pest camp, a graveyard!" the doctor exclaimed.

But he had no medicine, no food, and besides, everything was already settled. The chiefs had gone to the last conference at the agency with their few guns hidden on their warrior guard, for surely now the protesting ones would be killed. It was a tumultuous meeting, and one of the young warriors forgot himself enough to speak out in the council. "We are sickly and dying men," the slender young Finger Nail told the agent there in his soft Cheyenne. "If we die here and go to the burial rocks, no one will speak our names. So now we go north, and if we die in battle on the way, our names will be remembered by all the people. They will tell the story and say, 'This is the place.' "

There had been a roaring of *"Hous!"* from many of the young southerners too, and to the agent's angry order to draw the troops closer Dull Knife rose with a hand lifted for silence. He spoke of the many Indian complaints: peaceful people shot by soldiers, the buffalo destroyed, the lands taken, with too little of the pay promised in the white papers, and now nothing at all. No food, no houses, no cattle or wagons or plows. So they were going back north while some were still alive.

This too brought a roaring of approval from many of Little Robe's warriors. The agency chief had once been dragged back wounded from a Pawnee war charge by Dull Knife, but that was long ago, and now he rose and knocked the old chief into the dust with the butt of his leaded saddle whip.

In that moment every warrior was up, scarred breast against breast, knives and pistols against panting bellies, the white men pale as old paper in the silence that waited for the one thrust, the one shot to start the massacre, the soldier guns up, ready.

But almost at once Dull Knife was on his feet and the warriors were ordered back, all going except one who gashed himself and held up his bloody knife, shouting, "Kill! Kill the white-man lovers!" As Little Wolf had him dragged away, Dull Knife shook the dust from his blanket and, with it folded about himself, looked down at the agent, his lips curling proud.

"My friend," he said, "I am going."

Slowly, majestically, the man feared by Crow and Shoshoni and Pawnee for forty years walked from the·council, his warrior son and his band chiefs around him. Afterward Little Wolf talked very earnestly for peace, for permission to go home in peace as they had been promised. He could not give the young men as hostages never to be returned, and if the agent loved their food too much to give them any, he must keep it all. "I have long been a friend of the whites. The Great Father told us that he wished no more blood spilled, that we ought to be friends and fight no more. So I do not want any of the ground of the agency made bloody. Only soldiers do that. If you are going to send them after me, I wish you would first let me get a little distance away. Then if you want to fight, I will fight you and we can make the ground bloody on that far place."

⊑⊧   ⊑⊧   ⊑⊧

THE ORDEAL BEGINS

IT WAS a clear, cold night, the moon so large and shining on the snow that it seemed one could see to the horizon, to the circle of the four Great Directions. Only once before had a moon seemed so much like day—the time these Cheyennes had slipped out of their guarded camp in the North Fork of the Canadian. Now, exactly four months later by the white man's figures, the ninth of January, once more Dull Knife's people were preparing to flee, this time to fight their way through the log walls of a prison house and the soldiers and the winter cold.

At first when everything was shut off at the barracks,* there were still the benches and floor boards to be burned. The women had a little grain and tallow put away, and when they were taken to the brush below the stables, they managed to hide a little snow in their blankets for the thirsting children. Not too much, for one woman had looked so suddenly fat that a soldier bumped her with his gunstock and the snow slid from the folds of her blanket around her feet and she stood there, her sunken eyes down upon what was lost.

Now almost everything was used up, and the below-zero cold that sat among them like a wolf grew stronger from the frost crawling in between the logs, the women huddled together, the children crying out in their cold and hunger from the troubled half sleep as they would not have dared if awake.

The young men had long planned for this day that Hog promised them the night they were brought here. The council chiefs were pushed aside even more now than usually happened in warring, this time by younger leaders like Black Bear, Little Shield, Bull Hump, and the southern Pug Nose. There were older men among them too, like Great Eyes and even Bridge, who had never gone armed except by his healing power, and the wilder young sons of the chiefs, Little Hump and Young Hog, following Roman Nose and the Little Finger Nail, the one who had grown so strong these few moons past.

Behind the blanket-covered windows the plans were approached with the old formality now. In the prolonged desperation of the barracks the killings down in Kansas by any avenger seemed suddenly the work of a foolish and faraway time, like the things of hot youth seen from the responsible years of the council fire. Here everyone must work together for the surprise, the power they did not have in guns or numbers.

Little Shield, the leading warrior of the Elks, the lesser and so the guest society here, was given the place of bravery. He

---

* Last food and fuel, Saturday, January 4, 1879; last water, January 8, Captain Wessells told Board of Proceedings. Other military and Indian sources put both at varying but earlier dates.

would head the outbreak on his end of the barracks, be the first
through the window there and upon the walking sentries with
loaded guns to be taken, every gun possible. Those on the opposite side would be led by Little Finger Nail. The work of all
the others was well planned too, who would step into a man's
tracks as he fell, the younger women also in it this freezing night
that was like day. Always the weather was against them now,
with storms to hide the attacking soldiers, moonlight to reveal
the fleeing Indians. Truly the Cheyennes had lost the sacred
way somewhere, long ago.

With the moonlight and a cold to freeze the grouse, they
must go very fast, and for that the ropes and the few elk-horn
saddles and pads must be taken along. Two good horse catchers
would run ahead to Bronson's ranch on Dead Man Creek, the
nearest herd. Some day their friend would be paid for what they
must now take, and if not, no man would grudge the taking less.

Dog soldiers, experienced in this duty, would guard the
rear, fight to hold the soldiers back while the other men ran
with the children and helped the women get away. Some were to
carry a few things of the old times, old medicine objects, although the best they had brought, the Chief's Bundle, hung
under the arm of Little Wolf. But they had the stone buffalo
horn sacred to the Dog soldiers, the lance heads of their tribal
bands, a few pieces of fine old quill work—something to hold
to, to remind those who might be left after tonight of the greatness of the past time; to remind them that they must always be
Cheyennes. It was in this planning that Great Eyes took out his
fine old shield, with the triple tail of eagle feathers and the claws
of the strong-hearted grizzly, and called his nephew, the thirteen-
year-old Red Bird, to him.

"You have no weapon, not even a broken knife, my son,"
he said. "You have grown too small in the hungry times to help
other people much in the fast fighting of this night, so I give
you this shield to care for. You know how old it is, how many
arrows and bullets it has turned away. Take it, my son, and
run hard. Pay no attention to anything, do not stop for a drink
from this long thirsting or for mercy for anyone. Run very hard

and keep hidden, and if you must die, die with your body protecting this. . . ."

The tall, thin boy stood shamed by this honor, feeling foolish and weak, unable to reply. Gently the man passed his long hand over the shield cover once more, as if to remember all its form and feel all the greatness of its power. Then he put the wide rawhide band of it over the boy's shoulder, and turning quickly, he went to stand at the blanketed window, looking for a long time where one could not see.

As evening neared, the young men became restless, some walking up and down, their moccasins soft on the bare earth where the boards were gone. Some were like drunk with firewater, talking, talking, staggering a little; some cried out suddenly, "Open the door! Let me charge against the soldiers! I want to die right now . . . ," until older men led them away. And if one young man here in the barracks now wished to give up, he did not put the words to his tongue. Not a young man or any one.

So it was like lying on the hill for the vision, the dreaming, the exaltation. None had eaten or drunk or warmed himself; none had been with a woman for a long time, or the women with a man. Now they were prepared for the ordeal in the old, old way, and it was as if all the foolish things had fallen from them and ahead was the greatest thing in their lives, the greatest test of all.

That morning Wessells had sent for Hog because he was the one the warriors had seemed to follow at Chadron Creek. Hog refused to go, thinking of the hanging post where a man swung from a rope. Besides, no one chief could speak for the Cheyennes, and whatever was said someone must be there to hear it, so the whites could make no lies of it later and his people never know.

"I cannot go alone," he said. "I must talk where all can hear."

When he was told he could bring a man along, Old Crow consented to walk beside him to the adjutant's little building,

but the warriors cried out "No! No!" and stood against them at
the door. Only Hog's growing power kept them from actually
putting their hands upon him. Even his own son, Young Hog,
shouted against him. "Those two blinded men will never be allowed to come back!"

"Wait!" the father said again, as he had two days ago when
Young Hog drew his foolish knife against a sentry and had to
be held back so he would not die right there, heavy on a bayonet.

But now Hog's sick wife saw he was going and she began
to moan, rocking herself back and forth, and so he had to stop
and go to her with a few quieting words.

"They will kill you!" she cried.

"We have these other people here," Hog said, in the long-
known chieftain's reply to such protestations. "They are given
into my palm to care for now, to shield. . . ."

So with Old Crow beside him, he went slowly through the
blinding glare of sun on snow to the little adjutant's building
that was full of whites, several officers sitting around the chunky
red-faced Captain Wessells, and many of the soldiers packed in
there too. When Hog said once more that they could not go
south, the guards sprang upon the two Indians from behind,
with irons ready for their hands. Old Crow was subdued first,
and easily, but the still powerful Hog, grunting, with soldiers
hanging to him all around, managed to bend and twist and get a
hand to the knife in his belt as he lurched himself halfway out
through the door, his old shirt torn away, his naked shoulders
heaving to throw these puny whites from him. One of the men
was cut a little in the struggle, as with a great roar to those over
in the barracks Hog got his hand up. But as he drove the knife
quickly downward against his own belly, the jerk of the panting
soldiers deflected the blade, and the iron rings were snapped
upon the Indian's wrists.

It was done very quickly, and perhaps even Hog's cry
would have been lost in the blowing wind, but a Cheyenne
woman was out talking to her brother from Red Cloud trying to
get her released to him. She saw Hog burst out with soldiers on
him like dogs hanging to a grizzly, and the irons on his hands.

She threw her head back and gave her penetrating woman's cry of danger, high and thin on the wind.

Immediately there was great excitement in the barracks. Some of the Indians made a rush for one of the doors and broke past the guards, but were driven back by a company of mounted troops charging in around them. Young Hog, with his sheet blanket over his head, shouted for everybody to get out of the way, for he was coming to get his father. But there were so many guns against him, their bayonets meeting together over his gaunt belly, that he was pushed back and finally the door was closed on them all.

A long time Hog looked where his son had had the sharp steel of the soldiers pushed against his flesh, so close to the place where their relative Crazy Horse had died of the lance-pointed gun. With the water of sorrow jumping down his dark, stony cheeks, Hog held out his manacled wrists. "Take them off," he said. "I will go back and tell my people it is hopeless. They must give up and go back south."

But the little *veho* Wessells gave no such order. Standing silent before the powerful Indian, he stared up into his face, the soldiers who came from the barracks stopped by the long looking. After a while the officers around Wessells began to move a little, uneasily, making noises with their boots on the frozen ground.

"I cannot let you go in there," the captain finally said. "You would not be permitted to come out again."

So the two Indians stood together beside the shoveled drifts, their old blankets whipping loose, now that their hands were ironed, waiting for the ambulance to take them to the soldier prison down at the encampment. Once there was a disturbance at the barracks door and Left Hand came hurrying out. "I cannot see my brothers taken away with the irons on them and stay behind," he said, as he held out the hands that could fell a buffalo with a thrown rock.

At the barracks the roaring increased; the noise of boards ripped off somewhere and hammered across the doors; the sound of digging, breastworks thrown up, holes made to protect the women and children even now if the soldiers charged the

building. Then there was drumming, dancing, and singing, singing that those who knew Cheyenne said were songs of war and
strength and death.

"We have quite a powwow started now," Wessells said casu-
ally, as another company of troops came up on the trot to take
over the guard. He had the inside doors from the barracks to
the cook and guard rooms boarded up too, and then he rode
after Hog and the others to see that they were manacled foot
and hand, safe, in the tent that was the encampment's guardhouse.

At the prison the three Cheyennes were turned over to
Lieutenant Chase.

"I am grieved to see what has happened," their young
friend said, when water had been brought them and he saw
the men drink cup after cup, jerking themselves back harshly
now and then, as they would long-thirsted horses, and then
drinking deeply again.

"Ahh-h, it is a bad thing that has been done," Hog finally
agreed. "They all want to die up there now. They will break out
tonight and die fighting."

This was repeated in the presence of Wessells at Chase's request, with Rowland interpreting and many soldiers around to
hear, so everyone could know and be prepared and there would
be no excuse to butcher the people like fleeing buffalo. Then
the three Cheyennes were fed and told they could go back up
there and call their families out.

There was talk of Wessells taking the handcuffed men into
the barracks but Hog was against that. "No! Then the warriors
must make a fight and everybody will be killed," he said sternly,
as though in command here.

And truly it was dangerous to go in to the Indians now.
That morning before Hog was taken, a Cheyenne living with
Red Cloud came into the barracks room to talk to his relatives
and he would have been killed if his friends had not hurried
him out. And when the Sioux scout, Woman's Dress, came in,
even Tangle Hair shouted against him.

"You want to get us killed like you helped kill Crazy

Horse! We have been told how you did it, coming to spy, sneaking around, then telling lies!"

The young men lifted more than their voices against Woman's Dress, and he ran from the door with his arms about his head, the Cheyennes quirting him clear out to the guards, even though he had relatives among them here, and they knew that this would not be forgotten.

When Hog would not go shackled into the barracks, they talked through cracks where the chinking was gone from the logs. After a while the wives of the prisoners and some of their small children were allowed to come out, and two very old women, but only after much angry talk and noise. Young Hog stayed, and the elder of his sisters, the one called Hog's Daughter. She would not leave her brother.

"Tell them all to come out," Wessells urged. "They will not be harmed."

Hog said this, but held his hands out before him, showing the iron that bound them together. He received no reply. Rowland talked to Great Eyes through the blanket-covered window and asked him to let his nephew, the young Red Bird, come out. The boy's angry voice answered for himself. He would stay and die with the rest.

Once Wessells tried it himself. "Dull Knife! Dull Knife!" he called. "Why don't you come out?"

Without waiting for the interpreter, the old chief answered that he could not, and knowing that this would not be understood by the whites, who would think it was the warriors who were against it, not the strong wall built by his own heart, he said it once more: "I will die before I go south. . . ."

But it was the captain's request that Tangle Hair come out that brought the greatest excitement, a roaring and shouting against his going that was unusual, coming from the soft-spoken Cheyennes, who were suddenly as noisy as Tangle Hair's own born brothers, the Sioux. It seemed very strange to the white men who knew that the Hair had said little in the troubles at Chadron Creek, and then was not heeded.

Finally Little Shield made himself heard outside. "It is plain this man cannot go out." he called to Wessells. "He owns us now like a silver dollar in the *veho* palm, and he can do with us as he likes! Most of us are Dog soldiers and he is the leading chief of the society. With Wild Hog taken from us we now must follow this Sioux. We cannot let him go!"

When it was night the Indians in the dark barracks saw the post blacksmith come over the moonlit snow dragging heavy chains and make a hammering as he fastened them across the doors that led to the cook and guard rooms of the barracks. The outside doors he fastened more securely too, one with an iron bar screwed down. Now the Cheyennes were shut in tight, not in a stone house as in Florida but in wood that could be fired, burned to the ground. Some of the warriors said this among themselves, whispering it over a little glow of fire to warm their trigger fingers. The women had heard the hammering and huddled closer together in the darkness, their eyes where the doors were—watching for the coming of the guns. Perhaps no one would be allowed out any more for any purpose. Perhaps they were meant to die here, humiliatingly, in the smell of imprisoned people who had no privacy and no room for it. They were to die of thirst, trapped together like antelope in the pits, with no one coming to slit the throats, none to make it quick and easy.

But one woman back in the dark could think only of the chained doors. She began to rock herself, "We are to burn!" she moaned, softly at first, then lifting the words louder and louder as she repeated them. "They will put fire to us all here!" she finally cried, thin and high, like a hunting panther, over and over.

The others tried to stop her, to quiet her, doing it gently, remembering that she had seen her baby thrown into the flames at the Sappa. But suddenly the woman sprang up and felt for a sleeping child in a mother's arms, those around trying to hold her back, take the knife from her hand in the darkness.

"No, no! Help me!" she pleaded. "Quick, your knives—let us help the little ones here to die easily, before the burning soldiers come!"

Now the old men hurried to the woman, Dull Knife speak-

ing so harshly to her that she crumpled down, sobbing. Quickly
Red Feather and Brave One forced her helpless against the wall
and twisted her wrist back until her knife dropped in the darkness, while Bridge started his sleep chant and his slow rattle to
quiet her. Gradually she settled down to the floor, her head in
Medicine Woman's lap, and seemed to sleep, but the fear she
saw was still there in the night and the silence.

So Little Shield called the warriors together. "You see how
the people sicken. They cannot wait longer, not even to midnight," he whispered. "While some watch that the building is
not fired, the rest will dress in our best clothing. We will die
outside, fighting."

Stooped over the little fires that had been saved to light this
preparation, they painted their faces and put on the few good
things left. Dull Knife drew the beaded lizard outside his shirt,
and Little Finger Nail put on his shell-core collar and tied the
watchful, clear-voiced bird in his hair, the bird that brought
him the sweet singing. Most of them had new beaded moccasins that the women had made, or were presents from the Sioux.
Then they tied their blankets at the neck and around the waist
to leave the arms free, but they took no other notice of the cold
that made the smoky logs creak and was a sparkling of frost
along every chink and knot in the light of the little fires.

So the 130 Indians prepared for the going, only 44 men, including the eleven-year-olds, and with very little in their hands.
They brought out the five guns hidden in the holes and the pistols too, nine of these, and one more that worked part of the
time. Then they divided the cartridges as well as they could,
and the lead and caps and powder. It was so pitifully little; one
man had only two cartridges and one of those so poor in powder
it was only for the noise. Dull Knife sat down by himself when
he saw how it was, brooding alone. But Black Bear had his lucky
Custer carbine that his wife had carried through the searches,
and others the two good ones that had been found in the brush
of the White River by the women where the warriors from Little Wolf had signaled them to look. Now even the knives were
divided, those with broken blades whetted to points these last
few weeks. Four men had war clubs to use in the Sioux way,

clubs made from wood out of the barracks with spikes from the floor driven straight through until the points stuck out of each club head like spines from a great cactus.

As silence settled over the post and there was only the far howl of the coyote and the slow clump of the sentries on the stony winter earth, one man after another went quietly to the women's end of the room, whispered a name here or there in the darkness, touching a braided head perhaps, or a child fretting for water. Then at the signal they took their places at the windows, with Little Shield and Little Finger Nail to lead, but good men at the other windows too and one ready to get into the guardroom for a gun or two, if possible. Behind them waited such men as Singing Wolf with his Sharps rifle, the powerful buffalo gun, to stand against the soldiers when the first warriors went down. Next there were a few men without guns but carrying children. These were the fast men. Whatever happened some of these little ones must get away, some must live as seed so the people here would not be lost forever. With these a few women were to run too, strong women like the wives of She Bear and White Antelope, to rear any children that might be saved in this pitiless light of the moon, teach them the Cheyenne way. Perhaps somewhere they could find the good path, walk with the Great Powers once more.

Older men like Dull Knife and Noisy Walker, without guns, would go with the women to help them, as was always their duty, someone to help Lame Girl too, for this last one of her family must not die easily. Behind these would be Sitting Man, where his healing leg would delay no one. Two young warriors would come last of all, to get everyone out, out and running.

Piva, so it was planned, and if it was not good, it was the best they could do, with so little, and so many against them here.

When the stars that the white man called his drinking dipper were turned past the ten on the *veho* clock, there was a single shot from the dark barracks, the explosion like fire in the night as the guard at the corner of the building fell. The boom rolled loud over the snow in the still cold moonlight, followed by three fast shots, so fast their echoes came back together, into a scattered firing. Two more soldiers went down and two in the guard-room were wounded, but truly the Indians had thinned the powder too close or there would have been more than the two guns they got before other guards were upon them and soldiers poured out of the company barracks doors, looking white as the snow in their underwear from the sleeping.

The first Indians through the windows were followed by the rest in close file, like a string of bulky antelope leaping a bank, some of the last ones falling from shots inside the barracks. Then there was faster shooting from outside, dropping the Indians as they ran over the snow toward the river, the men shouting, herding the people together, hurrying along those with children under their arms, and the women with the saddles and the little food somehow saved, heading them all toward the bridge. Below the stables five Dog soldiers led by Tangle Hair dropped in a line behind a snowdrift to hold the soldiers back. They were coming fast now, many of them still not dressed but shouting and yelling, a trumpet blowing, the horses neighing and running, and the powder smoke stinging the eyes with the breath-biting cold.

When all the people were past the stable, all who would ever come, the five rear guards started jumping around, whooping, firing into the faces of the soldiers to hold them back a little longer, just a little longer. But finally the last of the five Dog men was down, dropped in the old-time honorable way—covering the flight of their people.

One of those who never came by was Sitting Man. His leg had broken again as he jumped through the window, so he sat there against a high drift singing his death song as a soldier put a gun to his head and blew his brains out, splattering them dark against the moonlit snowbank. Nine men were killed before the Indians reached the river and twice as many wounded, one— Tangle Hair—injured more than his feet could carry away. So he dragged himself out of sight and called to some soldiers who knew a little pidgin Sioux. They recognized him, took him to their quarters, and sent for the doctor. No other man was left wounded in the stretch of snow to the river. If they could not run, they died and were shot many, many times by the trigger-hot soldiers. Two women and some children lay back there too, and so many were wounded that the fleeing path was plain as far buffaloes scattered to sleep along their trail, many dark things on the crusted snow, the powder smoke creeping in white clouds along the ground, a stink on the biting air.

The Indians that were left struck for the bridge of White River, with thin, snow-drifted brush along the banks, the water low in the little ice-locked center channel. Some had to fall flat there to drink if they died for it. The rest crossed and, turning up the south side, ran toward the sawmill on the second bottom, the faster men getting far ahead of the foot soldiers. But now more came on horses and a few Indians stopped near the saw-mill to make a little stand. But when they were charged by a wide line of cavalry, the warriors broke and scattered, all except three men. These fell back a little and held again, desperate, wounded, but firing so long as they could lift themselves. After that no more stands could be made, without the ammunition and against the hundreds of soldiers plunging through the crusted snow almost upon them, and more on the gallop from down at the encampment, the trumpet blowing there.

It was plainly useless to try to get to the horses of Bronson's ranch, so quickly had the Indians been overtaken, so many shot, and there were no shielding bluffs close along that open road. Instead, they dropped their saddles and turned toward the river again, and the cliff-steep bluffs beyond standing in a dark wall for miles against the north. At the frozen stream the swift center channel was open, but the people plunged into the icy water, through it, and on, their clothing frozen at once and hammering like iron against their running legs. The soldiers overtook fifteen, sixteen more on the deep-drifted slope toward the bluffs. All the wounded men were killed with pistol shots through the head because they might rise up with guns. The women were to be captured, but it was not always easy to tell them in the blankets, fallen, sprawled out, or fleeing like shadows over the moonlit snow.

A few, very weak from hunger, had hidden in the narrow tangle of drifted brush and grass along the White River, slipping down the stream a way, or up it, but only a few, the men driving the rest out and on, one woman crying, "Run, my sons! You can save yourselves. I am played out." Others were found by the soldiers there, the troopers plunging their horses after every moccasin track, with everything so plain on the bright snow.

In the first half mile, half of their fighting men were lost. The women and boys grabbed the guns and ran, not stopping to make any stand now. A little soldier chief who slipped down into a snow-filled washout near the sawmill stumbled upon two Indians hidden there. They attacked him with knives against his revolver and went down. Then he saw that they were women. Another one was shot to pieces. She was without hope or will to live, with her man dead there on the ground, and so she stood up, but she was behind a stump and a line of troopers charged her, thinking it was a man. The bullets tore the blanket from her as she fell.

It was along there that Dull Knife, Bull Hump, and their families struck off across a hard-crusted drift away from the others, with two warriors and the young Red Bird, still carrying his shield, close behind. Because one of the Knife's daughters was hurt and had to be left, Little Hump had dropped back to help make a delaying stand. Another daughter stayed with him until it was too dangerous and then she picked up one of the children of those already on the ground and ran with the women toward the bluffs.

The young men had fought bravely with what was in the hand. Dull Knife's son had a pistol, and when he was hit, he threw it to another as he went down. Later some civilians came along and he lifted himself from the snow and made one lunge at them with the broken-bladed butcher knife from his belt. Then Little Hump too, another of the Beautiful People of Dull Knife, lay dead on the ground.

By now there were many civilians following the Indian trail, some from the trading stores, like Dear and Clifford, and cattlemen, Bronson too, all going close past The Enemy, who had walked north with the Brave One. She was hidden in weeds and brush under a snowbank, cramped and freezing, not daring to move. Some of those passing were afoot, others horseback or in wagons, all with guns, shooting the wounded, the children too, stripping them, taking the scalps. An officer who was sending the wounded and the prisoners back saw the white men up on a knoll and shouted against them. But then he went on back toward the bridge with his soldiers who carried two bad-hurt Indians in blankets, and the other whites moved on along the path of flight, taking everything, their guns making bright flashes, the reports rolling over the broad moon-hazing valley. After the looting men were past, The Enemy had to come out, too, or freeze and die. But perhaps it had already happened, for she seemed cold as the snow over which she moved from body to body and looked at them all, dropping like a dead one among the others when anybody came past. She looked into one face after another of her friends and relatives, seeing them as she saw her loved ones at Sand Creek and the Sappa, but somehow these seemed strangers long dead and scalped, some of the women too, their skirts thrown up over their heads, and indecent things done.

Although the soldiers were very close, most of the Cheyennes had to stop a little when they reached the drifted pines and rocks at the bluffs, resting in their weakness, their clothing frozen and their eyes turned anxiously back upon their trail that bent down the valley of the White. Even in the hazing moonlight they could see dark blurs along it, unmoving, with many troopers hurrying close and spreading with the scatter of moccasin tracks. There were several quick shots along the bluffs, first the flash and then the sharp report of the carbine, where soldiers overtook the played-out and the wounded. It was hard to endure this, when those too were very close to the rocks where no horse could have followed.

White Antelope was one who fell before the hurrying troops. He had stayed back to help his wounded wife and some other women, the baby like a sack under his arm. None of them could run any more, even with the soldiers charging, and so Antelope left the baby and turned upon the pursuers with his short knife. He fought there a little while before he was brought down, the women he was trying to protect all wounded now, two of them dead.

But White Antelope was still alive, and when the soldiers went on, he crawled to his wife and saw that the baby was dead and the woman dying too. They spoke a little, a few words in their soft Cheyenne. Then he stabbed her twice, very fast, with the poor knife, and himself, too, six times, but his strength now was too little, for when the wagons came to collect the wounded they were both still alive, although their clothing was frozen to the bloody ground.

"The will to live runs very strong in these people," Dr. Moseley said at the post hospital as he stooped to listen for a beat in the man's torn breast, but now suddenly White Antelope was gone, and an hour later his wife also. Their names were added to the surgeon's list, the wounds tersely described: "GSW in thigh and knife. . . ."

Then they were taken from the wounded that stretched in a double row across the hospital floor, for others needed their places.

As the soldiers spread along the bluffs to search out the hiding Cheyennes, Little Finger Nail gave his gun to another and slipped back, silent as the tufts of powder smoke that clung to rock and bush and tree. He kept behind the soldiers, trying to find everybody he could, particularly old Bridge, the man who could slow the bleeding wound, bring healing sleep to the paining ones and the afraid. In a dusky place the Nail discovered five hurt women together in some rocks and pines, with three dead children on the shadowed, bloody snow. Among the women was the daughter of Dull Knife who had stayed behind to be with her brother, now down there at the river, his face turned to the moon. She was leaning sideways against a tree, somebody's baby tied to her back, hit too. The girl was still alive but unable to answer the whispered question: "Sister, sister— Are you bad hurt?" But the warrior's propping arm felt how shot she was, almost falling to pieces as he lowered her gently to the snow and smoothed back her hair once. To this one Bridge need not be brought.

A mile farther along the band of bluffs he saw a lone man afoot in a buffalo coat—the little Dutchman who had shut off

the food and everything from the children, the *veho* who had
killed all those helpless ones back there. If there had been a gun
in his hand, the young Nail would have shot. But it was good
this way, for the captain had a small Cheyenne child in his
arms, carrying it until some soldiers came along to take it to
the post.

Carefully Little Finger Nail watched Wessells and a few
troopers follow the tracks of two more Indians up to a high
rocky place. There six soldiers were sent in. They found a
Sioux woman that some of them knew, and an old Cheyenne
warrior. To the call for surrender the Indian charged out with
his revolver, right into the firing guns. When they were empty,
he still came on. The soldiers dropped back to reload and this
time the Cheyenne fell, and Wessells and the rest went to stand
around him in a dark little circle.

"A man so resolute should have lived . . . ," one of the soldiers said, and went to bring back the woman who was climbing
away. But she turned on him with a piece of stove iron from
the barracks, fierce as the dead Cheyenne had been.

There was nothing the Nail could do here, and too many
more soldiers were coming, their voices very close on the frozen
air, so he had to turn back. His feet were senseless with cold and
he would surely slip on some icy spot, perhaps set a loose stone
rolling into a foolish noise, and be caught. But he must look
just a little more, up very close along the bluffs, moving from
shadow to shadow, making the little winter-mouse squeak signals. But no one seemed alive any more to hear. Then he saw
that many of the injured up here would have to die because
their medicine man, the one who could heal them, was lost.
Bridge lay dead, face down, a reaching arm out ahead of him.
It seemed he had been crawling toward the women where Dull
Knife's daughter lay. With his rattle out and ready, he had left a
trail of blood stretching far behind him on the snow.

For a while Little Finger Nail stood in the still shadow of
the pines, his breath making a cloud around the blanket drawn
up around his head. He looked down to the pale frosty points of
light at Fort Robinson and to the lanterns moving here and
there over the trail of the fallen Indians, and suddenly the Nail

knew that his warrior days were done. No longer could he think of this as a fight, unequal, but still a fight, one in which he and the other warriors would gather honors for boldness. Now he saw only that he must get the people away, hide them and himself with them, creep away like frightened mice into the crevasses of the frost-cracked rocks, hide and hunt for meat and shelter and healing—do anything now that would save lives.

Truly it had happened that he was no longer a man of the warpath. He broke the frosted breath from the blanket around his face, and holding a fold up over his stinging nose, he stumbled away to follow those who got up into the bluffs.

With a few fresh soldiers Captain Wessells was moving farther up the White River valley, scouting afoot for a place to get troops over the bluffs, the horse holders following below. Several miles out they found three Indians in a drifted pile of rocks and brush, with only the sheer cliff wall behind them. The men charged down at the soldiers, whooping, swinging war clubs, one with a Sharps carbine that he used like a club too, the frozen walnut stock breaking like glass when it glanced from a dodging soldier and struck a rock. But the Cheyenne would never need it again. He was already down, and then the second man too. The third escaped and no one followed him because the recruits had let the horses get away in those first whoops that broke into echoes along the bluffs, a stable-wise old bay gelding leading them in a run for the post. So Wessells had to walk back several miles. But some Indians hidden along the bluffs tried to stop the horses, and then shot after them, hoping to crease at least one to catch it. Snorting, the horses had turned back, and were finally cornered by the troops in a rocky washout, miles away.

Once Wessells passed the crippled Stubfoot and his nephew. They were dug back under the drift in a pocket, very cold but afraid to have even a handful of smoldering grass for warmth because the smell would carry far tonight. The Foot had his revolver down on the soldier chief once, for the wounding of his wife on the run to the bridge, but he never pulled the trigger. His hands were very cold and there was too much killing already. Later the two followed the trail into the bluffs and ran into their friend Lieutenant Chase coming around a rocky point alone. The Foot and the young white man stopped almost against each other and all three could have died there in one beat of the excited heart, but Chase spoke *veho* words in a friendly tone and held out an empty hand. So Stubfoot put his revolver into it, butt first, in surrender. Then they waited together for the troopers. A man who had been in the sandhill fight down south and lost his first wife in the Sappa killings waited, a prisoner.

"Enough have died . . . ," he said to his angry, protesting young nephew.

Many soldiers were already dismounted and skirmishing along the bluffs wherever there was a snow track or a drop of blood on a rock. One place they were close enough to Pug Nose, Bullet Proof, and a dozen others to see their darkish figures creeping like bears up through a snow-filled crevasse in the 75-foot cliff that had looked impassable to anything except the soaring eagle.

"Look at 'em mountain goats!" one of the soldiers shouted in astonishment, and in admiration, but already the others were sending bullets that kicked rock upon the hurrying Indians. Instantly the graying light up there was empty, and several shots came down upon the soldiers from the top of the bluffs compelling them to fall back.

By now the civilians had reached the bluffs with their wagons and the buckboard that carried the mail on the Sidney-to-Black-Hills stage line. They were taking everything from those on the ground, even robbing the ones Vroom and Chase's troops had covered with their frozen blankets until the six-mule death wagons could gather them up.

By the next day thirty Indians, twenty-one of them warriors, half of all the men Dull Knife had, were laid out in rows down near the sawmill, and probably some frozen ones, particularly children, not found. The post hospital was filled with the wounded, mostly brought in by their young friend Lieutenant Chase. He had shot Indians—killing people for pay was his soldier work in the curious *veho* manner—but they were glad to see that he did not shoot the wounded. For that, and his gentleness with the hurt ones, the Cheyennes would remember him.

By daylight the scouts signaled of soldiers riding everywhere: up and down the White River, on the roads from Camp Sheridan, Fort Laramie, and Deadwood, out past Crow Butte and around northwest on the Hat Creek road, the road the Indians must cross if they would reach Red Cloud or even Little Wolf, although without the horses from Bronson they could never hope to get to the one they still called their Strong Man. The herd down on the Dead Man ranch would be watched now, and no signals came from the two men who still tried to get there.

But it was almost six miles around by a place where the soldiers could get the horses up on the bluffs in the snow, so those on top were safe for a little while to bind the bleeding and build fires for the frozen hands and feet—safe for a little weary chewing at the dried meat left in the rocks for them by Woodenthigh. There was not much, for the Little Wolf people were poor too this winter, and with the soldiers watching they had to travel very light. Yet the meat helped put a little hope into the starved stomachs here, helped to keep some of the bereaved ones from running back to die against the guns.

Little Finger Nail and Roman Nose went several miles along the top of the bluffs to see who was at the fires. There were some old people and even some small children, and the young girls like Singing Cloud and Hog's Daughter, with perhaps some others still hidden. Everyone at the silent little fires thought of those down there on the ground. No one asked about Dull Knife and the ones to go with him or spoke of his dead son and daughter down there and another daughter shot, perhaps dying too.

The day divided the Indians in their hearts between welcome and anxiety. The sun might warm their freezing a little, but it would light up every moccasin track, show it from far off, lengthened and curled and darkened at the edges in the thawing. Always the Cheyennes had to think in these two ways, between the warmth of day and the shelter of night. Before the bloody path out of the barracks here it was the trail from the

south, and all those other trails. But few had seen a night as bad
as this one, or such a morning.

And now there were signals of new soldiers coming close,
many more soldiers out, to reach for the Cheyennes like a great
grizzly clawing at the rocks for hidden mice. So the people had
to rise and start over the broad white glare of tableland, without
a stone or a tree, before they struck the breaks toward the north
and the sheltering stream beds that led away. Bent from their
wounding and lamed by frost, leaning on each other, some carried, one man with crutch sticks for a broken shin, the thirty-
four Cheyennes—children and old and all—moved out toward
the timbered breaks of Hat Creek, the far pines a black smudg-
ing on the snow. The Indians went in a dark straggling file,
winding around the softer drifts, their weary moccasins driven
faster and faster as they left the protection of the broken bluffs
behind.

                        ⊂╞ ⊂╞ ⊂╞

THIS REMNANT

AFTER THE LONG waiting for permission to go to Red Cloud, at
last the Cheyennes were to be taken there, the crippled remnant of them. There was soft keening for all those who could
not climb into the waiting wagons, for the living as well as the
dead. Then the wheels broke from the frozen ground and the
little queue started down the White River road to the encampment where Hog and fourteen other men were in irons. Here a
few more women and children would be loaded in too, all except those who must go south with their men to the trial for
murder. These left-behind-ones were gathered on a little hill

back of the camp, and as the wagons started away toward Red Cloud, they set up a wild wailing and gesticulation, Hog's wife leading them. Keening in sorrow for her lost son, she threw her bony, shriveled arms in supplication to the Powers whose winds blew her loose mourning hair and her rags as she moved in a sad dance of despair, half a dozen others circling with her, naked butcher knives flashing in the sun.

One of the Sioux scouts was ordered to take Hog's wife to her tent and search her for weapons besides the knife she surrendered. He had the Indian's reluctance to touch a woman not his wife, and when he finally made a move toward her, she struck her breast quickly with both hands, half of a pointed scissors hidden in one and in the other a table fork with only the sharpened middle tine left. She stabbed herself several times more before she could be disarmed, blood streaming down upon her moccasins. Even then she broke loose and tried to kill one of her small children and stamped on another, fortunately with the soft soles of Cheyenne moccasins.

Before she was quieted with morphine, there was a shout from the prison tent. Her husband, the powerful Hog, lay in blood too, unconscious, stabbed four times about the heart although his hands were ironed and he was apparently disarmed.

"It seemed best to him, when he is to be killed by the whites. If he dies here, his wife and children can go to their relatives with Red Cloud," was all even Tangle Hair would say.

That night the reporter from the Chicago *Tribune* went to see Hog. The chief's eldest daughter lay on the bare ground of the prison tent, sleeping heavily from her wounding and the exhaustion of the long flight over the winter bluffs. She had crept very close to the fire, her face almost in it, as though she could never be warmed again. The white man looked down upon the worn and haggard girl who had been so lovely to see only three weeks ago, and then to her powerful father, lying head to head with her. Hog breathed heavily and moaned under the morphine, his handcuffs rattling as he tried to move, the big silver peace medal from the Great Father in Washington sliding on the black kerchief about his neck. The attendant gave the chief another pill and spoke kindly in some pidgin Indian to him.

The mother, her eyes wild and tortured, sat at the tent door as protector, an old gash above the right eye swelling her face, her stabbed breast hunching her awkwardly upon herself. Suddenly the wounded girl awoke with a low moaning of pain, and seeing the soldiers through the smoke, she screamed as though she were once more in that last murderous rain of bullets in the hole out from Hat Creek bluffs.

The proceedings of the Board of Officers investigating the Cheyenne outbreak at Fort Robinson closed with two questions: Could not identification of the guilty have been tried at Robinson as well as elsewhere, and did the dignity of the government require removal of these Indians back to Indian Territory without full investigation into the merits of their complaints? In his report General Crook wrote, "Among these Cheyenne Indians were some of the bravest and most efficient of the auxiliaries who had acted under General Mackenzie and myself in the campaign against the hostile Sioux in 1876 and 1877, and I still preserve a grateful remembrance of their distinguished services, which the government seems to have forgotten."

If there was a helpless sort of anger against Woman's Dress and Shangreau, there were those among the Sioux who were not too friendly toward some of these Cheyennes either—Sioux who had lost their relatives and friends in the last fights under Crazy Horse, when the soldiers were led against them by Cheyenne scouts. But when the men who rode out to meet the wagons saw these people now, they whipped back in angry excitement, and so the whites were sent indoors as the young Sioux came roaring up in paint and arms around the building where the Cheyennes were unloaded, threatening the little troop escort. Even some old agency-loafing scouts drew their guns in anger to see the wounded people, sometimes only a boy or a girl or a crippled old woman left from a whole family. The Sioux divided their poor rations with them, gave them blankets and moccasins and ornaments for their hair, making the guests feel welcome as the Indians had made the white man welcome once, long ago, when he first came.

A week later more wagons carrying Cheyennes, with soldiers riding ahead and behind, started from Robinson, this time the prisoners going to Sidney and the special railroad car that would take them to Leavenworth, Kansas. Among these were Hog, stooped and ponderous in his unhealed wounds, Tangle Hair, Left Hand, Old Crow, Porcupine, Blacksmith, and Noisy Walker with their families, most of the men still in irons, Hog holding his manacled hands out at the stop in Omaha and all along the way for the crowds to see, proudly, arrogantly, it was thought. But there was no Little Wolf or Dull Knife to exhibit at any station. The Wolf was reported to be many places between the Platte, where horses were being stolen as always, and the Canadian border, where raiders from Sitting Bull slipped down to hunt and pick up anything they could.

"Dull Knife is dead," the captives were now saying. "He was killed in the fighting of the first night."

But none told where his body lay.

"These here church folks is sure doin' a lot 'a yellin' in the papers about them Cheyennes bein' cleaned out," one of the cattlemen from the White River country complained. "I been corral-feedin' my stock horses over a month now—waitin' fer the troops to round up the last 'a them wily bucks. . . ."

But now the last of the Indians were gone, and most of the soldiers had ridden away from Fort Robinson to look for Little Wolf. Then one afternoon an Indian boy, young Red Bird, came hobbling out of the bluffs toward the house of a man he knew down the river from the post. The boy was so starved he seemed no thicker than the forked stick he used as a crutch for the dragging leg, but on his back was a painted rawhide case. Inside was the shield he must save by running hard and keeping hidden, to protect even in dying if need be. It seemed he was very young for such a trust, and played out, hungry, and very sorrowful, for all the other Cheyennes must surely be dead.

No, he did not know where Dull Knife was; he knew nothing.

By this time the Sioux around Pine Ridge knew. Dull Knife had left the barracks with Pawnee Woman and the

daughters. Behind him was Bull Hump with his wife and a child
and his father-in-law, Great Eyes, and the young Red Bird with
the Eyes' shield on his back. There were three young warriors
along to help in the flight, including Calf, the Knife's grandson. Strung out but together, they got through the first run past
the river with only one of the daughters hit but crying for them
to go on, go on. That was when Little Hump stayed back to hold
off the soldiers, close enough to hit now, and another daughter
stayed too. The rest could not wait to argue this but had to go
fast to get the old chief away. North of the river they turned
from the direct path toward the bluffs to a frozen drift that had
no friendship for tracks. From there they moved up a shallow
gully, stooping low as they ran, keeping to the moon-glistening,
the hard-crusted snow. At the bluffs they slipped carefully
through the shadows, clinging along the rock face as much as
they could so no snow would be touched, no track remain.
Once when the soldiers came close, there were a few hasty snow
steps that they could not hide and one *veho* shouted, "Here's a
trail, leading off this way!"

So Great Eyes, as rear guard, turned back. Stumbling out
into the moonlight as though seriously wounded, he made a
great whooping and singing as he dodged awkwardly back and
forth among the boulders and brush, moving away from the
others, firing an old revolver loaded with very little powder, but
making his defense last as long as he could, until he was finally
dropped dead on his face. By then there was no picking up the
tracks that his moccasins had covered and confused. So the others
got safely away, except that young Red Bird was hit by a glancing bullet and dragged a leg.

Dull Knife led them to a great hole in the rocks that he recalled from his young days in fights with the far-traveling Crows,
a hole that showed no opening at all two steps away. The soldiers never found the trail again and so these Cheyennes were
safe as long as they stayed inside. They almost starved waiting
for a good time to come out.

Ten days later the soldiers were all moving out in long col-
umns to the western Hat Creek bluffs, as Bull Hump could
see from a hidden place high up, with the field glass Pawnee

Woman had carried through the barracks. The snow had melted to patches, and before it was all gone, there would be more to show their tracks. Now, if ever, they must start for Pine Ridge. All but Red Bird. He could scarcely walk with his forked stick; he could never get over the long miles of the high open country where they must go very fast.

So the boy sat in the back of the cave alone, singing a strong-heart song to give himself courage as Bull Hump led the others away into the night. They moved very carefully, traveling in the moonless dark, setting no moccasin down in snow or soft earth, keeping to the high, drier, well-grassed slopes, but where the cold burned the breast, and not even a bush offered protection.

"It is better to be very cold than dead . . . ," the blunt-spoken Bull Hump told his little daughter when she whimpered in the freezing night wind.

So long as the sick old chief had the strength to walk, they kept going, and when he began to lag, they hid in one little draw or another little gully for the day, in places so shallow and bare that none would think to look for such foolish hiding. They ate any roots and prairie rose hips and buds they could find, the two rabbits the Hump snared, some sinew one of the women had hidden, and finally the tops of their moccasins, chewing the rawhide like buffaloes working at their cuds. Then one night, half a moon after they left the cave, when Hog and the other headmen were already far on their way to the stone prison at Leavenworth, Dull Knife reached the place of a man he recalled from around the old Red Cloud agency near Fort Robinson. Gus Craven, married into the Sioux, was a man known as unafraid, and so not one to be feared. This *veho* cried out when he saw the bare, frozen, and bleeding feet of his old friends, their gaunt and sunken faces. His wife made the little sorrowful wailings as she fed them hot beef soup and fried bread, and buckets of coffee with sugar in the bottom of the cup. The next night they were taken to their interpreter friend, Rowland. So these people were slipped in with the Sioux, their presence to be unseen, their names unspoken.

Dull Knife was taken to a lodge set up for him under a

little bluff off out of the way on Wounded Knee Creek, with wood and meat, and blankets for the long sleeps. When he had rested two days and eaten well at his own fire for the first time since he left the north country, he finally demanded to know what had been done down there by the chasing soldiers. So he had to be told how few were left besides the handful of prisoners taken to Kansas. His wounded daughter was brought to him, and one of the women who had lived through that last day in the hole. Slowly, speaking as with lips still frozen, they told what they had seen.

Once the old chief rose in a towering self-rage. "I am an empty man!" he cried to the Powers. "I have become so weak that I cannot even die with my people!"

Before his sorrow, everyone slipped away, some afraid of a blaming word, afraid of seeming to blame Dull Knife for splitting off from the rest of the Cheyennes down there north of the Platte because he trusted to his old-time wisdom and the old-time reliance upon a man's word, even the word of a *veho*.

After a while Dull Knife went to sit up on the bluff. Almost it seemed like the time foretold by Sweet Medicine, a time to happen here in the north country. Many people were to die, perhaps all the Cheyennes. For that time Sweet Medicine had left one instruction: "The last woman among you must carry the Sacred Arrows to a high hill and lay them down for the time when the people shall return to the earth."

But that was not for now, with the Arrows not here. Besides, the sacred objects had failed when the soldiers destroyed the Powder River village and left so many dead on the ground. Yet how is a man to lead his people when the old holy things, the old, old wisdoms fail?

A long time Dull Knife sat up there, silent, alone, without his pipe, his hands hanging helpless between his knees, as helpless as in the cold iron shackles of the whites.

IN THE AFTERTIME

BEFORE the Little Wolf people were well settled in the soldier tents at Keogh, there was news of raiding Indians up the Mizpah River. Two soldiers repairing the telegraph line over that way were attacked. One of the men was killed; the other, wounded, had crept away into the brush, and was picked up by travelers on the Deadwood-to-Keogh road. Troops took up the trail and followed it fast for five days before they caught the Indians. It was Black Coyote's little party; the soldier's horse and his revolver were still in the Coyote's possession.

The Cheyennes were brought to Keogh. Black Coyote and Whetstone were locked up with chains on their legs, as the men down south had been before they were taken away to the Florida prison, and here too the people were helpless. During the long months of her husband's imprisonment at the post, Buffalo Calf Road, the warrior woman of the Cheyennes, sickened and slowly died, some said of the white man's coughing disease. The herbs of her aunt, the cures and chants of the medicine man helped no more than the powders of the army doctor. Every few days the Cheyennes signaled her condition to Black Coyote who watched night and day, it seemed, at the little barred window. When he discovered that his brave Calf Road was dead, he became so wild no one could go near him. He did not eat or sleep and had to be overpowered and dragged out beside Whetstone for the hanging. There were angry words over this wherever it was known, even from army officers. Would the two soldiers have been hanged if they had shot Black Coyote or even

117

the whole party, including his wife and children? This was a
time of war.

The women keened on the hillside and the men sat dark
and sullen in their blankets against the log buildings at Fort
Keogh, but the bodies of their relatives were not given to them.

In the south there was a little more to eat, and the warriors
who had returned from the Sappa and the Beaver slipped back
as though only away on a hunt. Some of the Cheyennes
thought that Yellow Swallow died in the Last Hole beyond Hat
Creek bluffs, but the boy lived out his sickly way to seventeen at
home.

Long before then many other things were settled. In Kansas a commission sifted the claims for damages in the Cheyenne
outbreak. Cut down, the total demanded was still $101,766.83—
three beef claims for over $10,000 each, one for $17,760.

"Even at a fancy five dollars a head for them Texas longhorns, the Indians'd oughta been fat as badgers—around three
hundred Indians eatin' better'n ten thousand head a beef in
less'n a month," some of the settlers said. By 1882, $9,870.10 had
been ordered paid from the treaty funds of the Northern Cheyennes to claimants for damages in the flight through Kansas in
1878.

In the meantime ministers, newspapermen, and others
called foolish idealists by those who lived along the bloody
Beaver and the Sappa had taken up the cause of the Cheyennes. Attorneys came forward to defend them without charge.
By the autumn of 1879—a better one for the Cheyennes—Hog,
Tangle Hair, and the others taken to Kansas in irons had been
tried for murder and released for want of evidence. It would
have looked pretty bad for the whites who killed so many non-
combatants in the trouble, all those Cheyenne women and children, some said, if these men were found guilty. Afterward the
prisoners were taken back to the southern agency, but soon
they were allowed to come up with Little Chief as far as Red
Cloud's people. They brought the Sacred Buffalo Hat along,
and the few Cheyennes left with the Sioux went out to meet

them, singing the songs of reunion. Later all except a few rode away north to the Yellowstone country. But not the big, broad-faced Hog. He had sickened with pneumonia, a disease that struck deeper than any enemy's weapon, deeper than the knife he had thrust into his breast with his shackled hands in the encampment near Fort Robinson that cold January day. This time he died, very fast.

At the request of General Miles, Dull Knife had been allowed to go north long before. With his crippled, orphaned band he came to sit in this north country that had cost so much. But the beaded lizard of his medicine dreaming, of his power to save the people, no longer hung on his breast. Soon Dull Knife, the Morning Star of the Cheyennes, was allowed to settle in the Rosebud Valley that became a part of the Tongue River Reservation finally set up for the Northern Cheyennes. Silent, sorrowful, the embittered old man died there about 1883.

Little Wolf's followers found Keogh the good, safe place White Hat Clark had promised, but there was nothing for the Indians to do. A few scouted a little against Sitting Bull, but mostly there was not even much hunting, with the settlers and cattlemen coming in thick ahead of the railroad that crept up the Yellowstone, the railroad for which Custer had marched into the Black Hills in 1874. There were not even hides to dress or many beads for the women's work. So the Cheyennes talked over the glories of the past and played games, gambled, and drank the bit of whisky they managed to get now and then from the plentiful supply around the post.

The first winter Little Wolf obtained a little bottle. Hiding it under his blanket, he slipped away and drank it up fast. Then he went to a trader store and watched his daughter gambling for candy with Thin Elk there as always, looking on, talking and laughing in his bold easy way. The Wolf became angry to see this and tried to stop the girl, take her home. But nobody paid any attention. He was a little drunk, and this telling people what to do was not the Cheyenne way but the white man's, and so was ignored. Little Wolf brooded over this a while, the whisky heating the anger of his youth against this man that had lived in his heart such a long time. So he got a gun and shot Thin Elk. The report was like a cannon blast in his ears and at once he was sober. Slowly he put the gun down.

"I am going to the hill," the chief said gravely. "I will be waiting if anybody wants me."

He sat up there for two days without food or water, while down below, his lodge was cut up by the Elk's relatives and his possessions looted, as was their right. After a while Little Wolf came down and sat waiting beside a building for what was to be done with him. No Cheyenne came near him with the formal banishment; no one came at all, except an army officer.

"Little Wolf," he said. "You are no longer the chief."

The gaunt, bowed Indian did not lift his dusty head for this one small man of the people that he had defeated so long and so well. There was no need for a reply to him.

After the killing Little Wolf never smoked the sacred long-stemmed pipe again or sat with others who were smoking. He kept to himself and went everywhere afoot, often alone. He walked clear over to visit the Arapahos, the relatives of his father, beyond the Big Horn Mountains 200 miles away, his two wives along this time, carrying what they could on their backs, sleeping in the open or in the little brush shelters like those they made on that long flight north.

For twenty-five years Little Wolf lived so, the humblest of a reservation people. When he died in 1904, there were some who still remembered and still loved him. They propped his body up tall on a hill and piled stones around him, drawing them up by travois until he was covered in a great heap. There Little Wolf stood on a high place, his face turned to look over the homes of his followers and beyond them, down the Rosebud that flowed northward to the Yellowstone.

From several versions of a song by one of the Southern Cheyenne chiefs, winter 1876-77, while imprisoned in old Fort Marion, Florida, for resisting white encroachments on their treaty land. It was sung each evening from the highest wall, the Indian in chains facing the west.

Sun-Going-Down!
Sun-Going-Down!
From our prison we call you, O Sun,
Look in pity upon our barred faces,
   see our chained feet, our ironed hearts.

Sun-Going-Down,
Sun-Going-Down,
Soon you will shine
Into the winter faces of our deserted Ones.
Light them, comfort them, warm them
   with the love you see in my face,
   the water standing red upon my face.

Sun-Going-Down,
Tell them of this—but
    not of the irons trapped on my hands,
    the ball hard as the blacksmith's
    iron rock upon which he hammers,
    rooting my feet.

Sun-Going-Down,
Speak to them of the eternal earth,
Shine on them as they place my young son
    upon his first pony, teaching him to ride,
    selecting well the second father to guide him.

The time is long and we must learn a new road.

Sun-Going-Down,
Sun-Going-Down,
Touch the cheeks in that far country,
Touch the cheek of my wife,
    the brown cheek of my unknown son.

from THE BUFFALO HUNTERS

THE BEECHER
ISLAND FIGHT

THERE WAS TROUBLE in south Kansas this spring of 1868 now that the Indians knew another railroad, the Santa Fe, was coming up the Arkansas River. The new grade drew thousands of hopeful laborers from the unemployed in the east. The soup kitchens of the cities were only for the select few certified as the worthy poor by the police chief. Jobless men came to hunt buffaloes too, mostly tenderfeet, with perhaps no more than an old pistol and a jackknife. In a few weeks or even days many turned to outlawry, sometimes as Indians, with moccasins and awkward feathers.

Although the iron tracks crept steadily up the Arkansas, in the north the Kansas Pacific ran out of funds at Sheridan station, west of Hays City, and laid off most of the twelve hundred laborers indefinitely. These men had seen train loads of flint hides go out last year and heard of the money Wild Bill, Charley Reynolds and dozens of others made. Soon a few of them were found face down on the prairie, their backs full of arrows. There were rumors too, that the hide market was glutted, the bottom dropping out, and so after standing off a raiding party or two, many experienced hunters dropped their wagon tongues

125

at Ft. Wallace, or Hays or Sidney. Some of them sat around the saloons, getting into fights and shooting up the street while they waited for something to come along, or the troops to do something beyond guarding the trails and K.P. tracks.

By August there was raiding along the Saline settlements of Kansas again. The settlers protested to Washington and then sensibly built a few more sod forts and reactivated last year's private militias. Major George Forsyth, aide to General Sheridan and green to Indian fighting, decided on a little informal redskin hunt, maybe show up Major Elliott some said, although another man still around the country, one George Armstrong Custer, hadn't done any better leading the Seventh. With Lt. Fred Beecher and an army surgeon as the core, Forsyth raised a company of fifty civilians: scouts, angry buffalo hunters and post hangers-on. Sheridan's permissive order let him provide the men with Spencer seven-shot repeaters and Colt revolvers, put them on the government payroll and promised them all the plunder—horses, arms and anything else they could capture.

The first few hours the roster lengthened fast, but in the end Forsyth was still short a few men. The undertaking had its lawless aspects—a force of civilians going to attack all Indians on their legal hunting grounds because a few young men of one tribe or another committed depredations. Old-timers knew that success would only bring new raids against helpless civilians, particularly settlers, but more probably Forsyth's scouts would have to be rescued as with most civilian expeditions.

The major was eager to get started and out beyond the telegraph before the vigilantism of the expedition could be grasped in Washington. Few Indian fighters joined up, standing away, instead, from the big talk in the saloons, even at Drum's, where army plans were usually as welcome as a gold piece in the palm or whisky in a blizzard. Many troopers from last summer's campaigns were openly hostile, and some of the officers warned the tenderfoot Forsyth he should have a force of at least two hundred civilians. The Indians were well armed, the best horsemen in the world, and they knew their country.

But such talk was treason to the professed Indian fighters.

"Any man-jack of us is worth twenty a them sneakin' redskins," a broad-coupled man they called Whalen protested. "An' probably two Regulars throwed in."

"Two Regulars, hell!" a bluecoat roared and kneed Whalen to the sawdust.

So there was a little shooting. The bartender ducked the bullets and came up with his hands on a neckyoke that he swung both ways, suggesting that they reserve their gunplay for the Indians. Besides, Lieutenant Beecher, although lamed in the Civil War, was an experienced Plains soldier too and Sharp Grover, their head scout, was an old hand in the country.

They finally filled the roster with a quiet little Jew who had been, among other things, a frontier peddler and post handy man, but had little sitting acquaintance with a horse. Almost at once there was another volunteer, an outlaw but a fast man with a gun and not afraid of blood as the little Schlesinger would certainly be. But Schles couldn't be talked out of going now.

"Well, they got a little a everything, salt, pepper and gravel in the grease," one of the old scouts said as he watched Forsyth lead his little party out into the heat of late summer. They were a motley outfit and rode a ragged and awkward column, nobody wanting to eat the dirt.

"Yeh, Beecher there, the nephew of the Bible slingin' Hank Beecher, he's seen Indians before, and them hide men. But the deserters and the outlaws what's been rustlin' Indian ponies— I don't stake much on 'em. Mebby seven, eight real fighters in the whole outfit. I don't look to see 'em come ridin' back with much fight left," a buffalo hunter agreed, and settled himself for more waiting around.

Forsyth and his scouts passed small detachments of troops guarding the railroad and a scattering of buffalo camps. Everywhere the sunburnt men looked after the dusty column and pushed their sweaty hats back, maybe laughing a little. The hunters heard that the Seventh Cavalry was near an Indian village, and laughed at that too. But there could be a fight, with Wild Bill scouting for them, now that Custer was away from the regiment. Bill was filling in for Comstock, killed by Sharp

Grover who was riding with Forsyth. Sharp had done the shooting in a Cheyenne camp only a week or ten days ago and he
should be able to find the Indians again, although the buffalo
hunters along recalled uneasily that he was part Indian and
often in their camps, particularly the Sioux.

"That there bastard'll sure lead us into ambush," one of
the windy talkers complained when he saw that Grover was getting to ride up with Forsyth and Beecher. But there were half a
dozen fast men with a gun ready to shoot Sharp down at the
first sign of treachery. Besides, young John Stillwell was out
ahead and no one doubted him. Buffalo Bill Comstock would
have been better but he wouldn't have gone along on such a
wild dog-day chase, not any more than Wild Bill Hickok when
Forsyth sent him word, or Bill Cody.

And it was dog-day weather for early September. Remnants
of the grasshopper scourge rose in dusty sluggish clouds before
the horses where the grass wasn't eaten into the ground, even
the browned prairie sunflowers gnawed to the woody stalks. But
when the scouts approached the upper Republican streams they
suddenly found themselves stirrup deep in the late growth of
bottom grass that was ripening towards fall, with the gold of
black-eyed susans through it, and the circling flight of blackbirds gathering to go south. Everywhere the brush patches hung
dark with chokecherries and the sweet redness of wild plum.
Game was thick, driven from the grasshopper-eaten tablelands,
with the buffaloes in small scattered bunches now that the running season was over and the southward movements of the fall
had not begun.

But here there were no hunters. Beecher knew why when
Jack Stillwell picked up a wild travois trail at the Republican.
The trail thinned out but it seemed to head towards the shallow
Arickaree fork. Forsyth followed, and camped near a sandy island about two hundred feet long and forty wide at the broad-
est, with one tall cottonwood rising from its scrub willows and
the tangle of long bottom grass. Neither Grover nor Stillwell
discovered the two big Indian camps down the river about
twelve miles, the pony herds unconcealed for anybody who
might scout in that direction, the smoke of the evening fires a

pale line on the horizon. Forsyth would have ridden away up stream if the Indians had been as unobserving, but at dawn, September seventeenth, they came over the ridge into the bare little valley, whooping, their horses on a dead run upon the scouts, who were almost packed for the march.

"Indians!" everybody shouted, now that they were in plain sight and already sweeping upon some of the loose horses, running seven off immediately.

Forsyth hurried his men from the bare river bottoms to the brushy little island with its one cottonwood. While some worked to quiet the horses the rest threw their packs down for breast-works and young Stillwell and two others went to guard the un-protected lower end of the island. It was so bare that they slipped over to the south bank of the river and hid in a patch of marsh grass.

By then the Indians, painted and stripped for attack, were upon the scouts in a whooping war charge, the crack of their guns sharp as they came, the horses on the island jumping and plunging, the men among them ducking for the ground. As the Indians hit the shallow sandy stream in the blowing powder smoke, they split and swung both ways around the island. All except one bold Indian. He rode straight upon the island, his painted war horse crashing the tangle of brush and old drift-wood caught in it, into the face of the guns, the well-aimed guns of the buffalo hunters. His horse leapt the prone men, throwing sand over them, and then was gone, sending the shallow water into high fans of spray as he went through the stream. It seemed he was bullet-proof, both he and his horse bullet-proof as steel.

For a moment several of the men stared after him, certain he would whirl and return. The others had brought down some Indian horses and one warrior, but Forsyth's thigh was shattered and Lieutenant Beecher had taken two bullets and was dying— the two military men of the disorganized party. There were sev-eral more casualties before the rest could throw up circular breast-works from the loose soil, keeping down as they dug, the air thick with bullets and arrows that cut the brush and grass and even the cotton wood leaves, and hit among the horses with the dull thud of lead and iron on flesh.

In the second charge a warrior rode out of the dust and smoke over the island again. By now one of the mouthy Indian fighters was throwing sand like a scared badger and bawling like a settler's bucket calf all the while, unwilling to pick up his gun or even touch it at Forsyth's command. But in the dust and smoke the Indians had not noticed the three men in the tall grass of the river bank, and several were hit from there. In a pause, while the smoke lifted a little over the valley, they could see horsemen and travois carrying off the injured Indians and the dead, while a crying of sorrow came from somewhere on the wind, women keening for the dead.

The next charge was afoot, the wily redskins creeping over the rough ground and from weed to weed. Some ran zig-zag through the shallow water under the smoke and dropped into the grass of the island within a few yards of the scouts, digging their own hurried breastworks in the loose sand. Their guns hit among the men now, and particularly among the wild and faunching horses. Some went down, others broke away, until only a few were left, the men all forced to keep down and so unable to hold off the creeping Indians. Plainly those on the island had to be driven out. It cost additional hits among the defenders but it was done.

By now the little knot of white men was in a desperate situation. With four, five hundred Indians already fighting, more were coming up all the time, until a solid row, including many women, watched along the little ridge where the stream cut in towards it, and still more came, until the ridge top was dark as with a forest of trees.

On the island there was cursing, praying, and another attempt to get the big man out of his burrow for the next charge and to straighten out two others who were shaking like rabbits. By now Lieutenant Beecher was dead and laid aside, and they were left with only the wounded Forsyth to direct them, Sheridan's green aide, with no experienced advice, but dozens of contradictory suggestions, and their horses all down. He ordered the dead horses dragged into place around the breastworks of the circular little hole where the white men lay pushed so close together. Only one among them still seemed optimistic. Schlesinger, little Schles, crawled busily around, distributing ammunition, tearing bandages for the doctor, helping with tourniquets, hurrying to his gun when another attack threatened. The men had dug as deep as they could without striking wet sand, trying to prepare for the next charge, the greatest, and perhaps the last one, for the Indians were preparing it with great care and ceremony.

Waiting, the men took hard stock. They were afoot, with very little hope of standing off the Indians until help came. Nobody knew where Forsyth's scouts had gone and there was no chance of getting a courier out, a courier afoot in a region buzzing with angry warriors. Yet, although Forsyth's shattered thigh was bleeding badly and very painful even through the morphia, he was working to tighten his command over these civilians. But many were injured now, and the water was getting scarce in the canteens, although it flowed openly on both sides of the island, no longer clear and flashing as it twisted over the yellow sand but red-streaked and soiled by the gut-shot Indian horses, the current digging little channels around their carcasses.

On the island there was only waiting now, with the groans of the wounded, and anger and uncontrolled fear among others, an uncontrolled fear that might have brought a panic as with buffaloes if there had been anywhere to run. There was none of the trained cohesion to which Forsyth was accustomed, but grumbling, disobedience and open derision. One of the outlaws spoke of Fetterman, who had let his eighty-one men be surrounded and wiped out by the Indians up in Wyoming less than two years ago.

"Another goddamn cocky West Pointer!"

Even the hide hunters who could look so confidently down their gun barrels for the shot into the lights, the lungs, of a buffalo, and the frontiersmen who had evaded marauding bands of Indians for years were desperate now that all flight was cut off. Some of the war veterans, those with actual battlefield experience, were a little cooler but coolest of all was the little Jew, the damn fool little Jew Schlesinger.

"Don't you know they'll scalp you!" one of the hunters

roared in fury at the cheerfulness still plain in the dirty, smoke-grimed face.

"Ah, yes," Schlesinger agreed. "But it's a poor thing they will get compared to the luxurious locks on some of the frontiersmen here among us—" He managed to laugh a little as he said it, but his nervous hands shook, and his peaked face was gaunt and drawn, for now the surgeon had also been hit. It seemed that one little man called Schles had better kept his nose out of other people's business this time. "—Always I hated the quiet life," he said soberly, and for a moment even big Whalen forgot his terror in the unconscious humor.

As the charge was prepared Sharp Grover watched the slope with Beecher's fieldglasses. The leader seemed to be Roman Nose, considered the bravest of the Cheyenne warriors, Sharp told Forsyth. He was a seasoned man, long past a warrior's usual age, but when they wanted him to be a council chief he said a man who had spent so many years on the warpath was not gentle or fatherly enough for the council. Roman Nose would be hard to whip, Sharp thought. The Indians believed him bullet-proof, and the warriors would follow him to hell.

Once more Whalen and the other two began to cry, burrowing deeper, while Forsyth cursed that they weren't soldiers, to be placed under arrest. Despite his shattered swollen leg, he sat up staunchly through this first Indian fight, so new to it he even had to be told that the Indians who were whipping their ponies, running them back and forth on the far slope, were getting them their second wind ready for the charge.

Finally when it seemed the men on the island could not bear another moment of waiting, the Indians came, starting slowly, with the loud cries of the women carrying on the fitful wind. The smoke had cleared considerably and the scouts could see the approach of the formal array, the painted Indians, feathers blowing from the spears and shields, half a dozen men in long, flowing warbonnets. Then suddenly they whipped their painted horses, Roman Nose the spearhead of the whooping charge, with the bullets of the hunters hitting all around him in the rolling dust, in the thundering that shook the earth, until it seemed he truly could not be hit, or even those around him as they charged in great waves through the hail of lead. Even when feathers were cut from heads, and horses began to go down, Roman Nose still came on, heading the spear of warriors, their bullets throwing sand over the besieged islanders, cutting grass and brush and flesh. Even now the cowards among the white men could not be aroused to fight. There was cold anger in Forsyth's commands. He would have had them shot right there if they were in uniform.

Yet every man was needed, and so the guns kept booming in the little valley, some of the excited white men blowing their ammunition as though an arsenal were at their backs, and still Roman Nose came on in the stinging smoke, closer and closer upon them. It was true; he could not be hit. A kind of flat panic hit the men on the island, even Forsyth silent, the shooting almost stilled as Roman Nose led the charge, barely two hundred feet away. Then suddenly at the water's edge he went down, shot from the side by Stillwell and the others hidden in the slough grass. The Indian fell and lay still, and the charge broke upon his fall as upon a rock. The running horses split and, turning to both sides, were away. And as they were lost in the dust and smoke little Schles carried the good news around the wounded, whispering as though made voiceless by the roar of the attack.

After a while Roman Nose began to crawl a little, stirring the long grass, and some warriors dashed in to carry him away, the women making their cries as he was brought towards them, the cries that were for a strong man dying, Grover and Stillwell knew.

Young Jack knocked over one more Indian as the warriors worked to get the others who had fallen. Otherwise the Indians kept out of range now, watching from the slope, some smoking or seeming to eat. About sundown there was a great keening on the ridge and Grover said that Roman Nose had probably died. As always the Indians withdrew before dark, and Forsyth was told that they would not return tonight. They believed that night fighting was bad luck, perhaps because the dew stretched the bowstring, for it was said that the arrow does not travel in darkness, the time of rest. But at dawn—

Yes, at dawn; Forsyth knew that. His left leg was broken too, now; he had twenty-three casualties, and his surgeon dying, shot through the head. The men broiled horsemeat and afterward two messengers slipped out, hoping to get through the Indian line somehow to bring relief, at least let the world know how the men on the Arickaree fork died. There was no sound, no shot and when it was hoped they had got through the pickets, they were suddenly back at the island. The second pair sent out included Stillwell and they did not return. There was more fighting the next day, mostly firing at long distance, and the third day the same. A second pair of messengers had started for help and nothing was heard of them either. The horsemeat stank now, even roasted to a crisp, and it began to rain, a fine gauzy curtain across the prairie, giving the yellowed grass an orange transparency, chilling the men, the wounded. Through this only an occasional Indian was visible, humped together on his horse, a hide drawn clear over him.

"They hate rain as much as hens do," Schlesinger laughed. "See how mad they sit in it."

The next morning there wasn't an Indian in sight anywhere, but no rescuers either. Gradually the men dared to get off the stinking island a little ways, carrying the fevered and helpless Forsyth in a blanket between them, his broken legs swollen and festering. They didn't go far from the protection of the island brush, silent, mostly, or wondering about the men sent out. They ate the rotten meat as long as they could and shot a stray coyote who was drawn to the dead Indian horses out on the bottoms. At least his stink was fresh.

Nine days after Forsyth camped there, the cry of "Indians!" went up once more as dark figures came out along the sky. Hopelessly, automatically, Forsyth tried to prepare for another attack from his blanket. But there seemed to be a vehicle behind the riders, a prairie wagon, an ambulance.

Now even the little Jew cried some, his first tears, and made a joke of it, as a small man must in the presence of big bruisers. Soon there were several hundred troops at Beecher Island, as the battleground was now called, and Forsyth's little expedition was rescued.

By now the Indians were far away and no one had much heart for trailing them now. The Cheyennes had withdrawn because they lost one of their great men. Later they said that his bullet-proofing medicine was broken by the accidental eating of meat that had been touched by an iron fork and there had been no time to make the purifying ritual. Forsyth, with his legs swollen thick as kegs with infection, too, would make no call for volunteers for another such venture. Nor would the buffalo hunters, not for a while when few dared to hunt, with the Indians so arrogant in their success. Let the Regulars fight the Indian wars. There was talk around Hays that the Regulars were getting ready to do just that. The Cheyennes would be made to pay for the wounds to the body and the pride of Sheridan's courageous but foolhardy aide.

⊏⊨   ⊏⊨   ⊏⊨

THE ROYAL HUNT

JANUARY [1872] brought a thaw, but before the snow cleared off enough to lay the dead bare for counting, there was news of more company coming to the buffalo country. This time it wasn't just a few millionaires who might be coaxed to help finance a lagging railroad or a senator with high-toned lady guests in sidesaddles, red veils flying, or some second string nobility out for a summer's gallop after a few buffaloes. This was royalty, big royalty—the Grand Duke Alexis of Russia—and as was fitting to a true man of Moscow, he was coming in the middle of the hardest winter most of the frontiersmen could remember.

The nation was indebted to the duke's father, Czar Alexander, because he supported the Union side during the Civil War. Just when it seemed that England would back the Confederacy, he dispatched a large section of the Russian navy on a visit of friendship to America. England took the hint. Now President Grant could make a gesture of appreciation through this gay but troublesome son of the Czar's. The handsome Alexis had married the daughter of the royal tutor and his father had the marriage annulled, it was said. Anyway, he was concerning himself only with wine, women and cards now—just the man for a western tour with Sheridan and Custer of the Seventh Cavalry, the regiment already called the Cossacks of the western world.

With his light hair, blue eyes, downy young side whiskers and mustache, and a high white forehead under his fur cap, Alexis made a fine picture in the parade at Omaha in the open barouche with gold trim and drawn by four fine grays. There was another parade out at North Platte, an early morning one in the cold clear air, with the duke riding beside Sheridan and Custer in an open carriage headed off towards the buffalo country, the duke's entourage a gay show of colorful Russian uniforms and gold braid following along behind, the newspaper men a drab contrast.

Out a ways they were met by General Palmer and an escort of well-drilled cavalry. Bill Cody had been drawn from his scouting at nearby Ft. McPherson—a fine picture in his fringed buckskin and broad white hat. There were half a dozen others to help scout and guide, mostly buffalo hunters, including Lonesome Charley Reynolds, hired back from the north because he knew the region as no other white man did, once trapped it and then hunted it all for buffalo hides, mostly afoot, ducking the skulking Indians who pursued him. The officers who had given him trouble were gone, and Reynolds was needed to make sure that no hostile Sioux or Cheyenne got near this Grand Duke Alexis.

Fresh horses waited a couple of hours out, where a company of cavalry greeted the party with a presentation of sabers to flash in the bright, unseasonably warm sunshine of January. From there on they saw an occasional lone old buffalo, the first few pursued in single-handed chase by Cody or some of the other hunters. Loud bravos and another passing of bottles celebrated the death of each one as the great animal thundered to earth and kicked his last in the winter grass.

After four o'clock, with the sun slanting low, the party reached a bluff overlooking a new encampment in a bend of Red Willow Creek called Camp Alexis. The cavalry band played "Hail to the Chief" while the Negro troops who were in charge of the camp and the services for the guests stood at attention. Then there was a grand charge of feathered and painted Sioux whirling around the duke's party, with some fine daredevil riding by the warriors as they clung to the far side of their running horses, hanging on by toe and mane-hold, shooting blanks over the straining necks.

Ah, these were real Cossacks, the red-skinned Cossacks of the American steppes!

Under the low bluffs lay the neat encampment—wall tents for the guests and the officers, hospital tents for the messes and long rows of field A's for the troops and the servants. Three of the wall tents were floored, the duke's carpeted in deep royal red, all heated with box or sibley stoves. Off to one side was an expanse of new pole corralling; on the other were the circles of painted, smoky Sioux lodges, with their great herds of ponies on the hillsides. All the Indians were out in feathers and beads, and their brightest flannel and blankets to greet the visitors. The camp had been established some days ago, with a supply train for the troops and guests, and twenty-five wagons of goods for the Indians, including plenty of coffee, sugar and flour, a thousand pounds of tobacco and many other presents. A hundred Indians had been invited, at the most two, but as the officers of McPherson knew, the Sioux loved any celebration or event and kept coming. Now around a thousand Indians were there under the long-time peace chiefs, Spotted Tail and Whistler, the latter the man who had saved Wild Bill Hickok from the angry warriors a few miles southwest of here a little over four years ago. But Wild Bill was nowhere around now, not with Sheridan and Custer, although Duke Alexis had asked immediately about this Wild One of whom he had read. The nearest Sheridan had was Buffalo Curly, the expert young hunter for McPherson, the curly-headed youth who, some said, was the brother of Wild Bill —a twisted-nose brother with the same fondness for guns. But perhaps that was a mixup, and occurred because Curly sometimes called himself Billy Barnes, the name that Wild Bill's brother Lorenzo used around Hays, the name that Wild Bill himself had used when he wanted a quick alias. Some had also heard of Buffalo Curly called Jack McCall, although here he used the name of Bill Sutherland.

"Ain't no wonder folks thinks it's safer to ask 'What name you travelin' under?' " Charley Reynolds said to another old hunter as they watched Curly showing off a little for the duke. Once Sheridan started to say something of the complication of names on the American frontier, when the duke brought up the Wild One a second time. It might amuse him to hear that even the Wild Bill of whom he enquired was really named Jim. But the general had struggled with interpreters during his observation of the Franco-Prussian war a while back, and before the interpreter here, whose medium was mostly Parisian French, the general gave it up.

After the evening meal an artist along from Omaha made a few sketches of the guests and the scene, and then Sheridan announced that this was an early night to bed, for tomorrow the hunt would begin. So on the duke's twenty-second birthday he rode out into the wilderness sunshine of a January morning. He was on one of the Cody buffalo horses, dressed in winter hunting garments, very quiet in color compared to the bright uniforms of his entourage, "his kings," as the Negro troops called them. But their awe turned to laughter as these kings, one after another, fell off their horses, which had been selected for their showiness and spirit from all the surrounding army posts and grained up for weeks.

With the scouts, the guides, and some Indians ahead, and an escort of troops, the duke rode out toward the Republican herd. Beside him were the plains heroes of Indian fighting, Forsyth, who still limped from the Beecher Island fight, and Custer of the Washita. A few paces ahead of the duke rode Cody in his buckskin, his hair falling over his shoulders, shinier and longer even than Custer's, leading them out to the herd that Lonesome Charley and some Indians had located yesterday, and watched all night to prevent drifting.

The duke had a rifle in the scabbard and at his side the new presentation Smith & Wesson, one of the .44 Russian model revolvers made on a large arms contract for the Russian government. Following the example and directions of Cody, he brought down his first buffalo in grand style, Cody's hunting horse carrying him up very close to a big old bull, heavy and ponderous. Alexis was a masterly horseman if not a practiced running shot against the great bison of the American plains. Custer and Forsyth also distinguished themselves. The two-hour hunt left between twenty and thirty buffaloes scattered over the rolling prairie, depending upon who told the story. The butchers for the officers' mess came in to take enough fresh hump roast for all around, leaving the rest for the troops and the Indians. The duke supervised the skinning of his buffalo and the cleaning of the head for mounting. It should have a place of honor among the trophies of his palace. When it was unloaded from the pack horses in camp he was pleased to discover that the head was even finer than he had realized in his excitement, the horns less worn than usual for such an old bull—really the finest head taken in the hunt, although on the range it had seemed that Charley Reynolds had managed to shoot the best one, a very wild bull that had almost escaped. There was much expressed admiration and drinking of toasts, and much praise of this wonderful plainsman, this Wee-am Codee, this Bison Beel who led the hunt.

Later when Cody, who had celebrated a little too well, was taken away for a while, it was revealed that the duke and Sheridan, too, knew there was a woman in the party, brought by her brother who had homesteaded nearby lately. She had seemed sufficiently hidden in her brother's hunting outfit and by the forked saddle she rode, although the few settlers in the region already knew her as an excellent buffalo hunter. This Mrs. Raymond had taken a fine bull too, before the duke got his, but fortunately rather far from his run with Cody, so he need not notice it. But the young Alexis did notice that she was a woman, and when he discovered that she spoke French very well, he asked her to accompany him through the Indian camp to study the home life of these extraordinary aborigines whose children looked like some of their own Mongolian tribes at home.

Later there was great feasting and singing, Russian, Indian and then by the troops and the scouts, one of whom was a trained concert singer who had found times too hard and so came west to hunt the buffalo last year. In the morning the sun came out even finer and today Custer rode with the duke, Custer in his buckskin too, and General Sheridan along, but taking it slower.

Today the Indians, led by Chief Spotted Tail, made a neat little surround for the royal guest. They came up on all sides of a small bunch and started the running buffaloes into a frightened circling, winding it ever tighter and closer together. Bow-armed, with arrows ready for the strings, an extra one in the teeth, the quivers full, they brought them down, one after another, within a compact area not much larger than an acre. A huge bull broke for freedom and one of their noted bow men, a half-brother of the chief Whistler, sent an arrow clear through the buffalo, his horse thundering along beside him. The bloody arrow was left behind, to quiver a little as it stuck a moment in the frozen ground and then fell into the grass as the buffalo's running forelegs began to crumple under him. Then he went down, his head still outthrust.

The duke and his men gave the Indians a great Russian cheer and then another after the hunting dance that the Sioux made during the noon rest. In the afternoon General Sheridan took part in the shooting too, and watched the duke get two more buffaloes, but it was good that it was the final hunt, for too much recklessness was showing up. Mike Sheridan, the general's brother, ran his fine horse down in the chase, to be left flat as the buffaloes, and Custer's horse fell dead after they reached camp.

There was another interval of unpleasantness during the evening smoke when Spotted Tail rose to make a speech. It was not in the tone of unctuous flattery of the rest of the hunt. Old Spot looked grim and sober. His people were poor in the midst of all this wealth and show that the whites were making from the Indian's buffaloes. He was now allowed a trader, but one with few goods and they should have two to make for competition and better prices. In addition Spotted Tail wanted permission to hunt here south of the Platte until the farming the white man promised to teach his people fed them well. None of the things that the treaties promised came, only soldiers to chase the Indians around and kill anybody they could catch, particularly women and children. Even he had to move many times and quickly the last few years and none could doubt him as a peace man, always with a white sub-agent along to see that his young men made no trouble. Who watched the troops to see that they killed no one?

Little of this long and customary complaint was interpreted for the duke, although he inquired of Mrs. Raymond later. "The chief, he was of extremely serious mien—" the young Alexis persisted.

Afterward the royal guest was serenaded by the cavalry band, the Indians made a powwow with a little war dance at a great evening fire built before the young duke's tent. He gave the warriors fifty dollars in fifty-cent pieces and passed out twenty beautiful blankets and many fine hunting knives with ivory handles, made for the Czar's own men.

They returned to the railroad, still through the most unJanuary weather the old-timers could recall. There Alexis gathered his guests to his private car, the entertainment ending with a big dinner, complimentary speeches all around, and the presentation of a large purse of money and a diamond stick pin to Bill Cody. Then the duke and his escort of American generals went on to Denver and back on the Kansas Pacific. In eastern Colorado they stopped for one more hunt, this time guided by Chalkley Beeson, and without the show of Buffalo Bill or Spotted Tail's Sioux. Chalk was a former stage driver and hide hunter, in addition to being a good musician who was also interested in ranching and in investments along the new railroad coming up the Arkansas River. The hunt was a good one, and afterward the royal party stopped for a visit with the legislature at Topeka. A fine picture was taken of the entire party, and one of the duke with Custer, both in their hunting outfits and their pistols, against a romantic backdrop. From Topeka the party went on a brief tour of the south. By now the duke was wearing a buckskin shirt like Custer and Cody, even with evening dress. All these things were in the papers, and plainly the young duke had made other conquests besides those of the great American bison. Fifty years later there were grandmothers who spoke wistfully of the handsome warm-eyed grand duke they met in their budding days.

⊂ᗒ   ⊂ᗒ   ⊂ᗒ

THE END OF
THE DREAM

THERE WAS a phase of the northern herd that those farther south did not have. That was the sudden, the frenzied hope of the Indians that the buffaloes were actually coming back, not to replenish the regions of the fierce and ruthless hunt but back to the quieter prairies near the Indians, particularly near the Sioux agencies of Dakota.

The buffalo had been vanishing east of the Missouri River for a long time, and fifteen years ago most of the south half of Dakota Territory was cleaned out by the hungry eastern Sioux from Minnesota and northern Iowa, pushed westward to hunt as their cornlands were preempted by settlers. There were often equally hungry white men too, and other hungry Indians from down towards the Platte, as well as the robe hunters urged on by the Missouri traders. By 1882 the agency Indians, who were to be fed in exchange for their relinquished lands, were starving, and yet no chief could get a permit to take his people out on a hunt because plainly the buffaloes were gone.

Many Indians and even some breeds and white men who had lived close to the great herds a long time refused to believe that these multitudes had been all killed off by hunters. "Man never could have exterminated them; they went back into the earth from whence they came," an old Hudson's Bay Company employe said.

As early as 1880 rumors had reached the starving Indians, rumors that the buffalo was coming back. They were even louder when Sitting Bull returned from Canada in 1881, not only because of the stories of the Bull's great power in dreaming that helped his reputation as a medicine man, but because some white men told of seeing buffaloes in new places. In September 1882, an old plainsman saw a herd on the Riviere du Lac, which joins the Mouse River near the present Minot, North Dakota. This was well east of the Missouri, and no buffaloes had been seen there in a long, long time.

Sitting Bull and the other headmen listened to these stories, which were not of a few old bulls hidden out in the badlands but good little herds of young stock with silky pelage. The hungry widows of the Sioux wars heard the stories too, and were reminded of the old holy men who foretold a time when the whites would be driven from the Indians' earth. Then the buffaloes would return, and now there was this news that they were coming.

Scouts slipped out of Sitting Bull's camp in the night, not to shoot but only to look, no matter how hungry, for shooting might break the medicine, the holy spell. It was true as they had heard—not just a few leaderless old bulls that had wandered far from the regular path of migration or fled into rough country from pursuit. This was a real herd, with fat young cows and the darkening calves at their sides, very many of them fat young animals. As proof of this they brought back sacks of new buffalo chips, round as great brown maggots, firm, from young stock and plainly not dropped over five, six days ago.

The old men examined the chips carefully and peered into

the faces of their scouts to see what might cling there from all that the men had seen, all their eyes had laid upon. None of the scouts told what the old ones saw they were holding back—the number. And when the leader of them finally made the quick signs for thousands, the old faces broke into almost fearing smiles. At last it seemed good.

So there was a little of the old-time hunting medicine to make, and some dancing to lure the buffaloes, to welcome their coming as brothers are welcomed. Not with big ceremonials, which were forbidden by the white men, but small ones, and carried out in the remote reaches of the reservation, around fires upon which the medicine men threw bits of the buffalo chips and watched the old-time sacred smoke rise to the Powers who were bringing the dark herds back.

The news of around ten, twelve thousand buffaloes about halfway from Bismarck toward the Black Hills, between the Moreau and the Grand Rivers, brought out the whites too. Zack Sutley, a one-time meat man for Cody, Vic Smith and many other hunters and meat men gathered. With their improved rifles and the telescopic sights, they were set over the route the fleeing animals must surely take, to pick them off. Between eleven and twelve hundred escaped into the badland country. The rest fell.

Now the agent at Standing Rock, Sitting Bull's agency, got up a big hunt to help feed his hungry Indians. Some Sioux from the Cheyenne River Agency came along too, making around a thousand Indians, with an escort of troops, some publicity seekers and the white hunters that flocked in. Vic Smith was back, and Sutley with wagons along to haul the surplus meat to Deadwood. There was word that Bill Cody was coming too, looking for publicity, now that he planned to put a real Wild West show on the road.

By the time the party had made camp, the Indian scouts appeared on a ridge riding in the little circles that told of buffaloes seen, some buffaloes seen. It was sad for men like the Reverend Riggs, who had known his Sioux in better times to watch hope grow in the old Indians, and even sad for Sutley, who had seen the whole face of the Great Plains and its life changed

within less than sixteen years, the flower of its fauna exterminated, the native expropriated. Zack still shot true, but he
found himself hanging back a little with a few other hunters,
keeping out of the way of this last Indian buffalo chase, they
called it. Because the Indians had been disarmed not many
years before, all but the headmen had to borrow guns and Sutley and a few of the others loaned theirs out a while. Some of
the older Indians used bows, a little shame-faced before their
young men who talked so big about the fine rifles of the hunters.
But all this was forgotten in the surround, in the whoops and
dust and thunder of hoofs, the cracking of rifles, the crashing
of bodies, including an occasional horse and rider.

And by evening over half of the herd was dead, the rest
guarded by the Indians who still knew the use of wind and
man smell to hold a wild herd from drifting. In the morning
they finished the rest, all except a few old bulls who managed
to slip away into the breaks and badlands. The Indians packed
some of the meat across their horses for immediate use, the
green robes laid on first, hair side down, the meat on top and
the ends of the hide lapped over each way and tied securely
with new-cut rawhide strings. But most of the buffaloes were to
be dried for winter.

And in this last camp Sitting Bull sat alone much of the
time, his pipe cold beside him, remembering the great Indian
and buffalo country he was born into. It was just over on the
Grand River there, the year before the fire boat, the *Yellowstone,* came smoking up the Missouri. Now all of it was gone,
vanished like wind on the buffalo grass. True, he had known
glory, much glory, but his broad face was hard as the walls of
the upper Yellowstone when he thought about it, for what is
glory to a man who must see his people as he saw them now?

It seemed he could no longer believe that the buffaloes
would all return as had been foretold, and that the white men
around him here, the agent, the troopers and hunters would all
be swept away.

Suddenly now the alarmists who had long been predicting
the extinction of the American bison found receptive ears,

when only two hundred and fifty buffaloes were left on earth. A little investigation placed the figure higher: two hundred and fifty-six in captivity, some of these in the cross-breeding herds, and about eight hundred and thirty-five wild—all that was left of the fifty million, more or less, of 1867. But most or all of the eight hundred thirty-five wild ones might already be dead, for hunters no longer made their killings public. Once there was word that the wild buffaloes had been reduced to fifty. Surely this was much, much too close to complete extinction and at last some energetic men went to work.

One of these was William Temple Hornaday, chief taxidermist of the U. S. National Museum from 1882. He was doubly alarmed. He had no good group for his museum, and the noblest beast of the western world, only recently the most numerous ruminant known, was in immediate danger of extinction. He got his specimen in finest pelage in December of 1886, the hard winter that cleaned out the cattlemen from the upper Missouri down into lower Colorado, and he was largely responsible for both the preservation and the enlargement of the buffalo herds.

Off on the Indian reservations there was another kind of activity for the buffalo, for his restoration. The ghost dancing started by the Indian prophet out in Nevada was to help bring back the great herds and to set the Indian back into his proper place. It was an old dream, one that fostered the earlier rebellions against the white man, such as the pueblo uprisings, the resistance of Tecumseh and his brother The Prophet, and inspired the Shakers of the northwest. The new prophet, called the Messiah, was Wovoka, son of the Prophet of Mason Valley, who died in 1870. By 1881 a young Kiowa had made medicine to bring the buffalo back and stirred up so much excitement that the year was called the Winter of the Buffalo Prophecies in the Kiowa calendar and caused the agent to report his uneasiness to Washington. In 1887 another Kiowa revived the prophecy and infected the whole tribe. They abandoned their camps and fled to their new prophet, but the day of delivery passed and the whites were still there, with not one buffalo in sight.

Now they had heard of this new Messiah and so great was

their need that, in spite of the earlier disappointments, they sent a delegation to Nevada to see him. Other tribes also sent reliable men. They came back with news of great moment, particularly to the old buffalo country. They told of falling down on the ground in a dreaming in which they saw great herds of their brother, the buffalo, come running over the broken terrain, come from canyons and cuts and draws where not even a buffalo chip remained. As the headmen of the Sioux listened, they recalled the buffaloes that had appeared at the edge of the badlands only a few years ago, a whole herd to be killed for the hungry where none had been in a long time. And for those who doubted even now there was news. In September 1888, a hunter named John Whiteside had seen over sixty buffaloes while hunting off north from Bismarck. They were stampeding to water and he was almost caught in a ravine that led to the river while he stopped to shoot one. The buffaloes did not hesitate at the stream but swam across and when he saw them last they were going northwest, the first herd in the valley for many years.

"Ah, they were running, and they paid no attention to the white hunter," the old men said, and so they began to dance.

The agents everywhere were uneasy, and kept a close guard on the Indians but they knew little of the scouts that were kept out watching. Secretly these men slipped off to the rough country where the buffaloes would surely appear first, as those up at the badlands did in 1883; those first ones perhaps a sign from the dancing of the Kiowa prophet, and of Wovoka—a sign to get ready. It was true that no more came to answer all the buffalo medicine that the Sioux had made secretly, perhaps because the best, the sundance, was too big and a forbidden thing that the troops would surely break up. Now there was news of this little herd up north of Bismarck—once more buffaloes in a deserted region. Such things were not to be forgotten, no more than the memory of the meat they had tasted from the newcome herd they had helped butcher near the badlands, now that the hunger of the reservations had closed upon the dreamers once more.

They must think about this man out west, called the new Messiah, which was the name of the Christ that the missionaries followed. The Christ had come to save the white men and they hanged him from the crossed tree, as was clear in the pictures the priests brought, long, long ago. Now he had come to the Indians. But of this the Sioux who came back from him had very little to say. They admitted that the Messiah was not a stranger come from far off, only a man who had always lived around the reservations, yet he was the son of a prophet, and he became like dead before them and then returned and talked of what he had seen.

"What does he see?" the eager ones demanded, and those whose lips were still bitter from the treaty forced upon them in the stockade, the treaty that took their lands and the Black Hills with all their gold.

The Messiah told that he saw the Indians in a happy time again, free from the reservations, with the lodges full of meat and other good things, and with buffaloes all around. But for this happy time to be brought the Messiah said they must be peaceful and of good heart toward all people. They must make the dancing as he instructed, the ceremonials and the dancing, and soon it would all come.

Other men who had seen these dreams also spoke of the buffaloes on all sides, the white men gone as though they had never been, and all the dead ones of the Indians alive once more and right among them.

This last Sitting Bull and the others who had not accepted the Happy Hunting Ground of the whites into their religion could not suddenly believe in now. It had always been that the dead returned to the earth which fed them, as the flower returned, and the tree and the buffalo and all living things go back. They returned in gratitude to feed other growing things, all the grasses that fattened the buffaloes and the people. The spirit which is like the light in the coal goes out as the light does when the coal dies, returning once more to the light that is in the Great Powers, of whom all things are a part—the earth, the sky and all that lies between. To Sitting Bull and other old medicine and holy men this promise of the dead returning to life seemed thin as the morning fog along the creek bottoms, gone with one look from the sun.

But the Indians were hungry and very many of them sick with tuberculosis, trachoma, measles and other diseases. So they started the dancing again, men and women together everywhere, to last four days this time and then later again and perhaps once more. If they did everything in a certain way, with no hand or heart turned against any man, and persisted in this for some moons, not too many, the Messiah who had been hung to the crossed trees by the whites would bring all good things back to the Indians.

A tall tree trunk was set up out on the frozen winter prairie. The headmen stood beside it and the others in a circle around them and the tree, hands held together, moving, dancing, with the ghost shirts drawn over their clothing, the holy bullet-proof shirts that the Messiah showed them how to make. They danced from Friday afternoon until sundown on Sunday without food or water, each as he was led to do, alone or together with others, their moccasins whispering on the dead grass, murmuring on the frozen earth in shuffling, slow, steady supplication, the dancers perhaps becoming suddenly rigid, falling in trances. Revived, they told what they had seen. Many slipped into animal dances, bobbed on all fours like buffaloes, pawed the freezing ground, butted heads like the bulls, bawling, and then fell into the dreaming. Afterward they told of this place where the white men were truly rolled away, and all the dead relatives back among them, with buffalo herds coming dark over the horizon, and fast horses ready for the chase. So more joined hands and danced with the holy signs on them, danced on all the reservations of the buffalo country, singing the repeating songs of their dreams.

> *They say there is to be a buffalo hunt over here!*
> *They say there is to be a buffalo hunt over here.*
> *Make the arrows! Make the arrows!*
> *Says the father, says the father,*

an old warrior sang in his high thin voice, jumping on his gaunt legs, bare and painted below the flapping breechclout, numb in the December wind.

White men came to see them, many from everywhere. John

Cook came too, the Johnny Cook of the buffalo hunting down around the Staked Plains where he had wondered once how he would feel if he were the son of an Indian and saw his buffaloes killed. He was still in the Indian service. He watched the dancing at one place a little while and then went sadly away.

At the Sioux agency at Pine Ridge, South Dakota, there was a new agent, with some newspapermen nearby who reported the ghost dancing as an uprising. With a little encouragement, particularly from one New York newspaper, they began to send out sensational stories of massacres, of white blood to flow and indeed already flowing, the blood-thirsty Sioux off the reservations and ravishing the settlements. Nobody said that not one Indian had left his reservation, except the few scouts out to herald the buffalo's coming. They watched out towards the Black Hills and on the path from the north, the way the buffaloes used to come hurrying to the shelter of Pine Ridge and the White River bluffs below it. The newspaper accounts alarmed both the settlers and the greenhorn agent, Royer, so he fled the agency and telegraphed for troops. They came, with four Hotchkiss guns and headed for Pine Ridge.

Up north, on Sitting Bull's reservation, the memory of the buffaloes that were suddenly there in 1883 was particularly poignant to those who had taken part in the hunt and eaten the flesh. Sitting Bull had been afraid that the troops would stop the dancing as they had the sundance, but he was reassured by the promise of the Messiah that there would be no violence, and no one could be hurt, because they would be wearing the sacred, bullet-proof ghost shirts.

So they danced, Sitting Bull too, for he had been a strong dreamer not many years ago. The agent there was an experienced man, and although no lover of old Bull, he knew that the dancing would soon wear itself out in the sub-zero weather of Dakota. He maneuvered to get the notoriety seeker, Buffalo Bill Cody and his newspapermen put off the reservation. But the army was less easily managed, and when orders came from Washington to arrest Sitting Bull, he held the army off a while, predicting general bloodshed if the troops came for the old medicine man. But the order was not rescinded and so he had to send out a force of his Indian police under Sergeant Bullhead to make the arrest. Before the sleeting dawn of December fifteenth, 1890, the Sioux in the blue coats silently entered Sitting Bull's log cabin and dragged him naked from the sleeping robes. By the time they got him outside on his horse, the place was surrounded by the chief's old-time warriors, and even Sitting Bull's son taunted the old man for his quiet surrender. But the moment the police got rough with Bull, one of the warriors shot the leader of the Indian police. Bullhead fell, but he fired into the chief's body as he went down, and another policeman shot Sitting Bull too, through the head from behind, as though this had been prearranged.

So the most persistent exponent of the nomadic buffalo hunting life was dead. There was hand-to-hand fighting in that gray December morning light, but it was all gone for nothing, lost on the wind.

As the Indians heard that Sitting Bull was shot, they scattered, taking their women and children out of the way before the soldiers came and there was more killing. One group fled southward to Big Foot's band, and suddenly that chief's people were afraid too, and they forgot their dancing for the buffalo's return. Instead all ran together now, heading towards the badlands and then turning, struck south towards the Sioux on Pine Ridge Reservation. But people had been fleeing from there too, going north to the rough country, to Sheep Mountain in the badlands because there were troops riding up from the railroad just south in Nebraska.

Some of these troops overtook Chief Big Foot, with his one hundred six men and two hundred and fifty women and children, and ordered them to surrender. The Indians did this without protest. They couldn't fight; they didn't want to fight, even if they weren't practically without arms, and their old chief were not sick with pneumonia in one of the wagons. To show their good will some of Big Foot's warriors immediately enlisted as scouts to help bring in the Indians who had fled to the badlands camp, and started for them.

The troops were under Col. J. W. Forsyth, brother of the man the Indians surrounded with his scouts in the Beecher Island fight in 1868 on a branch of the Republican River. He had eight troops of the Seventh Cavalry here, among them a couple of grizzled old campaigners who were with the regiment since its organization twenty-four years ago, men who chased Indians with Custer back in 1867 around the Republican buffalo herd, men who had ridden upon the Cheyennes out of the blizzard down on the Washita, and who were surrounded by Indians up on Reno hill while Custer died on a ridge a few miles away.

But now it would be different than that last time. Even though the Indians had surrendered, the troops had the four Hotchkiss guns set up on a ridge that overlooked the tents as the grey winter morning dawned, and a company of Cheyenne Indian scouts to help them. With Big Foot's Sioux surrounded, the colonel ordered all the men out of the tents, leaving the women and children behind there unprotected, and motioned the Indians up close to the troops standing ready with their guns in their hands.

The men of the band came in a long slow file behind the sick chief, wrapped close in their blankets against the freezing wind. Slowly they squatted in a line on the winter ground facing the troops. It was only two weeks since Sitting Bull was disarmed and then shot down. The men who killed him were Indians, but the coats were the same, always the blue. Yet resistance now would mean death, immediate death, although perhaps that was all that lay ahead of them in any case, for it was well known that soldiers who come to an Indian camp bring the killing in their hands. They are not easily cheated by a pleasant surrender, like that of yesterday, or the waving of a white flag.

Almost at once the Indians were sent back to the tents to bring their guns, first one little group, then some others, and so on. Because only a few arms were brought, the troopers went to search the tents themselves, driving the frightened women and children out, to huddle together in terror, but with no place to run on the empty plain, the one ravine that was nearby too shallow for hiding. Their men watched helplessly, their dark faces hard and unmoving as the stone of the Black Hills. When no more weapons were found in the tents the troops prepared to search the warriors, but nobody knew quite how to do this dangerous thing. The Indian lets no one lay hands upon his body or the body of his people. There was a scuffle between two soldiers and a Sioux they were searching, and somehow a rifle was discharged. Then an excited young Indian shot into the sudden silence, and the troops fired a volley, so close to the Indians that their guns almost touched them. Nearly half of Big Foot's men went down before that one volley. Those left, mostly with no more than knives, clubs or perhaps a hidden revolver, charged into the carbines as though to smother their smoking mouths. On the ridge the Hotchkiss guns began their stuttering fire, but upon the tents and the women and children there, cutting them down, the tents jerking as if alive, with crying coming from the inside, and then going down in smoke, some of them blazing out in the strong gray wind.

A handful of Indians, mostly women and children, were left to run in panic, pursued by the blood-heated troopers and raked with the Hotchkisses swung upon their flight. The soldiers chased the Indians like rabbits fleeing over the prairie, some of the women left dead as far as two miles away where Indians had danced for the buffaloes' return only a few days ago.

The Pine Ridge Indians who had withdrawn to the badlands were surrendering when they heard the guns over at Wounded Knee Creek, and later they saw the handful of terrified and bleeding survivors. Some gave the desperate war cry of the Sioux warriors riding to their death and charged away from their trooper escort over to the battlefield, where, now, two hours after the fight, the soldiers were still hunting down the living. For a while the angry Sioux warriors drove the troops back, but it was only for a little while and with raw courage, for the Indians had no arms to fight off the cavalry. And in the afternoon snow began to fall, running in thin grey curls over the desolated ground at Wounded Knee, settling in little white drifts behind the bodies of the dead, the women and children, the chief and his men. As the snow deepened, they seemed more and more like great whitened carcasses scattered where they fell over the prairie.

Now the dream of the buffalo, too, was done.

from THE CATTLEMEN

Some Dedicated Men

Pulling for New Grass

New Breed

Ritual and Restoration

SOME DEDICATED MEN

MANY AN early Texan lived almost as wholly from his cow as the Plains Indian from his buffalo. She was meat, fat, soap, and candlelight to him, and her skin had even more uses than the buffalo's. Although it was less commonly the white man's dwelling, she often did provide his shelter and the cover for his wagon bows, the door to his first dugout, and perhaps the floor and the rugs. Early ranch and settler shacks were often lined with rawhide against the blue northers and the scorpions, centipedes, and rattlesnakes. Rawhide made the woven bottom of the Texan's springless bed and his chairs, stools, cradles, trunks, valises, baskets, buckets, dough pans, and even the settler's churn, although some thought it gave the butter a peculiar flavor.

Cowskin furnished the rancher his winter coat, his carriage and wagon robes, often his bedcovers as rawhide made his poncho and his chaps, his *chaparejos,* to protect him against brush and thorns and rain and cold. In addition to the regular leathern uses, rawhide often took the place of iron, cotton, wood, and even silver or paper. It was the rawhide riata in place of the surveyor's chain that measured off the Spanish land grants.

The horses were hobbled with strips of rawhide instead of iron, and sometimes shod with it, as were the oxen. In a pinch rawhide served as slates, blackboards, playing cards, and faro table tops. Portraits and holy pictures were embossed or burned on it. When the horrifying cholera epidemic of 1849-50 swept up along all the western trails to the edge of swift water, and reached San Antonio, too, there were so many dead in the town and the fear of infection was so great that the corpses were simply rolled into cowhides and buried. To the Texan the cow was all the things the buffalo was to the hunting Indian, except perhaps the center of his highest religious ritual that the buffalo occupied in the sundance of many Plains tribes, and perhaps that could come, too.

The restrictions in trade and money during the war made Texas even more surely the Rawhide State. The trail drivers used the skin of the cow as thread and twine, pins, nails, washers, screws, bolts, as well as iron and cloth. While hackamores and picket ropes were usually horsehair, the lariat was rawhide, of four, even eight long, even strands, round-braided into graceful length, stretched and oiled until the throw rope was just stiff enough to sing out like a fiddle string and just the right weight for deft and accurate aim.

While the Texas Ranger was turning to the Colt six-shooter, California vaqueros still lassoed and dragged horse-stealing Indians to death rather than shot them, as the early Spaniards of Texas had also done. Once duels were fought by horsemen with leather riatas, each man trying to dodge the rival's loop while trying to rope him, jerk him off, drag him to pieces behind a spurring run through the cactus. Sometimes more or less friendly chapping contests decided who was to escort the very occasional girl home from a ranch country dance. Even the winner would be stiff for a week from the spanking his saddle-leaned buttocks took from the rawhide chap leg wielded against him. A particularly keen rivalry between Negro or Mexican bullwhackers or cow hands was sometimes settled by bull whips at a certain number of steps, the experts snaking the whips out in powerful, stinging, flesh-cutting lashes that sounded like sharp pistol shots but carried farther on the wind. To admit defeat short of blindness or collapse was shameful beyond a man's gut. Sometimes the welted faces were carried with a little of the show-off of the German officer's sword-cut cheek. Even in Texas the welts were proof of a little extra Texas dash and sand, an ability to ride life to a finish even as it had to be lived in the San Saba country.

Perhaps it was true that the Texan of 1867 needed to be tough as whang leather and hard as a flint hide, with the darkness of defeat and ruin on all the South and, except in the vast increases among the Longhorns, as heavily upon Texas. In addition to all the rustlers there was the Reconstruction Act of March, 1867, passed by the Radicals over President Johnson's veto. By this the South was turned over to the carpetbaggers pouring in all the past winter and to the local citizens not "disfranchised for participation in the rebellion" called scalawags.

McCoy's promise of good facilities and a sure and fair cattle market at Abilene started a booming of hope from the Red River to the Gulf and out beyond the Cross Timbers. But he had no control over the depression in the East. The first trainload of Longhorns sold very poorly in Chicago and the second shipment, around 900 head, found no market at all and had to be taken to Albany, New York. Apparently it wasn't that no one wanted meat, even trail and railway-gaunted meat, and from cattle rumored diseased enough to sicken any cow that touched the ground the Longhorns walked on. There just wasn't much money around. Newspapers reported long queues of the unemployed being fed in the Tombs at New York City, and not with beef or even beef soup.

Surely these postwar years seemed enough to discourage anyone, but to many men of Texas the cow had been a way of life for a long time—dedicated men, dedicated to the cow with all their property, their time, even their lives.

One who was already an old-time cattleman by 1867 was Richard King, a New York Irishman. At ten he had stowed away on a schooner for Mobile. Discovered, he was made cabin boy and was on the steamer back in 1842 when the chief of the Seminoles and his principal warriors were lured on board for counciling and then told they were prisoners. Later, with a partner, King operated twenty-six small steamboats on the shifting, treacherous Rio Grande. Much of this time Captain King was also a cattleman. As early as 1852 he selected the Santa Gertrudis country of south Texas for a ranch, and bought the land as he could, land of many and sometimes doubtful titles: Spanish, Mexican, Texan, and United States. Some of it he had to buy twice. But it was coastal plain and seemed worth the effort. There was green-gray prickly pear, with the great flat ten-inch tongues or hands, reaching up to eight, ten feet. Most of the scattered trees of the sandy region had been brought in by the Longhorns dropping the seeds as they roamed the region. The most prolific were the mesquite and live oak, both able to exist without rain, both low, twisted, and often in clusters or *mottes* penetrable only to small animals or a determined man on foot. The oaks favored the coast, particularly the sandy belt, the mesquite spreading farther west on the black loam and clay as well as the sand. Willows came in too, and the huisache, the wild persimmon, the ebony and the brazil bush—all gnarled and thorny, mostly four, five feet high, seldom much above the mounted cowboy. This was the wild brush that the Longhorn favored, and therefore the cowman.

By 1867 King had bought out one partner for $50,000 and dissolved the agreement with another. He hoped to own all the land between the Nueces and the Rio Grande and, further, to control a strip of land three miles wide from Brownsville to the railroad in Kansas for a cattle trail. The King Ranch already contained a good portion of this land the captain coveted, and the Chisholm Trail promised to serve as a cattle highway when beef prices came back. In the meantime he started to fence his range with wooden planks, another typical King dream. But his cattle were flourishing and he had great plans for improved stock. For this the scrub bulls must be kept out, away from good blood.

In the meantime the glutted markets forced the Texas ranchers to set up hide and tallow factories, to reap something from the great herds, make a little northern money. King was one of the first to try the slaughtering sheds and pens set up along the coast at such places as Fulton and Brazoria. Here cattle scarcely worth the rustler's trouble were harvested for the hide, worth more than the whole cow alive. Some were mossy old steers with horns eight or nine feet across, rough, wavy horns so heavy they threatened to tip the steer's thin rump up into the sky. Here New England buyers gathered hides for their tanneries, tallow for candles and soap. Sometimes hoofs and horns went to glue and comb manufacturers and hair for plaster and padding. Only the meat was worthless, left to rot or to feed the hordes and clouds of gorging scavengers—the small skittering animals and the larger, the foxes and coyotes, the buzzards and magpies, with the flies gathering thick over everything, in clouds around the long sheds and the factories as thick as the stink. At Brazoria Negroes were hired to take what was wanted of the carcasses and then slid the rest down the chutes into the river, where fish fought obscenely over them, great catfish, evil-whiskered mouths slashing and crushing, the fish leaping clear of the water in the struggle. A factory down at the bottom of the Brazos attracted whole schools of fighting sharks.

This waste of meat distressed Richard King, who had known the hungry and saw this all as profit lost besides. He tried preserving the flesh of newly-killed Longhorns by injecting brine into the veins. The process failed but he brought in several thousand hogs to fatten on the meat. Many got away into the brushy country, where descendants of the King pigs were killed and eaten by cowboys for many years.

The factories weren't the only places where cowhides were taken. Mexicans scoured the country, hamstringing the fleeing Longhorns with machetes, stripping off the hides. Some fired the grass to herd the cattle together in unburned strips and pockets. After blue northers the cattle that had drifted into bunches and piles along the coast drew out everybody, even boys and some women, to skin the dead and the dying. Only the slaughter of the buffalo up along the regions of the railroad exceeded the hide taking here.

Yet even in this time so sorrowful for the cattlemen Richard King was laying plans for better cattle, with more meat and

with an immunity to the disease the North called the Texas
fever but which no Texan intended to admit existed. For this
better, this immune stock King was working out better range
methods, more efficient handling and care. His methods, all his
methods would be his own, and if there were those who objected,
he intended to be too high, too big to reach, for anybody, or any
power to reach. He was a dedicated man.

There were other men with determination in the cow business. Soon after the Mexican War James Olive had moved his
family from Louisiana to Williamson County, Texas, and
started in cattle. He and his wife were quiet, religious, church-
going, but there was trouble between the father and the eldest
son, young I.P., called Print, for Prentice. In Texas this grew
like the thorns, with the son's taste for bad companions, hard
liquor, cards, and gun play and the mother still shielding him
as she had from birth, keeping his actions hidden from the father when she could, standing before him with her broad skirts
outspread between him and the son when his misconduct was
discovered. Finally Print was drawn into the war, wounded,
and, recovered, made a mule skinner and captured at Vicks-
burg. Paroled in an exchange of prisoners, he was appointed
to garrison duty at Galveston. Here, in idleness, he found drinking and gambling even more attractive and more available, as
well as several shooting scrapes that involved no one that an
Olive could possibly have termed a damnyankee.

When the war ended, Print went into stock raising near
home. Pleased at what looked like a sober settling down at last,
the father and two of the other sons bought more stock. Print
and the other three had their farms separate but they ran a
ranch farther west on a large tract of state land together, each
with his own brand. Under Print's hard riding, hard cussing,
they built reservoirs to catch any water that fell, dug wells, and
later put up windmills. Their cattle grew into thousands. For a
while they neighbored with the ranchers around them, particularly with the Snyders, J.W. and Dudley, also of Williamson
County. It had been Dudley who trailed beef to the Confed-

eracy, swimming his herds behind the two oxen who drew his trail wagon but led the steers across the swollen rivers. Dudley Snyder was known as a good man to tie to, and Print Olive missed few tricks.

In 1866 Print had bossed the general roundup of the region, really only a great cow hunt for stock branded before the war, the unmarked, the mavericks, to be divided among the ranches represented. At night the men gambled in the light of brush fires with the unbranded stock, a top critter worth $5 in chips, down to a yearling valued at fifty cents. The Moore boy who was along watching for his father's strays kept the fires going for two bits a night. Print Olive furnished the grub: coffee, corn meal, salt, whisky, and all the beef a man could eat—so long as it wasn't Olive beef. But that was customary.

By the 1870's many were complaining about the Olives, not aloud, but among themselves. Their stock was shrinking while the Olive herds, particularly Print's, more than doubled every year. There were some complaints at the courthouse but nothing came of them except that a couple of the bellyachers seemed to quit the country. At least, as Print said, nobody saw them around any more. Then there were rumors of trouble with a new settler, a young man called Deets Phreme, who went into cattle. One spring day Print Olive, his brother Ira, and some hired help starting on a cattle drive ran into Phreme and a couple of his hands. It seemed that the Olives accused him of killing their cattle and pistol-whipped him until his face and head were cut and swollen, knocked him down, and told him if they caught him on the range again he would be shot.

Old-timers warned him to go, get out, but Phreme was determined to stay. He had a legal right here. He was still as stubborn when he heard the Olive version of the encounter, saying they had found some of their brands in the Phreme herd and while the men cut out their stock, Print and the settler had words. Later Phreme and his hired man had shot at young Bob Olive, Print's brother, tried to bushwhack the youth.

Plainly they were setting the young settler up for a target, the old-timers said.

A few days later Print Olive managed to meet Phreme out on the prairie. "Did you shoot at my brother Bob?" he demanded.

"No, I didn't," the settler replied, "but I sure as hell would like to take a pop at you!"

The two men fired almost the same instant and fell together in the stinking powder smoke, both badly wounded. Phreme died soon afterward and Print Olive was several years really recovering. This time he was tried for murder and acquitted. "Easier to move men than cattle," he was reported to have said after the celebration.

Now the rumors about the Olives were more open, some perhaps spread by them to scare the settlers from the range they claimed, and harder to hold with so many pushing into the San Gabriel and Brushy Creek region. This man or that one vanished, and while few in Texas reported their comings and goings, some were settlers or little ranchers who left families without so much as a pone or a spoonful of hominy grits.

Maverickers, as well as out-and-out rustlers, and anybody that Print Olive decided fit these terms, were given fair warning to keep off the Olive range, claimed by the only right possible on public lands—the guns to hold them. Cattle prices were coming up again and large rustling outfits followed the rise like the eagle's shadow follows him on the ground below. Some of the ranchers had been hiring tough, gun-fingered cowboys, men who didn't care whose cattle they burnt with the ranch brand or whose milk cow they whooped off into the passing herd. In return the little outfits and the settlers stole back as much as they dared, and a little extra for their trouble.

Here and there suspected rustlers drew together in gangs for self-protection by lies, perjury, intimidation, and murder. Not that these methods were unfamiliar in a country largely unorganized, and where many a man even in high position was traveling under a name that never belonged to his father.

An old man called Pea Eye because his eyes were squushed together, although apparently large enough to see one of these gangs stealing cattle, appeared in court as a witness against them. Not long afterward his faithful ox team drew him into his home yard, down in the bottom of the wagon dead, full of buckshot. It seems nothing was done about that, except that one man was found hanging to a pecan tree and another vanished. Some of this was not far from the Olives, grown into a powerful clan of farmers, ranchers, and even peace officers, as peace officers went on the frontier.

The pointed complaint that stock was still vanishing in the Olive region Print Olive switched as handily as a spinning bronc switches ends. "We mean to kill any man found skinning our cattle or running off our horses." He said this half-tipsy in a bar but even those on fair terms with the Olives stood away a little, silent, remembering some of the things told of this fierce-eyed, gaunt-gutted man.

In a little while everybody knew that Print Olive meant what he said. The *Austin Statesman* reported the death of Turk Turner and James H. Crow over near McDade, adding:

> Two beeves had been killed and skinned and in the absence of the parties who did it, the carcasses were discovered and watch kept to see who would return to carry away the beef and hides. Finally the above parties returned with a wagon and after having loaded up and started away they were fired upon by unknown parties and both killed.

It seemed the bodies were found by Crow's young son sent to look for his father after school. The dead men were several hundred yards apart, the team tied to a tree. Later it came out that there was more than the *Statesman* printed. Turner and Crow had been wrapped tightly in the fresh hides of the cattle they killed, while still alive, and left on the prairie to suffer the slow and horrible Spanish "Death of the Skins" as the burning sun drew the green hides tight and hard as iron about the men. The brands had been turned up conspicuously for everyone to see—brands of the Olives.

There was alarm in the region, the women afraid, their eyes filmed with the horror of what had happened to Turner and Crow when their own men rode away, for the skins drew as

tightly about the innocent as the guilty. Turk had been re-
garded as a desperado but Old Man Crow, though he had a son
in the pen, had been considered honest. Besides, there was a
courthouse and law here against rustlers.

Although Crow's son accused the Olives of the murder,
nothing came of it. They were still on close terms with two of
the region's most prominent citizens, Dudley and J. W. Snyder.
The Snyders had a newly-purchased herd over on the Olive
range. Young Moore, who as a boy had kept the fires burning
for the roundup gambling back in 1866, was hired to keep an
eye on the stock and was boarding with the Olives.

Early in August the brothers, Print, Jay Thomas, and Ira,
with four cowhands, including two Negroes, were branding a
new herd. Although they were working the stock at the ranch,
at night the men stretched out on the prairie beyond the corrals
to sleep, their guns ready, apparently expecting a raid on the
cattle. Around one o'clock, when the moon was well hazed, they
were awakened by shots, men setting fire to the ranch buildings
and shooting at anyone seen moving out on the dusky prairie.
All the Olive outfit except young Moore were well armed. They
fired from behind banks and bushes in the rising flames from
the ranch house. There seemed to be fifteen, perhaps twenty in
the attacking mob, some scattered in a wide circle around the
ranch, others closer up, apparently with shotguns. In that first
stiff fire in the light of the burning ranch Thomas was hit with
several blasts of buckshot. Dying, he thrust his rifle into young
Moore's hand and motioned to him to unbuckle the cartridge
belt. Print was struck in the hip and crawled painfully for better cover, growling his curses against the men who killed his
brother. One of the Negroes was dead, too, the other badly
wounded. Inside the corral the cattle were milling hard from
the shots fired into them and in terror of the flames rising high
from the burning logs of the ranch house, sparks, and rolling
smoke over them. As they surged against the poles of the corral, the attackers jerked the gates back and the big steers stampeded for the breaks, almost running over the defenders scattered behind the shadowy clumps and banks.

The fire of the buildings died rapidly and the lowering

moon was lost in the smoke that filled the valley. In the darkness the fight became a watchful preparation for dawn, but with the first graying that might show a known face, the attackers slipped away. The ranch hands got Print stretched out to ease his wound a little and covered the half-naked body of Thomas. Then they discovered from the wounded Negro, who had been the first to awaken, that the place had been robbed of seven or eight hundred dollars Print kept on hand as down payment on cattle delivered.

But plainly this was not just a robbery; it was a plan for extermination. Many blamed the Turner and Crow killings. Crow's son, who had served time, promised vengeance. It was known that he headed a lot of toughs and desperados, probably the mob that attacked the Olive ranch. But immediately another gang loudly claimed the honor in saloons and the country post offices. Not even Print seemed certain who the attackers had been, with a dozen enemy outfits long itching for a showdown. In addition the Olives still had the trial for the murder of Turner and Crow before them. When court convened, the Olive forces camped at one side of Georgetown, the county seat, with an estimated forty armed men ready to drag the jury out to the trees down along the San Gabriel if the verdict went against them. On the other side of town it seems another camp had gathered, sixty men against the Olives, determined to uphold the law of Texas, here so close to Austin, to stop this bloodshed practically on the capitol steps.

All through the trial the town was divided into these two armed forces, the main street a barren and dusty sort of dare line between the waiting belligerents. But in the end the Olives were turned loose and without bloodshed.

By now more dead men had been turning up. Two were found hanging by their picket ropes near the Williamson County line, with plenty of money still on them, so it wasn't robbery. Later in the summer another dead man was found in the timber, stripped naked except for a hickory shirt and a blanket over him. "Almost like he was ambushed in bed, like Thomas Olive was," some said.

The law-abiding people of the region were furious as a bull

at the smell of blood. Here, within a twenty-five-mile distance, ten or twelve men had been killed during the past few months, and more farther out. Newspapers agreed in their protests, pointing out that more men had been killed in Texas the last year than she lost during all the lamented war. The editor of the *Austin Statesman* suggested a remedy, "—instead of hanging, have horse thieves and robbers surgically rendered incapable of crime and of the procreation of knavery."

As Print recovered enough to get around in his buggy, the bold attack and the death of one of their brothers stirred the Olives to a revenging fury, particularly young Bob, and the eldest, I.P., Print, his small eyes always burning in one rage or another. The women of the region pitied his wife, even those who envied her the wealth of her husband's ways. She had been an orphan reared by her grandfather, and was now the mother of a growing family, including a son who roused his father's anger and contempt as Print himself had infuriated his religious father. It was said that both Print's wife and his parents begged for a quieter life, for peace for the children. But families counted very little in these days of cow feuds, and Print and young Bob were laying for the killers of Thomas. Then one day two Negroes stopped in at the home ranch and asked Mrs. Olive for a drink of water. Although Negroes outside of the army were not allowed to carry guns, Print saw they had pistols strapped to their saddles. He ran to the house for his rifle, for once not beside him. With it across his arm he got between the Negroes at the well and their horses. When they started to leave, he pulled down on them, ordered them to halt, to explain their business.

Oh, they were just out hunting stolen horses and needed a little water this hot day, one of them answered amiably.

"Then why was you asking my wife where her husband's at?" Print roared. "Don't make a move!"

Scared, one of the men jumped for the horses and was shot dead on the spot. The other surrendered and was driven off the place with a bull whip, so it was rumored, perhaps to explain the deep red and swelling cuts on his dark face and the bloody shirt slashed from his crusted back. Within a month Print Olive was tried for the murder of the Negro and acquitted.

"Just another of them biggety Lincoln niggers gettin' an Olive ticket to hell," a sympathetic southerner said, and counted the dead Negroes credited to Print and to his brother Bob on his fingers, moving to the second hand and grinning. But no one counted the white men openly.

Even those friendly to the Olives were getting uneasy about Print. He was drinking more, brawling more, too, perhaps with the Union vets who had returned to Williamson County but often with long-time associates as well, until one or the other of the more peaceful brothers or a trusted ranch hand had to coax him out of the bar. Not even his brothers were spared Print's violent tongue now. And there were so many ways to get even with a rancher, ways that didn't involve actually facing his gun. He had cattle to be stolen, scattered, or destroyed, range ready for the lucifer or even flint and steel. He needed some who passed as friends in the emergencies common in the wilds, not only in prairie fires, stampedes, or attacks but in accidents and sickness. Even in ordinary times he needed someone to offer a pleasant word not forced by the fear of a low-slung gun, particularly a man with children, with a growing boy. There were rumors that even Print Olive's wife dared a little gentle urging for a move to new, less-crowded range.

Perhaps the wildest section of all Texas was the Big Bend country of the Rio Grande. Most of it was barren earth and rock, the stream squeezed into a deep canyon by the dark and rugged mountains, like a great hard-knuckled fist thrusting the river toward Mexico. In the entire region it seemed that nothing could ever be found except by the eagle or the buzzard. Yet even here at least one man had dedicated himself to the cow. Milton Faver was from the outside, too, although few who knew him had any idea of his origins, but no one doubted that he was the first cattle king of the Big Bend, with vaqueros to work his cattle and a trooping of Mexican farm hands for his fields and gardens and his famous peach orchards. His wife was a beautiful Mexican, fitted to her courtly, educated husband who spoke French, German, Spanish, and English fluently. It was said he came to the region in 1854, and that while he brought no cattle with him he tolled a comfortable number to swim the Rio Grande and burned his little F brand on them. Others said Faver was from England, had come to Mexico and started in cattle by trading with the Indians and then moved to Texas in 1857. Another account was that he came much later, straight from the North somewhere for his health, and that the start in cattle came with his beautiful wife.

He established the famous Cibolo Springs Ranch, later a freight stop for his ox trains on the Chihuahua-San Antonio line. The ranch, in the Chinati Mountains, was good tillable land, irrigated from living springs that had watered the cultivations of prehistoric Indians there. Faver's peaches were famous, and his peach brandy, too, particularly at the roundups. He made it in his fifty-gallon copper still, with enough extra to trade to the Indians but never delivered until they were safely far away from the ranch.

As the herds of Milton Faver, Don Milton as his Mexican neighbors called him, increased, he built new ranches for cattle and for sheep, the first of the latter in the region of the wolf and the eagle. At Cibolo he built a fort against Indians and bandits, the walls twenty feet high, with tall lookout towers and portholes. The commander at Fort Davis furnished him with a cannon and some troops who took their orders from old Don Milton. But during the war-time shortage of men the soldiers were withdrawn from such frontier stations as Davis. Indians raided the region as they pleased, and while Faver's Mexican help fought well, he lost all his cattle except thirty, forty calves in the corrals at Cibolo. With these and what he got through persistent and careful trading he built up a new herd, much of the stock from the Indians who liked Mexican spurs, bridles, and so on, preferably silver-mounted, and knew where to find plenty of cattle for the taking.

Sometimes even the friendly Indians raided Faver's stock, particularly the sheep, with their astonishing panic that the Indians found so amusing. The raiders killed Faver's brother-in-law, who was foreman at the sheep ranch, and stole the man's wife and sons. They were never traced although some reported them up in Indian Territory a long time later.

Still Don Milton Faver stayed on, to dominate the wild Big Bend country for thirty years. His trade grew; he increased his string of freight wagons with their fast-walking Mexican oxen and set up five freight stations. Each had a good adobe house and a little irrigated farm so the station keeper could grow his frijoles, his chili, and corn, with his Mexican peaches ripening golden and red in the sun. Thousands of Faver's cattle roamed free and unbranded, not even with the small F, and when Don Milton died he was buried on top of the mountain behind his house at Cibolo. His origin and his past were as deep a mystery as ever, as much as the man's nature.

Charlie Goodnight was another man who made his whole life out of cattle. At nine he had ridden bareback from Illinois to Texas. It wasn't as far a piece as to Oregon in 1845, but it was a long, dreary overlanding for the family, with no good prospects and without solidarity, for Charlie's father was dead and the stepfather acknowledged as a pretty poor stick. Still, the boy got a fine bow to his growing legs all those miles, and soon there was another, a more acceptable stepfather. In 1856 the twenty-year-old Charlie Goodnight formed a partnership with his stepbrother, Wes Sheek, to run cattle on shares. At that time most of the ranchers penned their stock at night against Indians, the occasional rustlers, and against the persistent urge to go wild. Soon the herds were too large for corraling and after a year Goodnight and Sheek trailed their stock to Palo Pinto County, where the fall mesquite grass was like a golden buffalo robe spread over the earth and where the Comanches came riding with the full moon. Scouting the Indians led Charlie Goodnight into the Rangers. By the end of the war his herd was estimated at around 8,000 head but he knew they might not be able to collect more than 1,000 with the roundup difficulties in the Cross Timbers country and with the neighbors, near and far, who had stayed home branding diligently.

The protective association formed by the early cattlemen of

the region, to serve until law and order arrived, had disintegrated long ago and little unmarked stock within reach of a hot iron went unbranded. The Comanches were a constant threat and Goodnight and some other discouraged Cross Timbers cowmen went looking for new range, freer from Indians, the running iron, and the growing crop of carpetbaggers reaching out from Austin. The others headed across the Rio Grande into Mexico where a whole party of Rebel officers had gone. But Goodnight valued markets too much. He gathered up what he could of his remaining cattle, added a wild bunch of around 250 head he cut off at a watering place, and with a few cowboys to help, he moved 1,000 head farther up the Brazos, twelve miles from a settlement. He was freer of the mavericks for a while but he ran into immediate trouble with the Indians.

The buffaloes, never very fond of timbered, brushy or rough country, were probably always scarce up and down central Texas. They had become even scarcer after the Civilized Tribes were crowded into eastern Indian Territory, forcing the local Indians west and south, making more hungry people to feed. Before the cattle came in these Indians had to venture out among their enemies on the open plains for their meat. Then the white men brought their spotted cows, drivable stock, and the even more attractive American horses, meaning larger, non-mustang horses and much more valuable to keep and to trade to the New Mexicans, the *comancheros,* who dealt in stolen stock from the Indians The young braves took to this with whoops of joy, waving blankets to stampede them flying off west into the wild country.

Goodnight had gone back to gather up another herd of around 1,200 to 1,500 cattle. He started for his new ranch short-handed and was attacked by Indians who killed a wily old frontiersman he had along and swept away all the cow horses except those the night herders were riding. After that it was one raid after another in the region; many people killed and around 10,000 head of cattle run off.

Trail drivers had discovered early that herds of more than 1,800 to 2,500 were too difficult to water, to handle in stampedes, and to protect against raiders. Most stories of great trail herds of

5,000, even 10,000 and 15,000 head, came from liars while talking to a tenderfoot who didn't know that fighting a grizzly barehanded was a feat. They simply threw in another grizzly, even two. However, many reliable men were certain that in 1866 a party of around 100 Indians started west from the San Saba region with a herd of 10,000 cattle that they had stolen from the ranchers. How they got across the waterless Staked Plains to the Pecos, or if they went that way, wasn't known, but the cattle disappeared and some of them, some of Goodnight's, were found in New Mexico later.

By the next spring Goodnight was prepared to move again. With his partner he gathered up a beef herd to trail to New Mexico and Colorado—2,000 big steers and fat dry cows. But the Indians stampeded them, fought off the trail hands, and swept the whole lot away. Thoroughly disgusted at last, Charlie Goodnight gave up ranching in Texas. Too many Indians and no use begging for help from that Reconstruction gathering of scalawags and carpetbaggers down at Austin. In addition there was the news of glutted markets up in Kansas and farther east. But the mining regions of the Rockies seemed to have some money left. Besides, George Reynolds had taken a small herd no farther than New Mexico the summer after the war and found that steers worth at the most $8 or $10 in Texas brought $60 up there. Not only that, but his sister went along on the drive. Of course he could start from Fort Davis in the Big Bend country, on the other side of the Pecos, with no Staked Plains to cross and almost none of the Comanche country.

Even so, it was no Natchez promenade with ruffled parasols and crinolines for a lady, Goodnight was told.

No, but Sallie Reynolds could sit a saddle longer than most of the hard-bottom cowhands of the country. Besides, that drive was nothing compared to one from the Brazos. It would take real time, money, and sand to swing down an unknown trail through waterless country to get around the Comanches, or most of them. Yet Charlie Goodnight, an old cowman at thirty, insisted he was heading for Colorado and going around the south to do it. He gathered up little herds of loose, unmarked cattle here and there. Some objected to this, particularly the

Jacksboro Unionists, who had left Texas for the safety of south Kansas during the war and then come tearing back to their old stomping grounds to get a crack at the cattle before the Texans were out of their grays. Thieves, Goodnight called them, and they paid him back in the same coin a time or two, until it seemed the bad blood between them would break into gun play, especially now that Goodnight was preparing to quit the country with cattle he had run out of their herds, claiming they belonged to him but with no brand to prove it.

Old Charlie, as some called him now, was convinced by his wartime experience with the Rangers, and since, that any crossing of the Indian country of northwest Texas was to be avoided. To those who pointed out that the Comanches surely preferred fat young buffalo to trail beef, there was the reply that they preferred anything they could trade to the *comancheros* who were selling the stolen stock to the new ranchers starting up in New Mexico, the trailers to California, or to the Denver traders for the mines.

Goodnight also knew something of the country he would have to cross on the southern swing and the turn westward to the Pecos and up its briny, forbidding canyon and beyond. The reputation of the stretch to the Pecos was bad ever since the first cattle came to Texas with Coronado. The other two ranchers who were to go with Charlie Goodnight to Colorado got scared out just chewing it over. In the end the old rancher Oliver Loving, who had tried to talk Goodnight against it, too, asked to go along.

Oliver Loving, father of Jim of the Keechi region, was the most experienced cowman on the cattle fringes of northwest Texas. Back in the 1850's he ran a small, remote supply store on a military trail, with a few slaves and a good ranch herd. On the side he bought most of the minor lots of cattle then produced in the Cross Timbers and trailed them to Shreveport or New Orleans. In 1858 he and another man pointed a herd northward, swung around the larger settlements to avoid trouble, turned eastward, swam a dozen streams, and marketed the cattle in Illinois. In 1860, with John Dawson, he headed 1,000 steers to the new gold camps of the Rockies by striking the Arkansas

River below the Great Bend and following the stream up past Pueblo, where they wintered. In the spring Loving peddled the stock in Denver for good money but the Civil War broke out and the authorities refused to let him return to Texas. Only his friendship with Kit Carson, Lucien Maxwell, and other old-timers got him away, to help feed the Confederacy, as the Denverites had feared.

After the war he enlarged his roundups with Bose Ikard as his right-hand man. Bose was a former slave from the Ikard ranch, a good bronco buster, exceptional night herder, good with the skillets when necessary—an all-around ranch and trail hand, tough and lasting as rawhide, one of the most devoted men any rancher ever had.

Goodnight had planned his drive in the hope that there was some nice money loose for beef in Colorado and certainly there would be grass to hold any stock not readily salable. Now another and, by his planned route a more immediate, hope came up—the hope of selling beef to fill Indian contracts in New Mexico on the way. There was even a chance of cornering a little of the often-exorbitant prices that some Indian contractors seemed to get. True, the agent for the Mescalero Apaches at Fort Sumner was already charged with graft in cattle dealings, but there were other agents around the post for other tribes, and the government was advertising for steers to be delivered there.

So, in 1866, trailing a mixed herd of 2,000 steers, cows, and calves, with eighteen hands, mostly armed, they set out, the fifty-four-year-old tough and range-hardened Loving in charge of the herd, Goodnight scouting ahead. But neither of them had ever been over the route which had stretches that few except the Comanches raiding into Mexico for horses even attempted. Those Indians preferred to make the run early in the spring or in the fall, when there was some hope of finding water holes not dry mud baked iron hard.

PULLING FOR NEW GRASS

In the early years of the cattle drives most of the larger herds that marched north in the swinging walk of the Longhorn were steers, with some dry cows, all headed directly for the slaughter pens or perhaps by way of the fattening grasses of Indian Territory or Kansas or the broadening corn regions of the Middle West. But almost from the start there were herds with young she-stuff, the seed for new ranches. These were usually headed for the opening ranges of the north and the west, yet they had to cross the same Indian barriers as the beef herds, the Civilized Tribes demanding toll in cattle and, even before the war, in money. West of them were the reservations of the Southern Cheyennes and the Arapahoes, and of the Kiowas and Comanches, who still claimed vast hunting grounds in northwest Texas, where the Southern or Texas herd of buffaloes ranged. It was usually to these regions that the raiding Indians escaped with their loot and certainly no drover could hope to get a trail herd of cattle up through there. Besides, there was the Kansas summer quarantine, June to November, on cattle brought in from Texas. This one might avoid but if not, there was the expense of holding the herd to fall.

Goodnight and Loving gave no thought to these obstacles now. They were headed the other way, down the old Butterfield Trail, to follow it as far as seemed handy. Goodnight, out far in front on his short-coupled black, looked over his shoulder from a rise, back toward the Texas of the Palo Pinto country and the Brazos, almost as though he were making a last mind picture of it, bidding it good-by. Then he considered the long, dusty line of their herd winding toward him out of the breaks. They were already getting trail-broken, and moving pretty well. Perhaps it was true that in Colorado a cattleman could still make a living.

He let his impatient horse out, pointing his hat at arm's length before him, signaling the direction. So Goodnight scouted the trail for water, for range and bed ground, doubling back to give his signals. Loving, behind him, knew how to get the most from the men and the herd. All but the two point riders, the best men of the outfit, shifted positions daily to relieve those on the dusty side and those riding drag—always keeping the herd strung out well and yet close enough to let them feel each other, hold them in an unbroken file to crawl like a thin, dark, thousand-segmented joint snake over the rolling prairie. It was a pretty route through the mirage region, the Phantom Hill country. By then the herd was a fine traveling unit, the leader taking his place every morning, keeping it day after day. As in most beef herds, the steers had traveling companions and when separated they raised their heads to get wind of each other, bawling until they got together. Each strong young cow gathered her own following within the herd. As in most good-sized drives, there were a few muleys, born hornless, and within a few days these bedded down together, a little apart. As usual, too, there was a loner or two who went prowling up one side of the herd and down the other, apparently searching for the never lost. Sometimes there was an outcast, hooked at everywhere, with even the muleys making the horning motion. All these, unless steadied down early, ended up with the drags, with the poor, the old, and the very young. But the two-year-old heifers were the real flighty ones wilful as young Texas girls, and most difficult to settle down, to road-break. Some never settled down at all and these it was best to eat early, if the owner could bring himself to kill his own beef.

Then, with this mixed herd, every morning there were the newborn calves to kill on the bed ground. There would be hundreds of these dropped before the herd reached Sumner in New Mexico. Every morning one of the trail hands made a circle, disposing of the freshly dropped stock, who couldn't keep up anyway and would only weaken the cows. But all that day

the mothers would bawl and try to break back, and particularly
that first night. If the cow had smelled her calf, or sucked it, she
might have to be yoked to a steer, or hobbled, so strong was the
Longhorn's instinct for her young. But even with the best of
care they would have slow, difficult trailing for the Pecos route,
at the best not good for a mixed outfit.

Loving had the herd traveling very well in the heat and
dust by the time they reached the head of the Middle Concho,
where they rested and fed before starting over the dry, horse-
killing jump of around eighty miles to the Pecos, with twelve,
fifteen miles considered a good drive in the burning sun. Then,
after days without water, and the smell of it from the river to
drive the cattle wild, they would have to pass the poison lakes
marked by whitened bones long before the first Spaniard rode
through that way. They had been warned against the poison
lakes, the alkali strong enough to kill everything that drank the
water, and just beyond was the Pecos, with most of the bank
very steep, the crossing a swift, swimming current.

Goodnight and Loving watered the herd, steers, cows, and
calves, with all they would drink and filled the canteens and the
water barrels of the grub wagon to overflowing. Then in the
afternoon they pointed the herd to follow the sloping sun out
upon the pale baked earth.

They trailed late that first evening, made dry camp, and
pushed on early. While the Longhorn on the range often went
without water for three days, driving dried out stock as it did
men. The second night the herd was too thirsty to bed down,
many trying to break back as they walked and milled all night
so it took most of the men to hold them. Goodnight realized
that this wouldn't do—the cattle had walked enough on the bed
ground to take them most of the way to the Pecos. He got the
herd started very early, knowing that the cattle would have to
be pushed today, the faltering whipped up by the sleepy, worn-
out cowboys under the sun that shimmered in great rippling
mirage lakes ahead. The canteens dried up, the water barrels
began to rattle in the wagon, and the dust rose in bitter white
clouds that grayed them all. It cracked the lips under the protecting kerchiefs tied loosely enough to be drawn up over the

nose, almost to the hat-brim, the dust-rimmed eyes bloodshot and burning; it stung and burned in the sweated saddle galls.

The pointers had to hold the strong leaders back while the drag riders whooped and cursed and popped their down ropes to keep the weaker stuff up. The herd bawled and then moaned for water, until many grew silent, their swollen tongues hanging out dry and dusty, eyes sunken, their ribs like some old pole fence. Often a maddened one turned to fight, as a critter drawn from a bog will, perhaps with the same desperation of death upon it. Those, too, were left to die.

The men grew as raw nerved, on the prod, worn, without sleep, and what was worse for a good cowhand, helpless to relieve the suffering of the stock. Irritable and dangerous, swift anger lurked in them as in a rattler, and with guns handy at the hip.

Loving worked with the drags now, holding them together the best his long experience could manage, fighting the alkali dust and the thirst to save as much as he could from the stock they had salvaged out of the losses of the war years and all the thieving and the Indian raids since. Goodnight had pushed on ahead into the pale, cloudless night, the second without sleep. The cook boiled up black coffee to hand to the men as they passed on the shadowy prairie, trying to make the stock follow the bells Goodnight had put on the lead steers, keep them reasonably together, help prevent the stampeding at any whiff of water that tolled them to some long-dead wallow or pond perhaps off to the side. Each time Goodnight spurred hard to overtake the leaders, to slow them, avoid a disastrous pile-up. But long before the steers reached such places they had usually slowed by themselves, with only a hopeless kind of bewilderment as they milled over the dried mud, bawling hoarsely, unwilling to leave where water had been, the weaker cows beginning to go down, too, as even the strong calves had long ago.

The men were ready to drop in the rising heat of the day, swearing thickly, their tongues stiff and swollen, as though unaccustomed to words. But mostly they were silent except for the "Hi-ah! Hi-ah!" to keep the drags moving. Finally one of the men couldn't stop his call, going on and on until he fell to mum-

bling, saying "Damn-damn-damn," over and over to himself,
sitting his horse like a limp and leaking meal sack. At last Loving came to pull him from the saddle and push him under the
bank of an arroyo, offering a little strip of shade almost wide
enough to cover the man's gaunt frame. Tying the horse to a
hastily driven picket in the bottom of the cut, out of sight, he
left a precious half-filled canteen with him and went on. "Wait
till dark, then try to follow the trail," was all Loving could sug-
gest, without much hope, realizing that Indians were probably
sniffing around the herds.

When Goodnight fell back to look over the plodding
horses, the men swaying in the saddles, the stock falling all
along the trail, he realized something had to be done, and fast.
With the dry canteens strung to him like the gray and empty
hulls of some futile fruit he set out for the river, pushing the
plucky little black to stumbling, so he cursed himself for his
brutality, his own tongue refusing the words. He slowed down
but almost at once, he was urging the tired horse faster again,
faster and faster, while he wondered at the fools that cattlemen
were.

Back from the hard twenty-mile ride over the burning
earth Charlie Goodnight saw it was a case of saving what he
could of the dying herd or losing all. With the four men and
horses that had stood up best, he let the stronger cattle, around
two thirds of the herd, go as fast as they could, making no effort
to trail herd them beyond pointing the leaders for the Pecos,
trying to let the men take turns at a few minutes' sleep in the
saddle.

But there were the poison holes this side of the river to
avoid. The herd must be swung out so the first smell they got
would be from the Pecos itself. The old cowman watched for it,
saw it come: the lead steer suddenly lift his head, his dry tongue
out stiff as a stick of dark and sandy wood. He broke into a feeble, stumbling run, then the others behind him, too, in sprawl-
ing gallops, the earth thundering hollowish as the wind carried
the smell and the excitement back along the strung-out herd,
the men fighting to keep them so, to avoid bunching and piling

up in the swimming depths of the Pecos, stomping each other under.

In spite of all that the five worn men could do the cattle poured into the river valley in a broad, dust-gray blanket, the dried alkali rising in choking white smoke over them. The leaders went over the Pecos bank, the followers in a cascade upon them, thrusting them out and clear across the narrow roiling stream before they could stop for the desperate drink. Goodnight, ahead, turned the cattle back, and as the jam of the frenzied animals spread up and down the narrow river they blocked the current, damming it to rise halfway up the banks. Then they had to be quirted out, the leaders found and started, to keep the herd from foundering themselves. Slowly, falteringly, they backed out of the water, stopping to blow, lolling their swollen, dripping tongues, and finally started away slowly before the whoops and popping ropes of the cowboys, to stop in the grass away from the Pecos valley and the alkali water, the first grass they had tasted in days.

Here the men were set to hold them, working in relays, with plans to let them sleep, too, hoping there would be no Indian attack now while Goodnight was going back to help Oliver Loving. But worn down as the men were, they couldn't keep awake, and some of the cows broke for water again. This time they got to the alkali holes back from the river. Before they could be stopped three had finished drinking and fell in their tracks, some of the others dying later.

Back on the trail the weary Oliver Loving was still with the drags, around 500 of them able to move. The wind turned and carried the smell of water from a place where the Pecos ran between banks six to ten feet high. Nothing could stop the stampeding cattle and they poured over the bank, falling and going under, most of the horse herd, too. Many of the weak ones drowned right there, and some were swept into a quicksand bend. The cowboys worked for two days but in the end 100 head had to be left in the river although still alive, in the quicksand, and stranded under high bluffs at the water's edge, with no way to reach them. Three hundred others had been dropped on the way to the Pecos, not counting the newborn calves killed

—all those bones strung out to mark the desperate trail, the graveyard of the cowman's hopes.

After several days to recruit the stock and the men, the herd was pushed up the east side of the Pecos, through country where the only living creature seemed to be the fish in the stream. Not even one prairie bird panted through the shadeless noontime, no kingfisher flashed his blue as he dove straight down, to come up with a wriggling of silver in his mouth, no buzzard circled the pale and empty sky. But there were rattle-snakes, and of these one cowhand with eyes so crossed that they looked in two directions, and poor eyes at that, got seventy-two before the herd reached Sumner.

Fort Sumner was the center for around 8,500 Indians gath-ered to reservations, but the soil was poor, and fuel, even grass, scarce. The heat and drouth were particularly trying for the mountain Navahos who had been torn from their lovely home-land to live on the sterile plain among their traditional enemies. But it was a common misery, for all the Indians were on the edge of starvation, and Goodnight and Loving got the excep-tional price of eight cents a pound on the hoof for the steers, two-year-old and up. No wonder the Texas Indians went to such trouble raiding the ranches for herds to trade to the New Mex-ican *comancheros*.

Of course the partners still had the cows and calves, be-tween 700 and 800 head, but neither man had suspected there was such money in cattle these days, and both were happy even with all the cutbacks. Charlie Goodnight was suddenly less angry with Texas, less impatient for a look at the Colorado ranch pos-sibilities. He hurried back on the 700-mile trail to gather up an-other herd for the Indians before winter. He rode ahead, fol-lowed by a pack mule carrying the $12,000 in gold under the provisions, with three cowboys coming along behind. They trav-eled down the Pecos by night, sleeping hidden out during the daylight, and prepared to shoot a path through any Indians or holdup outfit who might have heard about the sale at Sumner and try an ambush.

Their real trouble came from one of the swift night storms of the arid country, the sky blazing with lightning—great, blinding forks of it crashing to the earth, the thunder shaking the ground so that the dust rose in a hazing in the rainless night. One bolt struck too close to the pack mule, and he was gone with the provisions and the gold. Goodnight had managed to get his hand on the neck rope and hung on while the mule ran, bucking and bawling like a bay steer, provisions flying in every direction. Finally the mule was worn out and Goodnight, too, scratched and skinned up. The money was safe but the food was lost and no telling how many Indians might be around, so they couldn't risk much shooting, even if there had been any game beyond an occasional catfish. Before they got through the 200-mile ride down the Pecos they would have been happy to trade a lot of the gold for a bait of even Yankee sore-thumb bread.

⊂╪ ⊂╪ ⊂╪

NEW BREED —

Now THE free-range days were surely done, and the dedicated men gone. A few old-timers hung on as buggy bosses, perhaps in the new gas buggy to make their rounds, with a couple of young mechanics to help push the city automobile out of the sand or off rocks and high centers. Even Charlie Goodnight had moved to town and up in Montana Granville Stuart, the grand old man of the cow business in the North, was puttering his time away as librarian of the city of Butte.

The old brush poppers were mostly gone, too, although an occasional stove-up old-timer still limped around the livery stables of the cow towns and was surly with the dudes awkward in their cheap slant-heeled boots and fancy shirts asking for "a cowboy horse to ride out," but looking uneasy even after they got a grip on the horn, the reins sagging.

It was a sad passing of the cattlemen who considered paying for the grass an indignity, an affront to their cows. Most of them knew they were dealt out when the settlers began to overrun the country, even many who hired range protection, or went broke defending themselves against the federal government, the invading government as they saw it, come claiming land that their stock, their cows had walked on for years.

But if the range had to be bought, taxed as deeded land, then ranching became a hard business profession, worse—no better than rooting a living out of the sod, or working on the railroad or mining coal. Every acre would have to produce the most meat possible, for the highest price. The northerners always claimed, and the southerners agreed at least tacitly by taking their stock north to finish out, that their range grew more beef, of finer quality, brighter in color and with the fat finely laced through the meat, making it more flavorsome, juicier, tenderer, and from better grade of stock in the first place. To be sure, the pastures of the South, if not actually lush and green all winter, were at least grazable. There was no call for hay and feeding crews, and no real winter loss of growth and weight, almost no loss of actual stock even among the new calves.

But the South did need a better strain of cattle, one free of tick fever and other insect invasions.

Frequent dipping was found to be one preventive of ticks as well as the spreading scabies, itch, but not if the neighbors were neglectful. The solution, if there was one, would probably come through an immune stock, perhaps by crossing with the coastal Longhorn, who managed to live with the tick. Unfortunately, when enough beefy blood for good meat was added, the immunity vanished. The first effective crosses came from the Brahmans of India. These cattle had been brought into South Carolina back in 1849 and only later were found fever-immune and fitted to heat, humid or desert dry—a tough stock but tough-meated. Long and imaginative experimentation was carried out on the King Ranch. The captain's great trail herds once spread ticks and hatred all the way North and even brought him and Goodnight, that other towering figure of the early Texas cattle period, into open conflict. Out of the opposition to King's bulldozing of settlers and stock growers along the trails came the need and the determination that eventually made a great experimental laboratory as well as a great beef factory of the modern King Ranch under the Klebergs, who worked in a fine racing stud, too, and an oil kingdom.

This first purely American breed, the Santa Gertrudis, named for the original location of the King headquarters, originated in the cross of the Brahman and the heavy, tender-meated, but tick-susceptible Shorthorn, fixed by patient and calculated breeding to carry much of the heat and disease resistance of the Brahman with a little of the distinguishing hump. Added to this was much breadth and bulk of good eating meat from the Shorthorn.

Kleberg put the first Santa Gertrudis bulls up for sale in 1950. Since then herds of the blood have spread around the world. A steer will grow big and grass-fat on an acre of good hot-climate forage, such as, say, the pasture lands of Florida, instead of the fifteen to twenty-five acres required on the King or in regions of Arizona, the Middle East, or the dry land of Australia. The Santa Gertrudis are good rustlers. The breed matures fast and at market age averages around 200 pounds more than other breeds of the same age and pasture.

But other Brahman crosses are already being developed by ranchers: with Angus, the Brangus; with Hereford, the Braford; with French Charolaise, the Charbray, and others. The stock often feeds on experimental plots of imported and hybrid grasses, another King Ranch field of experimentation. Of course these later cattle crosses are not restricted to the King Ranch, nor the South. At Lasater's Ranch in Colorado there is a fine herd of Beefmasters, half Brahman and a quarter each of Shorthorn and Hereford—beefy but proud and aloof red animals, fine for drouth regions. In fact, the crosses are spreading so fast all over the beef world that perhaps fifty years from now some of the standard breeds of 1900 will have to be preserved as the Longhorn is now.

Long before the free land was gone small outfits of cattle·

men hard pressed by drops in beef prices or die-ups from storms
or even tick fever tended to drift into sheep. Usually they received stern warning from any ranchers around, as the Richards did when they brought sheep into the Niobrara country
north of the Spade. Often the protestors went into the woollies,
too, perhaps even within the year. But most of the cattlemen,
while still fighting settlers, had drawn imaginary lines across the
free range against sheep because they ate the grass roots out of
the ground, cut up the sod with their small cloven hoofs, and
turned much of Wyoming into sage plains, helping to finish the
overgrazing begun by cattle. The cowboys usually whooped any
herds that crossed the lines into writhing gray piles at the foot
of some deep cut bank or in some canyon. The dogs and the
herders, too, might be killed if they were foolishly slow in moving, or refused the warning to take the herds off the range and
the water holes, which the sheep roiled so that only a sheep
horse would drink. But the rifles the herders carried against
eagles and wolves penetrated the flesh of ranch hands as well.

Yet even after violence and shootings, some of the sternest
resisters of sheep had to give up and go into the business to pull
themselves out of the hard times of the Roosevelt Inquisition
and the new depression looming up before the war, particularly
the years when the tariff on wool was high. Long before 1900
there had been conspicuous examples of cattlemen running
sheep—even in the special regions of Wyoming and Montana,
men like Senator Carey of Wyoming and the Richards, both De-
Forest, governor of Wyoming, and Bartlett, and in 1905 the
Swan Company.

The big weakness in ranching treated strictly as a business
or as a manufacturing process is in its curious long-range nature. A ranch can't be shut down like a pants factory or a mine
or even a steel smelter. Expenses for feed and care of the stock
go on, and increase, while the prime stuff ages into canners. If
the ranch is closed down, three, four years are lost putting it
back into running—that long from cow to salable steers unless a
ready-made, mixed herd can be bought, very scarce and expen-

sive in times of rising prices and probably much higher than the selling price of the herd turned off.

After the Spanish-American War beef prices fell like drifting cattle hitting the Chugwater bluffs or the cap rock of Texas, driven down, it was claimed, by the manipulations of the Beef Trust. The ranchers, through the American National Cattleman's Association, accused the big packers of violating the antitrust laws and insisted that the railroads were in cahoots with them. President Taft promised an investigation but it was left for the Wilson administration to show that the Big Five—Swift, Armour, Morris, Wilson, and Cudahy—together controlled 514 companies and had interests in 762 more, dealing in 775 commodities including nearly everything from the loans that paid the cowpunchers to the fertilizer and tankage left from the cow as well as dozens of other products that no one would expect to find in the packing business, including, of course, the newspapers of the packing towns.

"Yeh, it's not only take what they offer us or go to hell," a usually unprofane old rancher admitted, "but pay what they ask for any of the 775 commodities we got to have. And tell us what we got to pay to get our steers to Omaha or Chicago to boot."

It took a long, long time from the promise of Taft, but in 1920 the packers agreed to get out of everything except meat packing and closely allied lines, and to operate under the shadow of the U. S. courts.

By then there were only the ranchers who survived the Roosevelt recession of 1907, when banks closed all over the country, even if not for long. Beef prices didn't pick up until toward 1910, moving moderately until the boom of 1914, with the war demand for meat.

By then many, many who had survived the Big Die-Ups and the hard times of the 1890's, even the fencing and land-fraud trials, were gone. The Spur had closed its "Protection A-c" and sold its holdings in 1908, paid the debts, and had a little left over to apply to the twenty years of outstanding dividends. The Western Ranches, managed by John Clay since the

Swan outfit fired him, had passed dividends, too, and finally liquidated, to reorganize as an investment company. "Loan the cowman money and let him take the risks with blizzards and hard times," was the sour comment of a man who had to give them mortgages on every foot of land and every cow he owned to pull himself through the bad years, although no one could promise much future, with the growing ranges of the Argentine and Australia and fleets of ships rolling off into the water, cargo hungry. All this time the rancher operated on the open market while everything he bought and that his customers bought, except meat, was protected by the high tariff of the McKinley days, almost unchanged on anything except wool and hides.

There were more sour comments on Clay for other reasons besides the loan business. One was a speech he made before a feeders' convention in 1914 attacking the cowboy of his Wyoming cattle company days:

> The chief obstacle of the range at that time was the cowboys, who were mostly illiterate, uncivilized; who drank and thieved and misbranded cattle, and with a kind of rough loyalty, never told on one another in their crimes.

"Hell, he's still mad because none of them would join the Regulators, the Invaders, gone to clean up Johnson County," one of the feeders told his neighbor at the table.

Out on the Laramie and the Cheyenne, the Belle Fourche and the Powder there was a certain amount of laughing, now that most of the Clay interests were off the range. "The cowboys were good enough to make a lot of money for a foreign hired hand like old tight-fisted Clay-bowels, with his sly way of getting everybody in debt to him and then gouging them hard," one of the Whitcomb relatives said, speaking not only for old Pap but a dozen others around him.

One ranch owned by the Scottish groups that included Clay as a member was still running, due largely, many thought, to the years of Murdo Mackenzie's excellent management. The

Matador was the only British ranch to make a decent profit for its investors, although its dividends had almost vanished from 1903 to 1908. But with the upswing from the declaration of war they rose as high as 20 per cent, much of it from British meat sales. Mackenzie was the finest cowman the foreign ranches brought in, many thought one of the finest cowmen anywhere, foreign or American. A booklover, he was considered one of the West's most influential supporters of the government in the fight for conservation of national resources and for shaping the government's policies in the interest of the small settler and homeseeker, although not all agreed on them. There were those, too, who recalled the range protection that the Matador hired with the Spur, to keep settlers from running tick-infested cattle into the Matador herd, Mackenzie claimed, although that wasn't the story the settlers told, nor the Spur. When one of the hired killers proved a real troublemaker for his employer, threatening to kill Mackenzie, the rugged Scotsman went right on, unarmed.

But many of the old free rangers spit into the dust at any talk of Murdo Mackenzie's good will toward settlers. Yet they had to admit that he was a powerful man in the fight against the railroads, with his admiration for, and friendship with, Theodore Roosevelt, even through Old Four-Eyes Inquisition, which didn't affect the Matador much. Most of the southern land was deeded and the northern ranges usually leased from the Indians, through Roosevelt's intercession in the Indian Bureau, the other ranchers said. Mackenzie, with Turney, the Big Bend rancher who followed the Scotsman as head of the cattle association, called on the whole cow country to stand solid against the high freight rates. When the Interstate Commerce Commission decided for the ranchers, the railroads went to court against price fixing and won. In 1904, Mackenzie visited with the President and got a plank for railroad control into the Republican platform. That brought legislation for rate fixing by the ICC, and changed the entire conception of the government's right and authority to regulate.

Needing northern range to finish their excellent-quality steers for top market prices, Mackenzie had leased half a mil-

lion acres of Dakota Indian Reservation lands. But he struck
trouble up there, including hard winter storms for his soft
southern stock, also the problem of getting cattle across the Missouri to the Milwaukee railhead at Evarts, the old river town on
the east bank. Ferries ran in floodtime, really paddle-wheeled
flatboats like floating pieces of stockyards, with enough small
pens to hold forty to sixty head and keep them from sliding to
one side and dumping the lot into the brown, muddy depths of
Big Mizzou. To help the stockmen get their cattle to the crossing, the Milwaukee railroad provided a sort of trail, a leased
strip of land six miles wide between the Cheyenne River and
Standing Rock Indian Reservations. It started up near the slope
of the Black Hills, was lane fenced all the way, with watering
places about every twelve miles, natural or from big dams and
reservoirs built by the railroad, all large enough for several
herds of 1,200 each a day. Gates opened from the ranges of the
Matador, the L7, the HO, such Indian outlets as LaPlante's and
Narcelle's NSS brand, and the Turkey Track, and many others
with range neighboring on the Strip. When heavy shipping was
on, waiting herds might reach as much as twelve miles back
from the river.

Another problem was fires. One August day, with the sun
almost hot enough to ignite the dry, curling grass as from an
empty bottle concentrating the rays, the Matador was gathering
beef. They had about 1,000 head of steers on the divide between the two Moreau rivers, cutting out the shipping stuff,
when somebody happened to look up from the dust and sweat
to see a great boiling of whitish smoke on the horizon.

"Prairie fire!" he yelled against the wind. "Big fire coming
out of the west!"

Every horse was set back on his haunches at the uplifted
arm, the pointing gauntlet of the warning cowboy. The wagon
boss ordered the herds whooped away out of the fire's probable
path, started the chuckwagon off for water, and sent a hard-
riding puncher to the line camps for the fire drags. The Turkey
Track, gathering beef some twenty-five miles south, turned their
herds loose, too, and spurred in to help. The big drags, twelve-

foot squares, looked like great bedsprings of netted steel chains woven through layered sheets of asbestos, a heavy bar across the end for the lariats. Snubbed to the saddle horns they were pulled by six strong horses, the work so heavy and so hot that the horses had to be changed every two hours. But in a wild gale-driven fire like this one little could be done except to guess where the head tongues of flame might come and backfire there. The streams and even the larger canyons all ran eastward, and the fire was coming down between them like stampeding Long-horns down a country lane. There was no barrier against which extensive backfires could be set, to burn safely into the wind. If they got away, they would be as damaging as the one roaring in from the west.

Mainly the cow crew worked the drags along the sides to narrow the spread of the fire. But the asbestos soon wore out and steers were killed, split and piled, entrails and all, on the nets of chains while Indians and white men followed to beat out the remaining pockets and smolderings. But they couldn't help much. The fire had started nearly 100 miles west of the Missouri and spread to a twenty-mile front as it came like a Milwaukee express train before the shifting west wind, burning in zigzags for two days and nights on its way to the river. One prong turned southeast, jumped the Big Moreau, and ran to the banks of the Cheyenne fifty miles away, while the main fire swept this way and that, as though to clean up what might have been missed. Finally the last flames died along the worn banks of the Missouri—over a million blackened acres behind them, much of the Matador range gone, with the stock to hold fat for market, and strengthened for the hard Dakota winter.

The old outfits that couldn't make the economic jump from free grass were gone and with them most of the old ways, although some, like the Matador, clung to the horsedrawn chuckwagon, the open corral, and the throw rope instead of the squeeze chute and the cross fences, the smaller pastures. But new problems arose with the new times. The list of cattle diseases doubled, tripled, and more, particularly as the blood improved and the old hardiness of the Longhorn was lost. Some recalled that the coastal steers could keep going when they were gray with bloodsucking ticks.

The Plains were once as free of cattle diseases as any region new to a species usually is. Some kind of *rinderpest,* perhaps foot-and-mouth disease, had swept up along the larger streams a couple of times in the first half of the nineteenth century, destroying millions of cloven-hoofed animals. Some regions, like the Laramie Plains, were left stinking and empty. The salt licks of the present Lancaster County, Nebraska, were once the center of buffaloes, deer, and other salt eaters and they suddenly were left dark with carcasses and avoided as poison by the Indians for years. There was a scare of foot-and-mouth disease as late as World War I.

Epizootics came and went but the tick fever apparently was there from the first cattle, perhaps from the first cow. The South had the screwworm, too, infecting any break of the skin, particularly castration before the bloodless emasculator was put on the market. Then came blackleg, spread all through the cow country, fatal to great numbers of the finest young stock, the animal lame for a little while, the leg swollen, the victim down a few hours and dead. The disease was easily identified by even a range child. A thrust with a quirt handle or a boot toe on the swollen leg made a rushing sound. The disease was thought to be spread by coyotes, wolves, and dogs that had gnawed at a blackleg carcass. So in addition to dipping for ticks and itch there was the seasonal vaccination for blackleg and then for such diseases as pinkeye, *hemorrhagic septicemia,* and a dozen more. The antibiotics came into general use and saved many cattle, particularly calves. Increased weight in feed lots is produced by the addition of aureomycin and stilbestrol to the feed mix but there is some public concern about the overuse of the latter, a fear of effeminization of the traditionally very masculine beef eater. It is true that the Plains Indian lived almost entirely on buffalo cow, and the cattleman, even the trail drivers, preferred a fat heifer for meat, but perhaps the natural hormone is in less concentration. Besides, the Indian wanted his meat well cooked if there was time and fuel, and the cowman would eat his beef no other way.

There is still a constant struggle to clear out the infectious abortions, particularly Brucellosis, Bang's disease, which destroys many cows for calving and causes undulant fever in man through milk from the infected cows. Many fine herds have had to be replaced from the ground up because of Bang's. Now, however, a calf vaccine is coming into general use. But leptospirosis is rising.

Where, fifty, sixty years ago, "immune Shorthorn" meant immune to tick fever, now strains are watched for inherited susceptibility to eye cancer, say, with the recommendation that the eye be removed, the calf fattened, and both mother and calf sent to the slaughterhouse. The last eight, nine years a new problem, the "sinister gene," the carrier of dwarfism, has cropped up increasingly among fine beef cattle, the result, some think, of the overclose breeding for the blocky, squat, spraddlelegged look, the one that prize judges favor and that feeders pay premium prices for. If a bull carrying a gene of dwarfism is mated to a carrier cow, one fourth of the progeny will be dwarfs, one half carriers, and only one quarter clean of the taint, and who's to say which is which until proved out? A carrier bull mated to a dwarf-free cow produces a normal-appearing first generation but half of these will be carriers.

There have always been bovine dwarfs as there have always been dwarfs among humans, but with the recent alarming increase in the three main beef breeds—Shorthorn, Hereford, and Aberdeen Angus, this has become of great concern. Often the dwarf calves are born dead or short-lived, the year's work of the cow lost. If they survive, they are often killed to hide the blight on the herd, which has already, in some cases, reached as high as 12 per cent—far above the losses required to bankrupt a breeder if the loss continues.

The only solution now seems to be the radical one of clearing the bloodlines. To make certain that a bull, whether of $500 or $50,000 blood, is free of the taint he must be mated to at least fifteen carrier cows, which takes time and can involve the loss of the cow's year if he is a carrier. Other methods are being developed, the profilometer, to detect the slight bump on the bull's forehead which indicates that he may be a carrier, or examination by x-ray for the so-called crumpled vertebrae that some carriers have. But it is a slow process, and as the stock is bred lower and lower to the ground the sinister gene becomes more common—one more problem unknown in the days of the leggy Longhorn that could outrun a good saddle horse for a nice stretch.

RITUAL AND
RESTORATION

THE FIVE-WAY corral gate, the squeeze chute, and the stable-bred herd sire have just about retired the roper and the cutting horse from all except a few show places not concerned with the poundage run off or the extra hands on the pay roll. Even some of the smaller outfits have put on jeeps and light planes to round up the stock and hunt out strays that show little tendency to wander, with their heavy bodies and short legs, the balanced rations before them winter and summer, and medicated rubbing posts and insecticide oilers to keep flies and other insects off, water always in easy reach, as well as medicated salt.

Where once the Longhorns quit the country at the sight of anyone afoot, particularly a woman with blowing skirts, the later grade Herefords came running to see what this strange walking creature might be, a fine sweep of white faces charging up, sending the tenderfoot racing for the nearest wire fence, certain it had been a run for life. But if the walker had stood his ground, the cattle would have veered suddenly away, every whitefaced, horn-bearing head gone and only red rumps visible, fleeing. Now even the bulls are tame, particularly the placid Hereford sires who may come sidling up in any western pasture to have their bulging ribs scratched and the itchy places back of the drooping horns.

All these changes in breed and coddling care brought a realization by 1927 that the foundation stock, the Longhorn, had vanished, the blood existing only in crosses. Then the United States Government tried to locate Longhorns for two official herds, one in the Wichita Mountain Wild Life Refuge in Oklahoma, the other at the Niobrara Game Reserve in Nebraska. They combed the Texas border and started the Wichita herd with twenty cows and three bulls. Several showed Brahman blood but this has apparently been bred out of the off-springs. Selected bulls have been brought in from Mexico to strengthen the strain, and by 1957 the two herds totaled around 500 head. However, as Goodnight wrote Frank Dobie, the climate in the Wichita Mountains would grow a shorter, thicker horn, with the bodies of the cattle also more compact. The greatest length of steer horn was generally developed in fairly low brush country, perhaps west of the Guadalupe River and often under rigorous circumstances. So far none in the tame herds have the fine, wild spread of horn or the generally wild look of the early photographs. Presumably the life is a little soft.

Another and more daring restoration is that attempted in Munich, Germany. By selecting domestic cattle with attributes found in drawings and sculpture of the urus, the wild ancestor of the present domestic cattle, including the Longhorn, the start was made. In one variety used the bull was black, the cow chestnut, the horns powerful, the legs longish, the back straight. These were crossed with cattle from the Hungarian plains, the Scottish highlands, and Corsica, the latter with the ringed nose, a stripe down the back, and a high crown of coarse hair, such as the urus, the aurochs, had, and from these a "present-day aurochs" has been created.

But long before any restoration was attempted the great changes that made a pretty tame business of ranching brought a reluctance to let the romance and the old seasonal routines die, particularly as they were recalled through the sunset haze of time that gilded the dust, made gallant the drudgery and the endurance of stinging blizzard and saddle wolf. Out of this and the long and very deep relation of man to the cow came the great American circus, the rodeo, which has grown into the third American sport in number of spectators, outranked only by basketball and baseball. Both of these get their followers from the very wide participation by the young—baseball on the sand lot or the cow lot, milk-cow lot, diamond, basketball from the schools.

In almost every competition of the rodeo the cow or the means of handling, controlling, the cow as the rancher used the term, is involved. In the center is the bulldogging, now called steer wrassling, but the idea is still the same—the supreme test of man against the lord of, say, the Chamber of the Bulls at Lascaux.

Even the word *rodeo*, Spanish for a surround, a roundup, once separated the initiates, the people of the cow country from all the rest by the shift in accent at the first syllable in the good old untutored Anglo-Saxon way. But the rodeo as a contest did not start in Spanish America or in Spain. Much of it reaches back to early religious dances and combats, back into mythology. Midway through the Bronze Age, perhaps four thousand years ago, there was rugged bull grappling in the arena before the palace of Minos, king of Crete. Scenes from this have been preserved in frescoes, bas-reliefs, and statuettes showing the steps in the sport. The challenger was posted into position, the bull released, and when he charged, the grappler clutched the points of the horns to swing lightly, feet first, upward on the force of the bull's furious toss. With this momentum the grappler turned himself into a back somersault as he released the horns and landed standing on the bull, looking backward. There, if he was an accomplished grappler, he struck a momentary pose for the applause and then leapt gracefully to the ground behind the animal. It was proper and not unusual for women or even girls to join the ranks of the professionals in this acrobatic, ritualistic sport. There was also the twisting of the bull's head by the horns to make him manageable.

In Thessaly riders chased the bulls around the arena and then brought them down by jumping upon them, grabbing the horns and twisting them in the Minoan fashion, much as the modern bulldogger does. It was only far in time and not in spirit from the Thessalian bull throwing to the capture of good young Longhorns about to escape into the brush of Texas by leaping upon them and twisting them down, to be tied with the piggin string and left to grow cramped and subdued enough to follow the decoys to the pens.

From the fourteenth through the sixteenth century the English put on bull baitings by specially bred dogs with pushed-out underjaws. Such a dog couldn't be choked off or shaken loose from his hold on the bull's nose no matter how powerful and swift the thrusts and lunges or how high he was swung, or how hard. There was bull running, too, the bull turned loose by the butcher and chased by the townsfolk until both were worn out. Then the animal was slaughtered.

In the Texas region of the 1770's the bulls of Espiritu Santo and Rosario Missions were prized mostly for the "Days of the Bulls," with bull tailing, bull roping, and riding. Even the occasional castration was left until the animal was grown for the sport of catching him on the prairie. In Spanish California, before the big Kill-Off, the bulls were sometimes run by horse-backers at full speed, each man spurring and maneuvering to get the bull by the tail to throw him, as later some of the brush poppers of Texas did to capture the wilier of the Longhorns, particularly some fine young bull for the ranch herd or a sleek young cow of good bone and meat. In Brazil the bull that showed special fight during cattle work might be surrounded by dozens of men grabbing at him anywhere, and brought down. Then, with the conqueror's boot on his neck, he was given long-winded and oratorical hell in a speech. If the bull got up and away, it just meant another speech.

The Indian was driven from his romantic hunting life to sit morosely on some reservation, the buffaloes killed off, and

the law overtook the lawless. Wild West shows began to sell their
romantic versions of the vanished era to the east, and the come-
lately westerners, with spurious Indian fights, buffalo runs,
and stagecoach robberies. As ranching turned toward book-
keeping, with planned breeding and the gasoline-powered hay
sled not far off, cowboy shows were put on the road, although
there were some cowboys in the Wild West shows that got so
much spread in the magazines and newspapers and so little
money.

Back in the spring of 1883, at the height of the beef bonanza, A. B. Grady of Lockhart, Texas, had organized a company of cowboys to put on exhibitions of Texas cowboy life:
roping and tying wild stock and bronc busting and handling.
They bought silver-banded Mexican hats, fringed leather jack-
ets, Angora chaps, and great-roweled Mexican spurs. Their
horses, all paints, carried Mexican saddles, the stirrups covered
by huge silver and fringe-trimmed tapaderos. Gaudy and handsome, Grady's Cowboys helped set the style for all the show and
dude cowboys to come. They advertised themselves as record
breakers at roping and tying down wild steers, but at the show
at San Antonio the local boys took the shine off Grady's professionals by beating their time. Grady's boys were fine, the local
newspapers suggested, patronizingly, for the large eastern cities.

The same year along in June there was an argument at Pecos, Texas, about who was the best bronc rider and fastest roper
in the region. Although the talk got hot as the rusty stove in the
general store in a blue norther, nothing was settled. A contest
was arranged for the Fourth of July, out on flat ground near the
courthouse. There was no entrance fee, no ticket picker, no
grandstand, no chute. The steers were turned out in the open
for the ropers. The bronc was snubbed or tied down until the
rider was in the saddle, then he was let up, the blind jerked
away, with the circle of riders around to hold him from running off over the prairie and into some arroyo or over a cut
bank. If he broke out, and took off in a blind run, fast-
mounted hazers went after him, to turn him back or pull the
rider from the saddle and "let him go to hell."

Such riding and roping contests were being held all over

the range country, often made up at the moment, just because some riders happened to get together, or rivals from neighboring ranches, the spontaneous "ridings" out on some flat, or some pole corral in Texas or Colorado, Kansas or Dakota.

Three years later Albuquerque put on a cowboy tournament described in the *New York Herald,* the drawing card twelve wild Texas steers released one at a time out upon the open prairie, the cowboy, rope up, spurring after him to bring him down and hogtie him, the prize for the best time a $75 saddle. Afterward there was wild bronc riding, too.

The idea of the cowboy tournaments spread and with them dust, excitement, and broken bones. At Montrose, Colorado, in 1887 a bronc bucked into the terrified audience, trampling a woman. This kind of publicity helped bring the crowds out. At Denver the same month a tournament drew an estimated 8,000 spectators to fill the grandstand, spread over the grounds, and gather twenty deep around the corrals. Some couldn't see but all could whoop and yell.

Inside, the broncs and Longhorn steers kept running around the corral walls, trying to get a nose over, for where the nose went the rest could follow. With the contestant flipping his loop back and forth in the dust, ready, the manager pointed out a horse in the wild-eyed, wild-maned circling herd to the man. Then he was to rope the bronc, dig in his heels to choke him down, saddle him, get on and bust him to a standstill, for which he got a box of cigars and a chance at the prize. One cowboy drew a ready-made outlaw that kicked, struck, and bit, and was so hard-winded it was almost impossible to choke him, the cowboy getting madder and madder as the crowd hooted him. Brutal with fury, he whipped the horse to a frenzy but still unwilling to be saddled. After an hour he was ordered to give up and turn the horse back into the herd, give another man a chance.

One cowboy who had great influence on the rodeo during those formative years was Bill Pickett, the Texas Negro who was credited with originating bulldogging, all unaware that there were some very substantial developments in the sport, beginning back in prehistoric times. Bill Pickett took after the released steer in the usual way, spurring up alongside, and taking a grand flying leap to grab the horns, twist them over toward him and, with the critter's nose pointing up, Bill bent forward, sank his strong teeth into the animal's tender lip, let loose of the horns and jerked himself backward. The steer flopped neatly over on his side, bulldogged. Pickett became very popular as the only cowboy bulldogger. Later he joined Miller Brothers' 101 Ranch Wild West Show and was the star of their outfit at the Jamestown Exposition, 1907, and at the New York Stampede of 1916. Jim Dahlman of the race horses, mayor of Omaha by then, and former President Theodore Roosevelt of the old Maltese Cross, the man who pushed the cattleman land-fraud cases, were honored guests to watch the bull biter work.

Ironically, Pickett died of a skull fracture, but from a sorrel horse, one that pawed him down and was on him like a cat, much as an old-time sorrel mustang mare might. Even so Bill Pickett didn't die immediately, although his head was a pulp.

Texas also furnished the rodeo with the man that many consider the greatest bronc rider of all times—Samuel Thomas Privett. He was born in Erath County, Texas, back in 1864. Redheaded Booger Red was riding at twelve, orphaned at fifteen, and went into rodeo bronc busting back when there was no time limit on the riding. It ended when a man was off or the horse gave up, standing head down, finished, or lit out to run. While other champions often went in for flossy saddles and other fixings, Booger's favorite bucking saddle was a plain hull or tree. His last public appearance was at Fort Worth in 1925. There, going on sixty-one, he rode a bucking horse on exhibition, and died two weeks later, normally.

There have also been noted women in the rodeo field, although they usually drifted into the more fixed routine of the Wild West performers, trick riders, queens of the rodeo, and so on. But at seventeen Lucille Mulhall, daughter of Colonel Zack Mulhall, was a steer roper and better at it than most men. She busted them so hard they seldom got up before she could tie them. When Theodore Roosevelt visited Oklahoma she roped a coyote for him. In 1904 she was with her father's Wild West Show at the World's Fair in St. Louis and in 1905 in New York's Madison Square Garden with Will Rogers and Tom Mix in the outfit. The Mulhall girl roped horses, too, and could ride a mean bronc. With Homer Wilson she staged the first indoor rodeo at the Southwestern Exposition and Fat Stock Show at Fort Worth. This was the real start of big-time rodeo in the region. Lucille Mulhall died in 1940, at fifty-six, in an auto crash, and was buried the day after Christmas on the last pitiful acres of the once great Mulhall ranch.

Depressions were always hard on the Wild West shows because they had a pay roll to meet. In the 1930's they just about vanished. The rodeo, made up of contestants who depend for their existence on prize money, could survive and did.

The first real impetus to the rodeo as a complete show came out of Wyoming. As early as 1872, with the Sioux still lords of all the Powder River country and the Black Hills, the rising Crazy Horse just growing into the war leader to stop General Crook, Cheyenne already had steer riding the Fourth of July. A few months later there was bronc busting right on the open streets, the crowd falling back as the horses bucked this way and that, endangering the windows, too, and the barking dogs.

The first rodeo in Wyoming was apparently around the early 1880's. The Two Bar Cattle Company, with 160,000 cattle and 200 riders, claiming a region approximately across the Territory, put it on. The Scottish and English owners came out to Cheyenne, about 150 of them. Alex Swan met them there. With carriages, wagons, saddle horses, and camp equipment, they headed out to Laramie Plains. A great wild west show and barbecue was laid out for them on the prairie, with Indians, too, for color. Each man on the pay roll trotted out his specialty. There was horse racing, bronc busting, an Indian and cowboy tug of war, bareback riding of wild horses and steers, and a bullfight of sorts. In this fight a little Mexican stepped on the charging bull's head, was tossed into the air, and came down on the animal's back, slid off the rump, and grabbed the tail, to run along behind, fanning the bull at every jump with his sombrero as rodeo clowns were to do for years and years.

One of the cowboys, Butch Cassidy, known as Parker then, later the notorious outlaw, put on a fine bit of fancy pistol shooting. There was a bronc race—twenty-five men on horses that had never been ridden before. Mounted, the blindfolded broncs in a rough sort of row, the best that could be managed, the blinds were jerked away for the start on the 200-yard course. There was bucking and squealing, some going farther backward than ahead, but half an hour later one of the men made it, still with a horse under him.

After a second night under the stars, this one of deep sleep, the visitors started back to Cheyenne, some of them, particularly the very blond, badly gnat-eaten, their eyes and ears red and puffed up like dough. But it was all a great success, and, as the spokesman who thanked Swan at breakfast had said, was worth coming 6,000 miles to see.

From then on there were small rodeos through Wyoming and the adjoining territory as there were over the rest of the cow country. In 1897 the editor-publisher of the *Cheyenne Sun-Leader,* Colonel E. A. Slack, who had seen the Greeley, Colorado, Potato Day, whooped it up for a Cheyenne Frontier Day. He got it the twenty-third of that September, with blast of cannon and ringing of bells, everything from mule and sheep bells to a big one hauled in by the railroad. Even the blacksmiths whanged their anvils, and the Union Pacific shop whistles tooted. So Cheyenne's first Frontier Day opened to 3,000 spectators. Out of that beginning sprouted a dozen others, then hundreds all over the country. In the meantime the test of man against the wild, unconquered horse in a fight to a finish has been cut down to ten seconds, the horses mostly what the contemptuous old cowmen call "pullman ponies." The tips of the Brahman's horns have been cut off, too, but there is still danger enough for an occasional blood offering in these ceremonials to the cow of the old range days, and before. In 1957, by July 5, the great hump-shouldered Brahmans had thrown twenty-three of their twenty-seven riders in two weeks of rodeos around the country. At Prescott, Arizona, which claims to have the oldest Frontier Days Rodeo, started seventy years ago, one of the riders got his mouth full of blood and teeth when his bull butted him in the face. Another was thrown by his bull as they came out of the chute and was tromped mortally, to the moaning and horrified cries of the spectators and the unconsciously increased interest in the contests. The more serious business of the rodeo clown is to lure the animal from any thrown man and then run for his barrel, the bull probably hard after him. Sometimes the little man in the baggy old pants doesn't make it.

Great reputations have been built for ropers and riders and for bucking horses in these rodeo years. It is still true that:

> *There ain't no horse what can't be rode,*
> *There ain't no man what can't be throwed.*

Perhaps Midnight was really the king of all the buckers, as his admirers claim. He probably spilled more cowboys than any other horse in the world, and earned the monument over his grave. There are outlaw mares, too. Miss Klamath, who died in 1955, tallied up the greatest buck-off record of recent years. She had been ridden and used as a pack horse on a ranch in Oregon before she decided to sink her nose and rid herself of man or pack. Her owner refused $10,000 for the Miss the year before she died. Current top buckers are not for sale at any price and their publicity is managed as carefully as a Hollywood starlet's sometimes is. Buckers are getting mighty scarce these stable-bred days.

But the first of the great rodeo bucking horses of international reputation, and to many still the greatest, was Steamboat. He came from the Two Bar Ranch where, almost twenty years before, the big rodeo had been put on for the visiting Scotsmen and the English. By 1903 Steamboat was bucking off all the ranch hands and professional bronc peelers as fast as they could crawl on and yell, "Jerk 'er!" to the man with the blindfold. In 1905 Steamboat was entered at Cheyenne and came away unconquered, unridden. Apparently nobody rode him until 1908, when Dick Stanley stayed with him at the Frontier Days, the horse past his bucking prime. In 1913 Steamboat, a really old horse now, was ridden again. The next year he died of an injury received in the Salt Lake City Rodeo, still bucking. He had never quit and was as surely a dedicated horse as the bulldogger Pickett and the bronc rider Privett were dedicated men, dedicated to the great memorial ceremony to the bygone power and glory of the cow.

From late spring deep into October is the season of the rodeo, the contestants moving from the larger western ones: Cheyenne, Pendleton, Calgary, Fort Worth, Prescott, Belle Fourche, and so on into the smaller fields, splitting up, a few to each state fair and to the littler ones, counties, small towns, competing against local boys, and corn and hog exhibits, and pumpkins and preserves, with perhaps a rodeo queen and some Indian dances by the Boy Scouts in the dust before the little wooden grandstand in the evenings. But the rodeo people are working their way eastward, drawn to New York and Madison Square Garden for late September and the big prize money. Perhaps 200 cowboys and cowgirls will gather there, with the rodeo clowns, the current western moving-picture and TV stars, and perhaps some old standbys like the Lone Ranger and Lassie. There, before many, many thousands of partisans they re-enact their formal rituals, the bronc riding, bareback and saddled, the calf roping, wild-horse race, Brahman bull riding, and so on, always with the steer wrestling, wrassling, still the center of the events. But more and more there are pretty girls in few clothes, the girls of the arena, lightly draped, going through this formal ritual or that one, perhaps riding pure-white horses in a flying charge, almost a stampede, to applause that rocks the Garden.

But the cowmen are not there, no more than their kind would have been dancing around the golden calf at the foot of Sinai when Moses was late coming off the mountain, in the arena before Minos, or even in the great caverned ceremonial Hall of the Bulls. As always those who actually work with the cattle are out looking after the meat of the people. Perhaps some of the cowmen are thinking a little about their own shows, those of the state fairs, just past, where some of their calves might have gone in a Calf Scramble, or were shown by Four-H Club winners. One might have been a boy in jeans proudly showing his champion Hereford, or Angus or Shorthorn. Perhaps it was a girl, with her steer on display in some great hotel lobby while the evening-dressed crowd milled past, some glancing at the sight of the girl on a campstool calmly knitting a school sweater beside her great blocky young Angus who chewed his cud as calmly inside the velvet-roped little enclosure, his feet in the convenient hay.

Perhaps the cowman out there on the Great Plains is thinking a lot about his own livestock shows, Fort Worth, or Denver, or Chicago, as he takes the fall buyers out to his sleek grass-fat stock and prepares for the forty-foot haulers. They will come in long rows, more orderly than the wild strings of Longhorns trailing themselves to Abilene or Dodge or Ogallala. As the cowman works he keeps an ear out for the market reports and later for blizzard warnings. In the meantime there is branding and dehorning of the young stuff, and weaning time, with the voice of the cow loud on every wind.

And as for thousands of years past he knows that they'll all make it somehow, if they can make it to grass.

from OLD JULES

Spring

Mirage

Winter

SPRING

THE BORDER TOWNS of Rock and Cherry counties were shaking off the dullness of winter. Galloping hoofs, the boom of the forty-four, and the measured beat of the spike maul awakened the narrow single streets running between the tents and shacks. Sky pilots plodded from town to town, preaching a scorching and violent hell. But west of there the monotonous yellow sandhills unobtrusively soaked up the soggy patches of April snow. Fringes of yellow-green crept down the south slopes or ran brilliant emerald over the long, blackened strips left by the late prairie fires that burned unchallenged until the wind drove the flames upon their own ashes, or the snow fell.

All winter the wind had torn at the fire-bared knolls, shifting but not changing the unalterable sameness of the hills that spread in rolling swells westward to the hard-land country of the upper Niobrara River, where deer and antelope grazed almost undisturbed except by an occasional hunting party.

But now the grass was started. Out of the East crawled the black path of the railroad. Colonies of homeseekers in covered wagons pushed westward. From the plains of Texas a hundred thousand head of cattle came, their feet set upon the long trails to the free range lands. In the deep canyons of the Niobrara, wolves and rustlers skulked, waiting, while the three or four ranchers already in the hills armed themselves for the conflict.

And out of the East came a lone man in an open wagon, driving hard.

Jules, hunched down on the wagon seat, a rifle between his knees, followed up the north fringe of the river bluffs from the little town of Verdigre near the Missouri. For three weeks he had whipped his tired team onward, always with impatience, as though tomorrow would be too late. But there was really no hurry. His Swiss-made map showed the sandhills a wilderness with many small lakes and streams, remote, uninhabited—wild fruit, game, and free land far from law and convention. There a man could build a home, hunt and trap in peace, live as he liked.

Little about this dark-bearded young man in ragged, camp-stained clothing suggested the dapper student who swaggered the streets of Zurich three years before, whose shave was as necessary as breakfast. An old cap, greasy and scorched from service in pan lifting, sat low upon eyes as strange and changing as the Jura that towered over his homeland. They were gray, and glowed at a lusty story well told, withdrew in remote contemplation of the world and the universe, or flashed with the swift anger and violence of summer lightning.

At twenty-two, after four years of medical school, Jules instigated another of his periodic scenes. A larger allowance was the pretext. Three thousand francs was not enough for the son of a gentleman in the university. Would they have him clean his own shoes?

This time he aroused more than his mother's short-lipped anger that always ended in tearful yielding to this eldest and most beloved son. His father's anger broke through a military restraint. So the fine Jules would play the millionaire? Did he forget that there were yet five brothers and the young Elvina to be fed and clothed and educated? Perhaps it would be well if he learned to clean his own shoes.

The son stood up to the father. Were the summer months he had spent as railway mail clerk, a life fit only for the slow wits of a stable hand, as nothing? Yes, his allowance had been increased, but he knew why.

To separate him from the little Rosalie who worked beside him in the mail service, and who was not considered good enough for one of a family celebrating the four hundredth year of its foundation. They would have finer daughters-in-law. Very well. Let their favorites, Paul and Henri and Nana, bring them. He, Jules, would go to America. And he would take the Rosalie with him.

But, as his father predicted, the little Rosalie would not go. So he left his home on the blue waters of Lake Neuchâtel alone, crossed the sea, and came as far west as his money permitted, to northeastern Nebraska. There he filed on a homestead and became a landed man, with twenty dollars, a stamp collection begun as a boy, a Swiss army rifle, and a spade. Letters in French and full of this wonderful country crossed the sea to Rosalie. She answered affectionately, but she still could not bring herself to follow her Jules to an American frontier farm, pointing out instead their total unfitness for peasant life.

So—after three years of disappointment—Jules married the first woman that would have him.

When the young wife, Estelle, refused to build the morning fires, to run through the frosty grass to catch up his team, Jules closed her mouth with the flat of his long, muscular hand, dumped their supply of flour and sugar to the old sow and pigs, and loaded his belongings upon the wagon to leave her and Knox County behind him forever.

Because, in 1884, Valentine was the land office for the great expanse of free land to the west and south, Jules stopped there. The town was also the end of the railroad and the station of supply and diversion for the track crews pushing the black rails westward, for the military posts of Fort Niobrara and Fort Robinson, for the range country, and for the mining camps of the Black Hills. Sioux came in every day from their great reservations to the north, warriors who as late as '77 and '81 had fought with Crazy Horse and Sitting Bull; law was remote, and the broken hills or the Sioux blanket offered safe retreat for horse thief, road agent, and killer.

Because the town was probably full of thieves, Jules camped in the sparse timber of the river valley. After a supper of antelope steak he kicked the coals from his fire and climbed the hill towards the double row of lighted windows.

The flat plain of Valentine was dotted with the dark bulks of covered wagons, hungry oxen, picketed horses—settler caravans and freighters camped for the night in their push westward. Jules stopped to talk to a knot of silent men squatting around a fire—Germans, they told him at last, going to the north table, two days out. They stared curiously at the dark, bearded young man, tall in the gleam of the fire, fine long hands and delicate wrists dangling from shrunken coat sleeves. *Ja,* they had heard of the sandhills. They sucked loudly at their pipes when he said he would go there.

Seeing, Jules left them and went down the one street of Valentine. He dodged behind the horse-lined hitch-racks as a dozen galloping cowboys came into town, yelling, shooting red streaks through the darkening sky, stirring up a dust that shimmered golden in the squares of light that spilled from the tents and shacks. In the doorway of the largest saloon and gambling house between O'Neill and the Black Hills the homeseeker hesitated.

Despite the blaze of tin lamp reflectors along the walls, the interior was murky, heavy with the stench of stale alcohol and winter-long unbathed humanity. Restless layers of smoke crept over the heads of the crowd. Hats pushed back, their hands on their hips, the frontiersmen listened to a short, stocky man sitting on the wet bar, their narrow eyes moving covertly over their neighbors. Jules edged closer with the other newcomers to listen to the strange American words.

It seemed that the stocky man brought news. The vigilantes down the Niobrara were riding again. That meant, he reminded his listeners, a cottonwood, a bridge, or a telegraph pole and a chunk of rope for somebody. The vigilantes had come as far as Valentine before, taken men away and left them dangling for the buzzards. They took Kid Wade from the sheriff at Bassett only a month ago. Hung him to a telegraph pole and sold the rope at fifty cents an inch. They said he was a horse thief. That dodge always worked.

Now the vigilantes were riding again and all opposition would be taken care of in the usual way.

Jules looked curiously into the frightened faces of the land seekers about him and started away to buy a glass of beer. It was all just another joke on the greenhorns and soon the laughing would begin.

At the bar a half-drunken youth, several years younger than Jules, was talking big. "Let the viges come. We'll make 'em eat lead," he drawled, and spit into the sawdust at his feet.

"Shut that running off the mouth, Slip," a whisper warned, somewhere near Jules. The youth called Slip poured himself another glass of whiskey, running it over. He gulped the liquid and spit again.

"I ain't afraid of any goddamn viges," he told them all, his hand on his heavy cartridge belt.

A shot set the glasses and bottles to ringing and started a wave of relieved talk and natural laughter as Slip turned and set his glass back upon the bar. A mushroom of powder smoke rose from the crowd and crept lazily toward the dark rafters.

Jules laughed too now, not as the others, but with keen enjoyment. This was as the shooting through the darkness outside, a show, the Wild West of which he had read, with a great smell of powder and brag. It was fine. Then he stopped, a little sick. The youth was bending low over the bar and from his mouth ran a string of frothy blood. Slowly he went down, his fingers sliding from the boards.

The sun-blackened men about him melted back, their hands frankly on their guns now. A hunchback and a negro pushed between them, carrying the sagging figure out. The swinging doors came to rest behind them and still no boot creaked.

At a shoulder signal from the bartender two men finally pushed forward, pounding empty glasses on the wet wood. Gradually the front line crumbled; glasses clinked, while one after another the newcomers escaped into the night. A blond-bearded Polander climbed upon a barrel and pulled away at a red accordion. Two girls came out of the boxes at the back and slipped companionably into the double line at the bar. Gradually the crowd thickened again. Everything was as usual.

Bewildered and angry at this, his first death, Jules let himself down into the handiest chair. Across the pine table from him sat a man twisting a finger into his walrus moustache, engrossed in his own thoughts and a mug of beer.

"But will the officials not try to apprehend the murderer, lock him up?" the newcomer finally demanded, in the stilted English of the foreigner.

A heavy eyelid went up slowly and came down. " 'T ain't healthy, times like this, to be too interested in the remains nor anybody what mighta been involved." The man stopped, fished in his sagging pocket, and brought up some newspaper clippings.* Shaking out the tobacco, he handed them across the table. Cautiously Jules took them and read of the surprising activities of the vigilantes, while the man talked on.

TRANSGRESSORS DEALT WITH BY VIGILANTES.

Sioux City, February 5.—Reports have reached here from the upper Elkhorn country, in Nebraska, that Kid Wade, leader of the Nebraska outlaws and horse thieves, has been hung by vigilantes, who have headquarters at a place called "The Pen," at the mouth of the Long Pine. They have arrested a large number of men in various parts of northern Nebraska and taken them away to this place, where they are tried and disposed of in a manner unknown. But as they are never seen again, it is supposed that they are shot, hanged or conducted out of the country. The terrible earnestness of the vigilantes and the mystery of their ways cause men to shudder when their doings are mentioned. It is positively certain that they have lynched eleven men, and it is equally sure that others have met the same fate, but how many, or by what means, only the grim executioners can tell. "Kid"

* From the St. Paul *Phonograph*, February 15 and 29, 1884.

Wade was captured at Lemars three weeks ago. He seemed to realize the fate that awaited him, but manifested no more concern than if going about his ordinary business.

LONG PINE, February 7.—Kid Wade was found this morning hanging to a whistle-post ten miles east of Long Pine. Coroner Shofford, of Long Pine, held an inquest to-day and found that he came to his death by hanging by parties unknown. The vigilantes left this place yesterday morning with Wade. The sheriff of Holt county took him from them, but on the way to Holt county ten or fifteen masked men took Wade from the sheriff.

VIGILANTES' LAW IN CHERRY COUNTY.

SIOUX CITY, February 16.—Sheriff Carter, of Cherry county, Nebraska, has been notified by the vigilance committee to leave the county immediately. The vigilantes claim that he is in collusion with the Nebraska horse thieves beyond a doubt. Sheriff Carter announces fixed determination to stay, denies the charges made against him, and has sworn in a posse of thirty men for his protection. The sheriff and his men are all armed to the teeth, awaiting hostilities. The leader of the vigilantes has posted up a notice that no man living can escape their vengeance, least of all Sheriff Carter. Further developments are anxiously awaited.

"Kids like that Slip there what steals maybe a hame string and shoots off their mouth got no business in this man's country, Frenchy. Of course, most of it's just likkered-up track hands and cowboys and soldiers or reservation bucks. But there's horse stealing, rustling, and skin games going constant. Then—" dropping his voice—"of course there's our viges."

"It is so?" Jules tapped the clippings.

"Yeh, claiming the courts is run by crooks, no protection for their stock or lives." The man turned his head over a thick shoulder and looked about. "I guess 't ain't no secret, but the county judge and the sheriff is supposed to own every sliver in this goddamn dump. The viges has ordered the sheriff to leave the county. He swears in a posse of thirty men with Winchesters and awaits developments."

Could this be so?

Wondering what his father would say, the recent citizen of the orderly, uneventful little Swiss republic leaned upon his folded arms and considered these people more closely.

In that packed room only one man stood out. He was alone at a corner table, with a rifle standing in the crook of his arm, the barrel against his young beard, his dark hair turning up in silky drakes' tails under the large belly-tan hat. His legs were exceedingly long, so long that his fine soft boots extended out upon the floor beyond the small table. But no one bumped against them and no one sat with him. Undisturbed, aloof, he sipped a small glass of whiskey.

"Yeh." The old freighter made the most of his fresh audience. "Like the paper says, the other morning they's a notice tacked up on this shack, mind you, saying that the viges gets what hair they's after. So far nothing's happened, as I knows, unless—" He jerked a stubby thumb towards the doors.

"But do the people here believe that the vigilantes are always right?"

The man choked, sputtering beer through his moustaches.

"Right? Who's stopping to ask about right if they has the crack shots on their side?"

So that was how it went here. Jules ordered two beers.

The country west the old-timer dismissed with a grand sweep of the replenished mug. "No-count, unless you got money enough to start a cow outfit and guns enough to fight the rustlers off. Starve to death farming. Never rains, cold as blazes in winter. They brought a feller up from the lake country south of here last week. Both hands froze, fingers rotting off, crazy as a shitepoke."

Jules, who never listened to what he would not hear, rose abruptly and took a turn through the crowd, wishing he had brought one of his guns with him instead of hiding both the rifle and his secondhand ten-bore in the buckbrush along the river.

He pushed away a girl who put her arm about his shoulders. There was no telling—probably diseased. He took no chances.

The man with the rifle was still there, turning the tiny glass between his lean brown fingers, watching the light in the amber liquid. "One-man outfit," the freighter had called him, "not running with no pack here."

Jules was not quite certain what these phrases meant, but there was something about the man. Not even the women, wandering about with large-mouthed laughter in search of pay dirt, went near him. In the glare of the tin reflectors the blued barrel of his Winchester gleamed, a repeater, a beautiful weapon, as true steel is beautiful.

To avoid the milling, dusty street Jules cut around the corner of the saloon and stumbled over something—a man, stiff and cold. Probably the youth who defied the vigilantes, chilling for shipment home.

The homeseeker pressed his back against the board wall for a moment. Inside, the Polander was still sweating over a fast polka. Boots stomped, while far away a revolver echoed twice, followed by a faint "Yi-hoo!" Jules touched the dark bulk with his foot. Sometimes the sparrow, like the eagle, dies far from his nest.

But only a most important man, a general or a senator, would be shipped across the sea. He scratched his beard. Surely digging would be easier in the sandhills than in the stony graveyards of Neuchâtel, and if there was none to wield the spade the wolves would clean the bones well.

Shivering a little, he slipped away into the pitchy darkness.

Back at his wagon, Jules pulled his Vetterli from its hiding place in the buckbrush. He raised it to his shoulders several times. The gun came up well, but it was only a single shot. Heavily he crept into his bed roll.

The next day he tried to trade the old Swiss rifle for a secondhand Winchester, but such guns were in great demand on the border and there were other needs for the forty dollars remaining from the relinquishment of his Knox County claim. There would be much to buy,—farm tools, seed, food, ammunition, shoes, drugs,—all the things of life in a new land.

The old storekeeper puttered about among his stacks of gaudy Indian goods, the thick woolens he kept for the freighters and the leathers for the ranch hands. Finally he took Jules into a back room and showed him the bales of furs caught up the Niobrara by Indian and white trappers—beaver, mink, an occasional otter, endless muskrats, not worth more than eight or ten cents, skunk, coyotes, gray wolves, and badgers from the bluffs and hills. But beaver and otter—those were the furs.

So Jules added a dozen steel traps to his supplies, and a book on trapping and first aid for the frontiersman. He obtained plats and information at the land office, listened with interest to the story of a hard-land region west of the sandhills, and made arrangements to have all mail held until he returned.

"That may be a long time, feller. Lots of things kin happen out where you're going," the postmaster commented dryly.

"I am a crack shot," Jules told him stiffly.

"Oh, are you!" The man looked the camp-stained homeseeker up and down. "There's other things catchin' where you're going besides lead colic."

But he made a note of the mail instructions and stuck the paper on the last of the long row of spikes jammed full of similar slips. Jules wrote letters to his friends in Knox County, young professional men: a doctor, a lawyer, an architect, all who had come across the sea in answer to his earlier letters. They had been disappointed in America, but now he would lead them to a better land. And last he wrote a letter to Rosalie, dropped a blob of red wax upon the flap and pressed it down with his grandfather's seal—a man with a seedling tree standing on newly ploughed ground, facing the rising sun. Then once more Jules set his face westward.

Every day the country grew more monotonous. The gash cut by the Niobrara sank deep between sandstone and magnesia-white bluffs; the grass was longer, yellower, less washed by the winter snows. Because the bluffs crowded close to the stream the homeseeker kept out of the valley, only descending into it for water and wood. The washed ruts of the army trail leading west to Fort Robinson did not interest him. There would be less game along the trail and less freedom on land within sight of troops.

The days brought pale, wind-streaked skies, yellow coyotes slinking into gullies, and endless small game: rabbits, grouse, quail. Wedges of wild geese honked their way north, and along the river the swift wings of ducks whistled over the brush and the clear, sand-bottomed stream. He saw many antelope and deer, and one morning a large, dun animal with high shoulders and broad pronged antlers grazed peacefully against the higher reaches of the sparsely timbered hillside. An elk. The young hunter's Vetterli came up, then dropped, stock down, to the ground. Arms crossed over the muzzle, Jules watched the beautiful animal, so nearly the color of the grassy slope that it vanished unless silhouetted against the dark green of the pines. At last he slipped away.

Towards noon a yellowish haze crept up the horizon. The wind rose in panting gusts, settled into a steady push, almost as tangible as a wall. The flying sand cut the man's face. Despite the sharp-lashed whip, the horses turned their tails into the wind. Finally Jules gave up, unhitched, and slept away the day behind a sandstone cliff over the river. The next morning was still and clear, and the rested horses set off on a trot that soon slowed to a walk in the loose sand, hock deep, blown from bare stretches over the grass. But the wind-uprooted trees, the denuded knolls, brought only a grunt from the homeseeker. He refused to see any significance in them. Instead he considered the coming Presidential election. Cleveland, the governor of New York, was an aggressive young Democrat. If nominated he would carry the election, build up world trade, bring good times for the poor man. Without tariff there would be no international conflicts, no wars. That reminded him of Estelle in Knox County. Lazy, good for nothing, didn't want to raise children. So long as there were wars it was woman's duty to make soldiers.

In the meantime an iridescent, bluish-yellow streak began to smudge the northwest horizon. It lifted like a delicate puff-ball, spread, trailing across the hills. Jules pushed his cap back and pounded his team toward the Running Water. At the first whiff of smoke the team plunged forward, down into the steep river canyon. The sudden lurch threw Jules forward, almost over the dash. The wagon seat bounced off, the bed roll whirling after it. The wagon teetered on two wheels and then went over, throwing the man into the shallow, sandy river. He got up, flung the water from his eyes, and looked to his team, heaving, down in the harness on a sand bar, but unhurt, while on the bluff above them five antelope ran swiftly before the fire.

Jules looked after them, pulled his wet pants ruefully from his thighs, and started the disagreeable task of untangling the team.

"Whoa—whoa—whoa," he kept saying nervously, only confident of his command over such powerful muscles as those of a horse when seated in the wagon and armed with a long-lashed whip. When the horses were free and the scattered goods collected, Jules built up a big fire and wrapped himself in a blanket like a Sioux Indian he had seen at Valentine, while his clothes steamed on the leafless chokeberry bush near the flames. He heated a pail of water and poured it boiling through his guns. The Vetterli, particularly, must not rust.

All next day the homeseeker pushed on through the fire-blackened region. Here and there a soapweed butt twisted a barely visible thread of smoke into the still air. There was no game, not even a snowbird, and for three days Jules had had no word with a fellow man. He was following the army trail now, but it stretched away before him as empty as the burnt prairie. Once he looked back, contemplating return to Valentine. Then he swung his whip and pushed onward.

Suddenly the country was grassed again. The homeseeker climbed off his wagon to kick the soil, to smell it, feel it between his fingers. Carefully he measured the dried sunflower stalks that rattled in the wind, and went on. Finally he saw a little half soddy, half dugout, beside the trail. No horse, no cow, no strip of breaking, only the little door and half window with a crooked, rusty stovepipe pushing up through the sod-covered roof. A middle-aged Swede looked out reluctantly at the man's knock.

"Aye don' spik Anglish," he kept repeating through the crack of doorway.

At a particularly level little flat about two miles long Jules stopped again. Good ground, but only enough for one. He would go on. What was the time? Not yet May. Too cold for growing crops.

Every day the wind's song was louder, the air drier, the sun glare brighter on the sandy stretches. Squinting his eyes over the map he fought to hold together in the wind, he moved his finger westward along the Niobrara. The country was getting high, approximately 3500 to 4000 feet, and still the sunflowers grew and the grapevines were knotted with flower buds along the river. He developed a tendency to undershoot and let a yearling antelope get away before he could reload. A little lift to the sight remedied that. A good rifle this Vetterli, for now, but a Winchester repeater—that was the gun. With it a wolf or a man could be killed a long way off; never know what hit him. Who needed the protection of law and government with such a gun?

He knew it could not be far to the hard land beyond the hills now. With the rifle barrel against his shoulder as the man in the saloon at Valentine held his, the homeseeker sang "Marguerite," a love song he used to sing to Rosalie in the cool green woods of Switzerland on Sunday afternoons.

With a sudden sputter he stopped. She had refused to come with him. She wouldn't be any use to him, no more than Estelle.

But there was no denying that she was the best comrade he had ever known. Long, fine hands; dark, curly hair clustered at her neck; a sharp, clear mind. It could not be that he would never see her again.

The horses trudged on in a slow walk, the yellow sand following the iron tires and dropping back into the tracks with a soft song.

Twice the next day retreating wagons crept eastward toward Jules. Both times the defeated homeseekers stopped to warn him.

"The cattlemen will have this land—all of it."

Jules patted the lock of his gun. "Heah?—I won't scare out."

But it was most dangerous to remain. Two settlers who refused to scare out were hung and then burned to death.

"Oh, you mean Mitchell and Ketchum—killed down in Custer County." Jules spit into the sand. "Where you hear this?"

"Cowboys, at the Hunter ranch, twelve miles up the river."

"So—" Jules scratched his beard, stopped, took the shell from his gun, and looked through the barrel carefully. Not a speck of powder soot marred the gleaming chamber. It seemed that the cowboys were only scaring the greenhorns, but he had thought the same thing in the saloon at Valentine. Clashes would come—when men would be needed—men who could carry Winchesters and shoot straight, and to kill. Jules gathered up his lines. He would camp at the Hunter ranch that night.

An hour later he saw a small bunch of cattle grazing along the hillside, and for a moment a rider stood black against the light horizon. Later he saw more cattle, and finally he struck the traveled army trail that dipped deep into the river valley past a log house and some outbuildings snuggled against the bluffs, half hidden by bare trees. As he opened the wire gate an eagle circled high over the bluffs, a tiny splash of black in the evening sky. He shot once and watched the eagle slant and fall.

A man at the barn looked up at the report.

"Not bad, old-timer, not so damned bad," he called. "Unhitch!"

There were only two men at the ranch until after dark, both of them old Texas trail drivers, and while they did a lot of laughing at this foreigner who expected to grow corn here, they made no attempt to scare him with murder tales.

"So you're goin' up to the Flats? Great farmin' country. Never get your crops wet there," the cook told the homeseeker as he lifted the pan of squaw bread off the stove and spit his tobacco into the fire. Jules speared a chunk of the brown, fried dough from the pan and laughed.

About dark the taller man took a lantern from a rafter, lit it, and went out.

"Snubs it to a tree on top of the bluff so's them riders what's coming in can see where the ranch is. Can't git a glim of the light from down here fur as you can smell a lily in a nest of skunks," the cook explained.

"Oho!"

An hour later three more men came in, blinking narrow eyes in wind-leathered faces. Perched on their haunches along the smoky wall, they ate thick slabs of fried beef and squaw bread and drank tin cans of black coffee boiling hot, for the evening air was chilly. Then, with a few words and a lot of unjustified laughing, they told Jules to "turn in anywheres," and crawled into bunks at the far end of the room.

At daylight they were out. Soon after sunup all but the cook loped away. Jules left too, a little disgruntled. He had slept with his rifle by his side, but no one had disturbed him.

Now the sandhills flattened away to buffalo-grassed flats. Last year's sunflowers stood taller, their stalks thicker, sturdier. Jules climbed off his wagon. His study of government bulletins, his knowledge of botany in the Old Country, convinced him that where sunflowers grow corn will grow also. And except for the few cowboys at the Hunter ranch the country was open, free. The grass was almost untouched; cow chips rare.

About two o'clock on the afternoon of the twentieth of April, the day before Jules's twenty-fifth birthday, which he had completely forgotten, the hills gave way and before him was the silver ribbon of the Niobrara, the wooded slopes barely tinged with palest green, topped by yellowish sandstone bluffs. Farther on was a plain, flatter than the palm of a man's hand, and reaching into the dim blue hazes each way. Far off to the left was a flat butte, box-like. To the extreme right were low hills, similar to those left behind.

But the land straight ahead, the Flats, as the Hunter cook called it, was absolutely bare, without a house, even a tree—a faint yellow-green that broke here and there into shifting aspects of small, shimmering lakes, rudimentary mirages. There, close enough to the river for game and wood, on the hard land that must be black and fertile, where corn and fruit trees would surely grow well, Jules saw his home and around him a community of his countrymen and other homeseekers, refugees from oppression and poverty, intermingled in peace and contentment. There would grow up a place of orderliness, with sturdy women and strong children to swing the hay fork and the hoe.

Leaning upon his Vetterli, his cap pushed far back from his eyes, he surveyed the Running Water, his new homeland.

⊏⊟   ⊏⊟   ⊏⊟

MIRAGE

THE NIOBRARA, its sand bottom still soft from the flood waters of March, was smaller here than in Knox County. But the current ran swift and strong and its load of abrasive yellow sand had cut deep through sandstone and volcanic ash and lime rock, baring bones of mastodon and beds of petrified snails.

But the homeseeker had no time for these things today. Jules pounded his thin-necked team through the stream and up a snake-head gully to the horizon-wide hard-land table. Where the occasional sunflower along the soldier trail reached to his shoulder, he sank his spade two blades deep through the tough nigger-wool sod. The soil was black, smooth, smelling of spring. Here the settler dropped the harness from his team. When his fire of diamond willow crackled, he skinned a grouse, and fried it all. If a man would plan well, he must eat.

His long hands about his ragged knees, he looked into the red fire. Soon Rosalie would be beside him, Rosalie and neighbors, lights all over the Flats, friendly in the dark that was un-relieved tonight.

At last he lay down to sleep.

The next morning Jules took his traps to the river, and while a blue kingfisher poised over the stream and fell like a plummet, he set several number ones where the dainty tracks of a mink embroidered the mud. Two larger traps he hid cunningly where a gnawed young cottonwood lay half in the water. He caught two muskrats, a mink, and two beaver feet, chewed off at the steel jaws of the trap. It was too bad to leave an animal crippled to suffer.

Before the kerosene that had slopped against the grub box was evaporated and the coffee was tolerable again, Sol Pitcher, a surveyor from Verdigre, drove out of the dusk to the camp-fire.

The two talked over their supper. The cook at Hunter's had said: "You'll find Frenchy scratching the dirt on the Flats until July comes to cook his liver and lights."

"Trying to discourage settlers," Jules grumbled, over a leg of cottontail.

"Yeh," Sol admitted as he wiped the gravy from his catfish moustaches. He liked the country, was disappointed that the impractical Jules had put off finding the government corners* of his land while he planted young ash and cottonwood and box-elder seedlings from the river. A wave of population was due. There would be money in locating.

For two days they plodded their ponies over the table west-ward from Box Butte to a wide prairie-dog town, thousands of little crater-like holes, with the derisive dogs bobbing out of sight with a flirt of the stubby tails, to scold and bark as soon as the men were past. Jules shot one to examine it—a gnawer, with teeth like a little beaver. He spattered the head of a rattle-

---

* The government surveys in this region were completed in 1881. The section corners were marked with four holes, one in each of the cornering sections, the soil thrown together in a central mound, and a stake bearing the section numbers driven into this mound. The Homestead Act, effective January 1863, allowed each *bona fide* settler 160 acres of land. The entry was by legal description and the entryman swore that he had seen the premise before filing. "Squatting" had lost all legal status.

snake on one of the mounds. Then he saved his ammunition.

They found several fine, whitened buffalo heads and a few depressions that lined up with the compass, but no numbered stakes as the government bulletins promised. Hoping that the weather had brought them down, they dug in the holes. Finally Jules threw the spade from him.

"Damn the luck! Prairie fire burn me the stakes or somebody maliciously destroy them!"

"Yeh, guess you're right, Jule," the calmer Sol agreed, picking up the spade. The next day Sol headed north towards the railroad survey, where locating would be more profitable around the new town sites. Three soddies would make a town, with lots to sell.

After his friend was gone, Mirage Flats was suddenly empty, bare as a burnt-out world. When a small puffball of dust came down the army trail from Fort Robinson, far to the west, Jules leaned with folded arms across the muzzle of his gun beside the deep ruts, and watched them trot by: three light wagons, officers, educated men with a mounted escort. They barely acknowledged his greeting. Only one more granger scalp if the Sioux broke out.

Back at his wagon Jules set the rifle against the wheel and poured out a cup of cold coffee from the blackened syrup pail, looking after the troopers until the clot of dust dipped down towards the Niobrara.

Suddenly he flung the dark liquid and the cup from him, and piled his plough, his axe, and his spade into the wagon. In the morning he would go back, not to Estelle and Knox County, —to Neuchâtel and to Zurich, to his friends Surber and Karrer, —to Rosalie.

But that night, while, with the point of his pocket knife, he probed frying balls of baking-powder biscuit in antelope-steak gravy, tired hoofbeats pounded over the prairie. A covered wagon broke from the darkness, the lathered flanks of the horses heaving. A man leaped down, deep shadows of night on his naked cheeks.

Jules reached for his rifle and stepped back into the darkness.

"Don't shoot! My God, man, don't shoot!" the frightened youth begged. "My wife's dying—and I can't find a woman to help her."

Suspiciously Jules came forward, scratching his beard. "In thaire?" he asked, thumbing towards the wagon.

Together they climbed upon the doubletrees, Jules carrying his lantern and his gun. Inside, between boxes and bundles, lay a young woman, little more than a child, her eyes unmoving caverns in the light.

Jules pushed his cap back and clambered out. He set the pan off and began eating rapidly with his knife, mouthing the hot food, his rifle still in the crook of his arm. Behind him in the shadows hovered the stranger. Once more he searched the dark of the Flats, shielding his eyes from the campfire and lantern glare. There was nothing, only those in the circle of the light.

"You can't sit there—eating—and let her die!"

Without answering Jules speared another chunk of steak and put it into his mouth. Slowly the man plodded to his team and gathered up the lines.

"Heah?—Oh, hell!—Put on a bucket of water to boil," Jules ordered.

At a hoarse cry from the wagon he gulped a cup of black coffee and carried the lantern into his tent, his back a black, moving shadow. From a small bottle with a red skull and crossbones he measured the equivalent of a grain of wheat of white powder into a tin cup.

"What you giving her?" the husband whispered.

"Morphine. Kill some of the pain. Now make me room and get me some clean rags."

While the boxes and bundles came out of the wagon Jules thumbed through his doctor book, washed his hands carefully, pared his fingernails close, and pulled his blunt scissors from the boiling water with a stick. Then he carried out the instructions of the book as unfeelingly, as coldly, as though the woman were one of the animals he had so often seen his veterinary father care for, the father who still hoped that this eldest of six sons would be a doctor.

The woman was spent by long hours of labor and he needed all the ingenuity and recollection his Swiss heritage could bring to his strong, narrow hands and the pitifully scant equipment he had. But she had endurance, youth, and courage, and Jules was without knowledge of pain. The horizontal rays of the early sun found the camp asleep—one more potential tiller of the soil on Mirage Flats.

And this morning the discouragement of yesterday was gone. With the help of the young father, Jud Haskins, Jules unloaded once more and started a dugout, a place for his belongings, something to mark his claim. Almost every day pin dots of black broke from the obscurity of the blue-veiled horizon. Only the impression that his place was safely entered protected it from claim jumpers.

Two weeks showed that it was not good with the Haskins baby. Although the young mother ate much fresh game and every day a bit from their lean store of potatoes and flour, the little Jules cried all night, his mouth like a starving birdling's. The settler swore and thumbed the doctor book.

Then one evening he found a note pinned to his clean blankets. The Haskins hoped to find a doctor and cow's milk at Fort Robinson. The fresh bread hanging from the ridgepole of the tent was for him, and the big jar of grape butter. And God bless him.

With a curse Jules crumpled the note and threw it into the fire. He sat a long time with his hands hanging between his muddy knees. When the clean coffeepot boiled over, he stirred.

"Every man need a good woman," he told the Flats.

WINTER

Jules bought his liquor from Pine Creek now, once a community of congenial settlers who knew how to enjoy life without breaking the law beyond picking up an occasional unbranded calf. Now the region was torn by the suspicions, jealousies, and hatreds of rival still operators and peddlers. State booze hounds came out every few weeks. They chopped up a still at Emile's place, where the eldest son lived alone in the big, empty house. They took away Ferdinand's kettle and worm. The son-in-law of Eugenie and Louis Pochon was not disturbed. "If you got any scabby cows in the lot, turn them out," the sheriff was said to have telephoned him before the enforcement officers came.

Next they went into the hills. They searched the Frank Wildman place. The young Bohemian had worked for Jules for several years. Perhaps because Flora grew up even prettier than everyone expected, he endured the father's abuse. But he must make money fast. Jules sent him away, but bought his product. Hearing this, the officers came and searched the old settler's house, barn, and orchard. They found nothing except a fish net hanging openly along the wall of the bunkhouse. They took it and fined Jules a dollar a foot and costs. One hundred forty dollars for a rotten old net fifteen years old.

"How can they do that—when they were looking for Frank's still?" Elmer Sturgeon asked, even as he questioned Panhandle justice in the nineties.

"The country has not changed since we run Freese out. You got to fight for your rights—and I'm getting old."

"Well, anyway, you have the money to keep yourself out of jail. That's what you have to have nowadays."

"Hell, yes." Jules shrugged his heavy shoulders much as he did in the dugout on Mirage Flats. Government officials were a lot of crooks. Fall, Sinclair, and that outfit indicted. A cabinet member implicated and dirty tracks leading into the White House. But actually Jules was more disturbed that wild ducks were dying by the thousands around the south lakes. Too thick, got a strange disease, old-timers from down that way told him. Then there was always the pain in his chest, like a thin wire, cutting his lungs at every breath.

He went from one doctor to another now, but they could do little except speak vaguely of diabetes and arthritis, words he did not understand, and give him diet sheets he would not follow. In a thundering rage he limped out of the hospital at Alliance, went home, drank all the grape wine he could hold, and groaned and swore for two days and nights. It was all Mary's fault, making him sleep alone. A man needs a woman as he needs the earth, for relief. Now he was gelded by disease.

Other times he insisted he was being poisoned. Somebody was killing him with a powerful, tasteless drug. And as he made his venomous accusations his bloodshot eyes slid in suspicion over the faces of them all. Mary moved her cot into his room, kept a hot fire going all night, carried everything to and from him. There were few minutes of joy for the old settler. One of these was when he saw that the Spade was advertised for sheriff sale.

"Well, the cattle king who run me down in Chadron when I was on crutches is gone—and his land selling under the hammer."

But even joy brought pain, and so he drank himself into numbness, where he could neither read nor sleep, just sit within his barrel-round body, a frightened old man in a huge, malevolent house.

Once more at Alliance the doctors cut off all alcohol, put him on a light diet. When he disturbed the other patients, the nurses held his wrist and gave him a shot in the arm. In two weeks he was roaring to go home. He stole his pants, climbed shakily into them, walked the half mile to a garage, and hired a man to take him into the hills. That evening he ate at the table and was better than for months. In a week he was helpless again.

But now he took everything anyone suggested, answered the patent-medicine advertisements until his room was like a pharmacy. Because he needed money he sold part of the land he bought from the Spade to Fritz. Now he had them all about him: James and his wife, a schoolteacher from Gordon, in the valley where the big round-up was held: Jule, the only one who followed his father's advice and married a French girl, one from the colony towards Ellsworth, living a few miles west; and now Fritz coming home with his wife from down along the Burlington. It was good so, with the sons close about him, like young pines sprouting in the shadow of the old tree. Even the two girls in high school would teach near. Only Marie was gone, like a seed washed far by a flood, and that was not good.

With the money he got from the land he sold, Jules went to Rochester. But he was too impatient to endure the painstaking procedure of the clinic. At the end of the third day he left, got a bottle of spiked wine, and went to Chicago. While limping along the street, his huge overcoat fastened with a blanket pin where he ripped the button off in his impatience, someone stopped him, offered to take his picture for nothing if he would let one of them be used in a window display. He went, gave the man his address, and started home.

At Lincoln Marie cut her university classes and met him at the depot. She helped steady his huge body on the tottering, feeble legs, and listened to his wandering tirades. Bitter and violent he had always been, but not wandering.

"I'm a sick man, Marie, a damn sick man," he told her when she put him on the train again. "I give you the money if you come home Christmas, my last Christmas."

When Jules was home a week the photographs came, a dozen, without a bill. Mary looked into one of the folders, laid it down, and slipped away to the frozen feed ground, where she wandered among the chewing cattle. After a while she came back, blew her nose loudly, and stuffed her handkerchief away.

"Damn fine-looking man you got," Jules told her, holding out one of the pictures. This time she was prepared for the eyes, by some trick swept free of their load of age and disease, the live, piercing, far-focused eyes of the man she saw thirty-two years before across the smoky kitchen on the Running Water.

Jules thanked the photographer on his letterhead with his long list of honorary memberships. He received an immediate and apologetic reply.

"See—I always tell you you ought to look decenter. The man took you for a bum."

Jules started to chuckle, shaking his loose belly, but the pain brought gray sweat to his face, and with his arm over Mary's shoulder he limped to his bed, the wine bottle on a chair beside him.

The girls came home from school for Christmas, the boys brought their wives, and once more the family was together, with Solomon, the Syrian peddler, Andy, Sandcherry Charley, and an old Austrian Jules picked up in Chicago. They talked of old times. Elvina had had another stroke, the third, and couldn't talk. William was dead; Lena living in Hay Springs. Ferdinand was bootlegging again. Paul still lived in Oregon with his five sons. Henri, with a houseful of girls, had given up surgery and was a veterinarian in Neuchâtel. Henriette was out again, at Alliance, companion for an old woman in a wheel chair. At least she did not have to live alone with the past.

"Surber is broke, talking of coming back here and living with his girl who married an ignorant broncobuster. All he knows is talk and blow and has not a cent," Jules told Marie.

"Ah, can he help it then that he was born when there were no schools? A few years earlier and your children would be the same," Mary defended.

"They could never be so ignorant," Jules insisted, dismissing the subject and turning to his illness. "You work in a drug house part of the time, you say. What you think I ought to take?" he asked Marie.

The mother lifted her hands in her old dramatic gesture.

"Ach, it is a change before death! I never heard Papa ask for advice before, and from a woman."

"Well, the women of my family are the only ones that get any education."

"Not with your help or approval," Caroline cut in, her tongue as sharp as her hair was blonde.

"Oh, hell," the father groaned. "I ask Marie a decent question and I get a fight."

But there was nothing his daughter could say, except that it was probably best to do as the doctors ordered. "You have an iron constitution or you would have died at Fort Robinson or in the hills when you were snakebitten. And besides, you have luck —like that time in the Big Horns. If you keep to the diet you will probably get comfortable again."

"Get so I can hunt, eat, and drink like I did ten years ago?"

Marie looked down upon her fingers, long too, but a little broader, with the large joints of heavy work in childhood. "I'm afraid you'll always have to be careful—"

"Then what is there to live for?" he thundered, still the man who rose from his sleep and whipped a crying baby until he was breathless.

"Ach, Jules, don't fight with them and spoil Christmas for us all!"

"Let him eat and drink," James argued. They did. Marie had written to Rochester. It was only a matter of weeks, they believed. But she realized that the three days at the clinic were too short a time to find the man who still stood tall within the quaking house.

After a big glass of wine Jules's pouched and bloodshot eyes moved about the long table with the same pride he took in his young cherry orchard. "We got a fine, strong family, an improvement on the old folks—on Mary, anyhow," and his eyes twinkled for a second as they did the evening Mary first noticed his fine long hands and their way with chisel and sandpaper on walnut.

"There is nobody to carry on my work," he added, a little proudly, and yet regretfully, too. "If the Marie was a man she might—as a woman she is not worth a damn."

But as soon as the house was quiet the old call came again. "Oh, my lungs, my lungs! Quick, Mary, quick!"

And when he slept a little, noisily, a whistle in his breath, the mother sat before the fire with Marie, rubbing her work-crippled hands before the flame to take out the cramp of over-work that night brought to them. Where would it end with Papa? Alcohol, patent medicine, morphine when he could get it, doctors, hospitals, and more alcohol. It was costing them everything they had, all they worked so hard to accumulate. And as she talked the easy tears slipped down the long folds of her thin face. Now he wanted to sell more land, go to Mexico, where he might get morphine. Everything was mortgaged again. Even the stamp collection was gone. But what could she do? One wouldn't let a dog suffer so.

Now his people could go insane, commit suicide, murder and be murdered, even let themselves be driven from the coun-try, and Jules lay unnoticing in his dark well. At times Mary got him into his wheel chair and brought him into the warm kitchen. Other times he staggered out on his dropsical legs, car-rying his rifle. Demented by alcohol, pain, and disease, he sought still an enemy. To quiet him the gun must be kept hang-ing over his bed, so Fritz removed the powder from the shells, replacing it with sand.

Then one evening Jules called quietly. Mary ran to him, lifted the water-puffed body, tugged and pulled at it until she got him to the edge of the bed, his useless legs hanging over the side.

"Mary—" he gasped weakly through the thin beard, "Mary, we gone a long ways together. But now—I guess it is good-bye."

"No, no, Jules, talk not so," she cried to him in German. But his face was grayed, his beard lengthened as his jaw relaxed. She laid him back. A long time he was like that, his open eyes like milky marbles. Then slowly the heavy lids closed. When they opened the eyes were clear again.

The next day he looked through the papers and found a small item announcing a prize for a short story awarded to

Marie. He tore the paper across, ordered pencil and paper brought, wrote her one line in the old, firm, up-and-down strokes: "You know I consider artists and writers the maggots of society."

Then for several days he felt more like the old Jules. He shot a hawk circling over the chickens in the alfalfa, he even got to the orchard in the hired man's car. He tried to read the articles in the Sunday feature sections of the Omaha and Lincoln papers praising his work, calling him the "Burbank of the Sandhills." But the page cuts of himself and the trees tired him less.

Before long he was in the hospital again, at Rushville. His relatives came, strange, tall young people he did not recognize, until it seemed there must be over a hundred. Old friends stood at the foot of his bed. Ma Green, ninety, outliving her sons one after another, brought courage with her, even now. Westover and Wood were dead, but their daughters came. The sons of Freese, fine middle-aged men who never went to law and never talked of God, stood silently beside Jules's bed and thought, perhaps of the day a wagon left the Running Water, a circle of men with Winchesters watching in the rain.

Others came: the Schwartzes, the young Kollers and Peters, the woman from the County Council or Defense. Sometimes Jules talked as brilliantly, as exaggeratedly as ever, but any moment his mind might turn dark with the load of his body, a black night with no moon or star. And then even his enemies went quickly away.

One day the room was suddenly full of Indians. In the center was White Eye, an old man between two graying sons. It was bad, this, to find Straight Eye in the medicine house with women in black robes to keep friends away. Jules was pleased, but soon the old Oglala led his people into the sunlight. "It is the land of the Gone-Before-Ones," he said, and the young Indians looked at him tolerantly.

When Jules could sit up, Elmer Sturgeon came to talk of old times, of the early days on Mirage Flats, forty-four years ago. Yes, there were two of them left, Sturgeon and Jones, only two, but forty-four years is a long time and two such as these are many.

Jones stopped in for a greeting every few days. Once he sat a long time, running blunt fingers through his fine white hair, still curly as a boy's. "Why did you have to spend your whole life fighting over stupid things like post offices, Jules?" he said at last. "You're good shot enough to know you have to aim high if you want to shoot far. Why, man, with your ability you could have gone to the legislature, the Senate. I've heard you make some pretty good speeches beside the old stove on the Running Water. You had ability and courage. You knew a trick or two, and where was the man among us who wouldn't have followed you through hell if you had only let him?"

"But the damned cattleman stole me my post office I worked so hard to establish. Everybody worked against me," Jules roared, his face flushed pale red with anger and weakness.

Jones brushed his hair back, put on his hat, and went away.

Early in November, 1928, Jules, seventy-one now, was rushed to the hospital at Alliance, and Mary sent a wire to Lincoln and then huddled beside the bed to wait. At daylight Marie looked out upon the first low sandhills, huge sprawled bodies under dun-colored blankets. So they must have looked from the east in 1884, a little grayer from the winter wash of snow, when Jules drove up the Niobrara. But then there were still deer, antelope, elk, wolves, Indians, and white men armed to turn back the westward invasion coming with the spring. Now ducks swam in melancholy file on the summer-shrunken ponds. Geese circled high to catch the swifter blasts of the north wind that moaned a little over the frost-reddened bunchgrass. The sunflowers, Jules's index to good soil, bowed their frost-blackened faces and rattled their fear of winter winds. And sometimes for ten, twenty miles through the choppy country along the south road there was no house, not even a horse-backer—only the endless monotony of a stormy sea, caught and held forever in sand.

The train stopped a moment at Ellsworth where the old brick summer homes of Bartlett Richards and his partner Comstock waited empty-eyed, a door swinging open and shut. Past the shabby buildings a road led through the sandy pass north. At the fork stood a signboard: FORTY MILES TO OLD JULES.

At the potash towns the old plants loomed gaunt, fire-stripped, the boilers and pipings red-rusted, the large chimneys tumbled down to piles of brick. The tar-paper shacks were gone, the towns dead. And on all sides the hills pushed in.

With a loud shriek of the engine they were out upon the hard-land table, with large barns standing against the sky. Straight bare stretches of graveled road stretched across the prairie between telephone lines, reaching northward toward Mirage Flats and the Running Water, over deep, smooth black soil that raised corn tall as a man if the rain came. If not there would be other crops: flax, potatoes, cattle.

James and his wife and baby met Marie. Behind them was Mary, shrunken, tiny, her sleep-weighted eyes light as the windy sky. They took her to the hospital room where an old, old man lay, his face a thin gray shell of wax with a few straggling beard hairs like wire. His faded eyes opened. They slid over Marie without recognition and closed, but not quite. Behind the slits he watched that they did not leave him alone.

The sight shook the eldest daughter. From such a being, helpless, without personality, without fire, a man had grown as from a tiny cloud a storm spreads, to flash and thunder and roar and bring rain to the needy earth, in the end to disintegrate, to drift in a pale shred of nondescript cloud.

Two days later he seemed no worse. James and his wife had gone home to care for the stock.

"Beer, bring me beer!" the sick man moaned, his voice trailing into incoherent fussing, a constant stream fretting the thin ice of his sleep. Then he saw he was alone.

"Oh, the fools!" he complained. "Run away and leave me."

Marie, clipping rose stems in the bathroom, came forward with the flowers in her arms.

"Where they come from?" Jules demanded, his eyes alight as by a candle, far off, but gleaming, the horticulturist in him living stubbornly on.

"Lincoln."

"Oho—you are Marie."

"Yes."

"Sit where I can see you when I wake up," he said drowsily. He slept, just a little. "Ah, I have a thirst," he mumbled. The nurse brought a bowl of broth. He gulped the liquid in huge famished draughts. Nothing like the leisurely drinking from Sunday-night glasses of wild grape wine on the Running Water, plates of bread and meat on the table and a dozen sun-blackened settlers about it. There were songs then, too, and good talk, for they were young and there was much before them.

"Where's Mama?" the sick man asked from his dozing. "I want Mama."

"She's gone to the hotel to sleep a little. She can't be with you every minute—after four years, day and night—"

"I know—" he said, without opening his eyes. "She has to have sleep. A good woman, your mama." But in a moment he moved a little, pulling himself higher. "You ought to come home next summer. I'm looking for a bigger cherry crop than ever before—and pears—and apples by the—by the truck-load—" The voice died to a whisper as of dark waters under thawing snow. The long fingers moved a little from side to side. Purple points came out on the man's neck. Grayish shadows sat on his temples.

Then once more he raised his head, his face alive, his eyes far-focused, burning. He began to talk slowly, as though his lips were metal, stiffening. "The whole damn sandhills is deserted. The cattlemen are broke, the settlers about gone. I got to start all over—ship in a lot of good farmers in the spring, build up —build—build—"

His voice sank deep into the caverns of his chest. He fell back slowly, his head rolling a little, his fine long hands flattening on the sheet.

Outside the late fall wind swept over the hard-land country of the upper Running Water, tearing at the low sandy knolls that were the knees of the hills, shifting, but not changing, the unalterable sameness of the somnolent land spreading away toward the East.

from THESE WERE THE SIOUX

FOREWORD

THE SIOUX INDIANS came into my life before I had any preconceived notions about them, or about anyone else. In our family no formal pattern of philosophical or religious thought was thrust upon the children, and I was left free to learn about our Indian friends as I did about the rest of our neighborhood of mixed beliefs, languages and origins—homeseeking immigrant Poles, Czechs, Irish, Dutch, French, Germans, Danes, Swiss, a few Serbs, a Bulgar, a Mohammedan, a Negro and a smattering of so-called native Americans, including Texas cowboys.

To me the dress of the Indians was just another folk costume, their language no stranger than English to my German-Swiss ear. But there was something most engrossing about these Sioux and their tipis, their campfires, their drumming in the night and their ways with thunderstorms, small children and the mockingbird in our woodpile. And as I grew older I began to catch a glimpse now and then into the meaning of the customs and beliefs of these brown-faced people, a little like the view from a high mountain as the mist begins to break over the far plains.

A NEW ONE IS BORN

BY THE TIME I was seven or eight I had begun to sense a special kind of individual responsibility among the Sioux, not only for oneself but for the family, the band, the whole tribe. Then one morning I saw something of the start of this. A small girl from the camp across the road came tapping shyly at our door, motioning to me.

"Ahh, I have a brother too now," she whispered, her dark eyes on the baby astride my hip. "He is just born."

I pushed the oatmeal back on the stove, glanced toward the stable where Mother was milking our cow and hurried across the road as fast as I could, my brother bobbing on my side. I slowed up at the smoky old canvas tipi, shy, too, now, but I did peer into the dusky interior where an Indian woman bent over the new baby on her lap. At the noise of our excitement, the tiny red-brown face began to pucker up tighter, but the mother caught the little nose gently between her thumb and forefinger and with her palm over the mouth, stopped the crying. When the baby began to twist for breath, she let go a little, but only a little, and at the first sign of another cry, she shut off the air again, crooning a soft little song as she did this, a growing song of the Plains Indians, to make the boy straight-limbed and strong of body and heart as the grandson of Bad Arm must be.

I watched the mother enviously. Our babies always cried, and so I had to ride them on my hip, but I knew that none of our small Indian friends made more than a whimper at the greatest hurt, even falling from the high limb of a tree. Now I saw what an old woman had tried to explain to me. During the newborn minutes, that newborn hour, Indian children, boy and girl, were taught the first and greatest lesson of their lives: that no one could be permitted to endanger the people by even one cry to guide a roving enemy to the village or to spoil a hunt that could mean the loss of the winter meat for a whole band or even a small tribe. In return the child would soon discover that all the community felt an equal responsibility toward him. Every fire became like that of his parents, welcoming the exploring, the sleepy or injured toddler. Every pot would have a little extra for a hungry boy, and every ear was open to young sorrows, young joys and aspirations. I also knew that never, in the natural events of this small boy's life, would he be touched by a punishing adult hand. If he grew up like the Sioux of the old hunting days he would be made equal to the demands of his expanding world without any physical restriction beyond the confines of the cradleboard. I still remember the closed, distant faces of the Sioux when I was whipped for staying out to watch the *heyoka* in the thunderstorm, and at other whippings as well.

The American Indian considered the whites a brutal people who treated their children like enemies—playthings, too, coddling them like pampered pets or fragile toys, but underneath like enemies to be restrained, bribed, spied on and punished, or as objects of competition between the parents, sometimes even to open quarrelings and worse over them. The Indians believed that children so treated could only grow up dependent and immature pets and toys, but with adult wills and appetites to be indulged—grow up designing, angered and dangerous enemies within the family circle, to be appeased and fought and be defeated by, perhaps even murdered. The Indians pointed to the increasing lawlessness and violence of the young people of the white man, a violence that was often turned against their elders. Such a thing was unknown among the tribes in the old days and very rare up to the recent expropriating days, when so many thousands of Indians were driven off their small holdings on the reservations into an alien society. Usually untrained and perhaps practically illiterate, they have drifted into hopeless tent and shack communities around the small towns and to the slums of cities like Chicago, with very few jobs open to them anywhere—nothing much but begging, thievery and prostitution, their white contacts too frequently the lawless and the violent.

⊂⊟ ⊂⊟ ⊂⊟

HIS SECOND PARENTS

IN THE old days our Sioux neighbors still had their traditional set of precautions against immaturities and resentments among their young people. They avoided overprotecting the young and saved the eldest son from the mother's favoritism that could destroy the parents as well as the boy. By custom every son and daughter, too, was provided with a second father and mother at birth—usually friends of the blood parents, or some relatives outside of the immediate family. The second father of a boy was often selected partly for excellence as hunter, warrior, horse catcher, band historian, holy man who listened and advised, or medicine man—either healer or one learned in rites and ceremonials. Still earlier the man might have been a maker of arrows, spears or shields, an outstanding runner or gifted in decoying and snaring animals. His wife, the second mother, was preferably known as warmhearted, and fond of boys around the tipi, the lodge. Sometimes the youth showed a special and unexpected talent as he grew and then a third father might be selected, one gifted in this new bent. Or if the puberty dream was of thunder, a *heyoka* might be added as a sort of uncle.

The second mother took over much of the small boy's care so he would never shame his blood mother by trailing at her moccasin heel, never bring the scornful whisper, "Little husband! Little husband!" as he usurped another's place in her attention and affection. The Indians understood the anger and resentment that could grow up in the most tolerant, fortitudinous man if his wife preferred the son over the husband, used the boy against him, brought him humiliation in the village circle. They wanted to avoid the retarded infantilism, the jealousy of the mother, the boy's inability to be a good brother to his sisters and to other girls and women, and finally a good husband and father.

In the second mother's lodge the boy could tease and laugh in a way improper in his own home. He could talk freely, so long as it was respectful. He never used profanity, however, for the Sioux language had no such words, and no obscenities except that practically any word could be made obscene by gross exaggeration. Sex was not a thing of shame or for snickers and embarrassment, although in a prolonged battle Sioux women sometimes taunted enemy warriors with gestures and shouted words indicating they were not men fit for the women of the Sioux.

And when a boy like Young One across the road went to war, whether in the old days against the Pawnees or the Crows, or later, to the Pacific or Korea, the women of his second home could show emotion and cry out, "Be careful, our brother!" and "Be careful, our son!" His blood mother could only stand off and sing the brave heart song for him. I saw this done as late as World War II, while an old holy man made medicine up on a hill for the safe return of these modern warriors of the Sioux.

I recall seeing the second father of the new baby across the road that first day, his white teeth shining in the sun with what seemed the same happy pride as the actual father's. That evening the little group of men smoked in the late sunlight and talked of other days of birth, and how the future was planned then, their words clarified by an occasional bit of sign talk because our father sat among them, passing his sack of Big Bale tobacco around. At the tipis the women bent over the cooking fires, boiling lamb's-quarters and mushrooms they had gathered and frying grouse the men shot that afternoon, with Indian bread, fried, too, and stewed gooseberries from our garden. The blackened coffeepots sent up a fine smell, and blue threads of fire smoke trailed off into the sunlight above the shadowing river valley.

In June a bad hailstorm up on Pine Ridge Reservation in South Dakota pounded the poor little corn patches and the gardens in the creek bends into the earth, so these friends returned to our region and stayed around most of the summer, until potato-picking time in October to make a little cash money. For a couple of weeks the wagons were gone from across the road and the nights seemed empty without the pleasant, nostalgic drumming of Bad Arm as he "threw his mind back" to the old days of his youth along the Powder River and the Tongue and the Rosebud. The Indians had pushed into the sandhills to gather chokecherries, sand cherries and wild plums. They picked up all the game they could find, too, the extra meat to be dried for winter, even if it was jackrabbit, snared and trapped because cartridges were very scarce. Rabbit was not the sweet, fat buffalo that once bulged the folding painted parfleche cases with enough dried meat to carry the Indians through the longest winter. Fall would bring ducks and geese but rabbit was available in the hot, drying time of summer and would taste pretty good boiled with prairie onion in the kettle those months when the blizzard roared around their reservation shacks and the teeth got long and the belly lean.

The women roasted some of the dried meat and pounded it with chokecherries and then stuffed this *wasna,* this pemmican, hot, into flour-sack casings instead of the buffalo bladders of the old days. It was a fine concentrated food, gritty to the teeth from the crushed chokecherry pits but enriched by the nutty taste of the kernels and pleasing to the old-timers like Contrary, whose swollen eyes watered a little in remembering.

By the time Young One was six weeks old he was little trouble to anyone, either in the cradleboard propped against a tipi pole or riding a mother's back while she went about her work. He would be up there some of the time until he was a year old or more, out of harm's way, seeing all the world from the high place and unpossessed by the mother's eyes. Before Young One was two months old it was decided he must swim, "before he forget it," the older mother told us, by signs. I took my baby brother down to see this. The woman carried Young One into a quieter spot along the riverbank and with her hands under the chest and belly, she eased the boy into the shallow, tepid water until it came up around him. Then, suddenly, his sturdy legs began to kick and his arms to flail out. The next time he lasted a little longer, and by the third or fourth time the woman could take her hands away for a bit while he held his head up and dog paddled for himself.

Winter babies, boys or girls, who couldn't be taught to swim early, were thrown into ponds or river holes in the spring by the father, the impact calculated to revive the fading urge to swim. Every Indian child had to keep himself afloat awhile if he slipped off into deep water, was caught in a cloudburst or in a river accident while the people were fleeing from enemies or a buffalo stampede.

The young Indian learned to make his own decisions, take the responsibility for his actions at an incredibly early age. When the baby began to crawl no one cried, "No, no!" and dragged him back from the enticing red of the tipi fire coals. Instead, his mother or anyone near watched only that he did not burn up. "One must learn from the bite of the fire to let it alone," he was told when he jerked his hand back, whimpering a little, and with tear-wet face brought his burnt finger to whoever was near for the soothing. The boy's eyes would not turn in anger toward the mother or other grownup who might have pulled him back, frustrated his natural desire to test, to explore. His anger was against the pretty coals, plainly the source of his pain. He would creep back another time but more warily, and soon he would discover where warmth became burning.

A PART OF
HIS VILLAGE

FROM BIRTH the young Sioux was in the midst of the adult
world. There was only one room in the lodge, and only one out-
of-doors. Back when he was small his cradleboard often hung on
a tipi pole or a meat rack, the wind swaying him drowsily, while
the children played and raced and sang around him and one
of his mothers or frequently several women worked nearby,
busy with the meat or the hides or perhaps beading the
regalia of the men.

But the little Sioux had to learn some use of his legs this
summer. He spent more and more time on the ground, perhaps on a robe or soft grass but often alone, free to discover his
body now and begin to get his discipline in the natural way, as
he must be free to take his ideals and aspirations from the pre-
cepts and examples of those around him.

When the thrust of the boy's growing legs took on insist-
ence, one of the fathers or perhaps an uncle lay on his back and
held the baby erect for a short walk up his stomach and chest,
laughing hard at the sturdy push of the legs, shouting that this
was a warrior son, this was a great and powerful hunter. Perhaps the man was a young war chief, or, if older, just out of the
evening council circle where any toddler could approach the
headmen unhindered. He could see them smoking quietly, de-
liberating the common problems of today and tomorrow or
planning ceremonials and hunts, perhaps selecting the warrior
society to police the village for the next moon, and protect it

from disturbances inside and out. The boy could hear the crier, always some old and very judicious and respected man, hurry through the camp with any news or with warnings of danger, or of a hunt coming up, perhaps carrying invitation sticks to a feast or a celebration, or proclaiming the council's decisions. And they were decisions, not orders, for no Sioux could tell anyone what to do. The only position a Sioux inherited was his membership in the tribe. He became a leader, a chief because some were willing to follow him and retained his position only as long as the following remained.

In the old days the small children traveled in their cradleboards or in skin sacks hung to the saddle, with other such sacks containing special belongings—finery and regalia, a hard-to-replace pot, perhaps, and seasoning and medicinal herbs, so many sacks that a woman's horse might look like some short, thick, fruit-hung branch. Older children sometimes rode on the pony drags in willow cages that helped keep them from falling out during naps or in flight from attacking enemies. Often an old man or woman was with them, one too feeble for a long ride on a horse or to run. But now and then even the gentlest travois horse took fright and ran away perhaps at the smell of a mountain lion or the flutter of a white petal blown from a giant thistle poppy, horses being what they are. The travois and its occupants might be scattered over the prairie, the willow cage turned upside down. It was very funny and generally only the women were concerned, the young people and the old men laughing hard to see it, those inside the cage, too, if they weren't hurt too much.

The young Sioux rode early. Sometimes before he could walk he was carried behind his father, clinging to the rawhide string of the man's breechclout. He learned to climb up the foreleg of an old mare like a tree, mounting on the right side as the grown Indians all did, the man with the bow in his left hand when he leaped on, out of the way, and leaving the right hand free to draw the bowstring fast.

In the old days Young One would have watched the war parties depart, the women singing them out upon the prairie, and then saw the men come back, perhaps with some missing, the bereaved keening their sorrow in the night. Afterward there might be a victory dance and feasting, the small boys pushing up among the standing legs to see the honoring, too, and later perhaps noticing the warm glances of the maidens for the young warriors, and laughing, as small boys do. Young One would have heard other exceptional services sung through the village—a successful hunt when meat was scarce, a disease ravaging the people stopped, a treaty made for peace and better times.

⊂⊑   ⊂⊑   ⊂⊑

HIS TEACHERS

FROM BACK before he understood the words or the wisdom, the young Sioux heard the hero tales of his people told around the evening fires, but in his early years he learned most from the other children. They took joy in showing him all their knowledge, and in practicing the latent parent lying deep in everyone, eager to care for any small creature or being around. But he learned much, perhaps most, from the scorn and laughter of these peers, and from another boy's fist in his face. Eventually he discovered how to avoid some of the laughing, and the blows, or to fend them off.

When Bad Arm, the man who had once carried me home from the plum thicket, was asked if there wasn't injustice in this discipline by children he drew on his old pipe awhile. All life was injustice, he thought. Lightning found the good man and the bad; sickness carried no respect for virtue, and luck flitted around like the spring butterfly. "It is good to learn this in the days of the mother's milk. Discipline from the young comes as from the earth and is accepted like hunger and weariness and the bite of winter cold. Coming so, it hatches no anger against the grown-up ones, no anger and hatred to sit in the heart like an arrow pointed to shoot both ways."

I remembered what the Young One would learn soon—that his grandfather, Bad Arm, was from the finest of Sioux lines, the old Man, Afraid of His Horse people, prominent long before the Indians had horses, when the family was headed by Man (the Enemy Is Even) Afraid of His Dog, the *dog* changed to *horse* later, perhaps because the new creature was called *big-dog* when it became the warrior's accompanying animal. The Man, Afraid name was handed down clear into the reservation days by songs through the village when a son or a nephew grew into the proper character and prominence. This line has been called the Adams family of the American Indian, brave and wise in war and in the council, peaceful, judicious and responsible, modest and incorruptible. Back in 1854 Man, Afraid of His Horse was asked to become the head chief for the whites after Lieutenant Grattan turned his cannon on the government-elevated Conquering Bear, whose death scaffold had stood on our home place for many years afterward, the Indians told us. Man, Afraid was promised fine presents and great power, but he told the government men sternly that the Sioux had no head chief. Instead, there was a council of headmen selected for regular, specified terms by the people, who retained the right to throw them one or all from their high place at any time. The white man's presents and power were not for him. Ruefully he reminded them that the man they killed had been in their high position barely three years. "It seems that the whites grow tired of their chiefs very quickly."

So the young Sioux learned from his peers, learned from their companionship, their goodness and the power of their ridicule, the same ridicule he saw used against those in highest position sometimes, for even great war leaders bowed in humiliation before concentrated laughter. And he saw men and women of his people walk in dignity through the village circle, the peaceful, orderly village where normally one heard no quarreling in tipi or outside, none except after the white man's fire-water came. In the old days the wiser chiefs kept the whisky wagons out of their camps and took their young warriors away from the white man's trails, from the trading posts. The occasional unruly youth or older one was called aside by some well-respected man, perhaps from the troublemaker's warrior society. The next time there was public ridicule, particularly from the women and girls and often from the Contraries. If necessary a humiliating lash of the bow across the shoulders was administered by the village police for all to see. Next his lodge might be torn down, and finally there was ostracism for a year or two, even as many as four. The driving out was done formally, by decision of the council, the man escorted to the edge of the village with his lodge, if he had one, and his other goods loaded on the poles and dragged by an old horse. Anybody who wished could follow the ostracized one and sometimes several did, even many—enough to start a new camp, particularly if the verdict seemed unjust. But if there was only one man and perhaps his family he went in great danger, for the tracks of a lone traveler, a lone tipi apparently wandering were soon stalked by enemies for the easy scalps, easy horses and weapons that would bring no reprisals. In any case the ostracism was a sad thing, a community failure, and often the women keened as for a death while the driven-out departed and grew small on the prairie.

"It is better to use ridicule early—to keep the young on the good road," Bad Arm and the *heyoka* agreed, telling me that in this, had I been a Sioux, I should have had a real place, for ridicule from the girls and the women stings like the yellow-striped hornet.

In the old buffalo days the very young Sioux learned to snare and track small animals, even the rabbit, with his trick of doubling back on his trail, teaching the hunter to use his eyes while other creatures taught him to sharpen his nose and his ears. As the boy grew he was drawn into the hunting games as he was those of the village: prairie ball, running and jumping contests, tag, snow snake in the winter, and always wrestling and horse racing, the boys riding sometimes so small they seemed like some four-footed creature clinging to the mane and back. Young One would have seen the men pile their wagers in goods at the betting stake before the horses were whipped home with dust and whooping. He would have learned to ride in a dead run while hanging to the far side of his pony with a moccasin toe over the back, a hand twisted into the mane, ready for war. He would have been along on raids against enemy horse herds as a young white man might study his father's methods raiding a competitor's customers.

As the boy grew he ran with his village kind as young antelope run together. He teased the girls, grabbed bits of meat from the drying racks when he was hungry. He went to watch the older youths and young men stand in their courting blankets at this tipi or that one for a few words with the young daughter and could hardly wait until he, too, was a man. He imitated the warriors and ran their errands, hoping to be asked out on a raid, as was done for promising boys, particularly by the war society of a father or an uncle, much as a white youth would be eased toward his father's fraternity, and often with little more bloodshed. Except in a few tribal struggles for hunting grounds, Plains Indian fights were scarcely more dangerous than a hard-fought football game. The first-class coup—striking an enemy with the hand, the bow or the coup stick without harming him—was the highest war achievement, more important than any scalp.

Occasionally the boy was taken out on night guard of the village and the horse herds, or to scout the region for unauthorized war parties trying to slip away, endangering themselves and perhaps the village with avenging attacks. An Indian who gave up the right to cry at birth because it would bring enemies upon the people must not do the same thing by rash and foolish acts later.

Understanding of the regular ceremonials and rituals came gradually to the young Sioux. Eventually he realized what old Contrary told us through the interpretation of his teenage granddaughter, who cheerfully turned all the *heyoka* said around to its rightful meaning. The Sioux camp of any size was always set in a circle because all sacred things were round—the sun, the moon, the earth horizon, as one could plainly see. Even the tipis were round, and their openings as well as that of the whole camp always faced the east, to welcome and honor the light that brought the day and the springtime. But the simplest and perhaps the most profound ritual that the young Sioux saw was the most common. The first puff of the pipe at a smoking and the first morsel of food at a meal were always offered to the Great Powers—the earth, the sky and the four directions, which included everything that lay within their arms. All things were a part of these Powers, brothers in them, and anyone could understand what a brother was.

THE MAN WITHIN
THE YOUTH

AFTER HIS seventh birthday the Sioux boy never addressed his blood mother or sister directly again, speaking to them only through a third person. When he showed signs of coming manhood he was prepared for his puberty fasting by men close to the family, including some wise and holy one. There were also holy women among the Sioux, advising and officiating in many of the rites with both men and women but not for the puberty fasting, which was the youth's orientation into maleness. When he was ready the boy was escorted to some far barren hill and left there in breechclout and moccasins against the sun of day, the cold of night, without food or water. The ordeal was to strip away every superficiality, all the things of the flesh, to prepare for a dreaming, a vision from the Powers. Usually by the third or fourth day the youth had dreamed and was brought down, gaunt and weak. He was given a few drops of water at a time and some food, but slowly, and after he was restored a little, and bathed and feasted, his advisors and the holy man tried to interpret the vision that was to guide him in this manhood he was now entering.

It was the puberty dreaming of the Sioux war chief, Crazy Horse, that predicted he would not die of a bullet, but that he must always walk as the plainest, the most modest of his people, without paint or war bonnet, without dance or song or voice lifted in the council. Years later, when he was made a Shirt-wearer, the highest honor possible, he took the further vow of selfless dedication to the people. Always it was their good that must come first. Now he would walk not only in plainness but the poorest of the poor, his heart turned from the seductions of personal gain and possessions, his ear closed alike to praise, ridicule or any abuse.

"If a dog lift his leg to my lodge, I will not see it," he vowed.

In spite of this dedication Crazy Horse later ran away with another man's wife, the girl he had courted in his youth but as a maiden she had been obliged to bring a man of greater importance, of more mature stature than a young warrior, into her family. Yet after faithful wifehood for some years, a Sioux woman was free to leave her husband, frankly and openly, and the husband, if a proper one, treated her decision with fortitude and composure. Unfortunately this husband was not such a man. He came roaring after the wife with a pistol and shot Crazy Horse in the face. The powder had been split in the cartridge, to supply two, and the bullet only knocked the chief into temporary unconsciousess.

The bullet, however, was powerful enough to split the Oglala division of the Sioux like a rock is split, and because Crazy Horse, by his impulsive act, had caused this, had placed his happiness above the common good, as no Shirtwearer can ever do, he was unshirted. He gave the woman back, and peace was made, yet the Sioux who camped across the road from us still carried the scars of that angry time, as Crazy Horse carried the actual scar of the husband's bullet to the grave.

THE INDIAN AND
HIS UNIVERSE

VERY FEW white men troubled to understand the Indian's notion of the earth and its relation to man even as real estate or, for that matter, the varying Indian attitude toward personal property. To the Plains Sioux nothing that was made less by division could be inherited. A good name, the art and craft designs of such things as the arrows and the regalia of the men, the patterns for beading and painting by the women, these were passed on to the heirs, those of the men to the male descendants, the women's down the female line. Everything else was distributed in a Giveaway Dance after the owner's death. Some special items went to friends or relatives, but most of the divisible property was handed to the needy and the sad and the unlucky, where it lifted the heart and was of use.

To the Indians, personal ownership of land was impossible to conceive. Food, arms, clothing, livestock could be owned, given, sold or destroyed. The tribe or band might give a man the temporary right to tell a particular story, to sing a certain sacred song or guard and carry a ceremonial object, such as the Oglala war lances or an ancient shield. With membership approval a man could sell or bestow his place in a warrior society. This was also true of some of the women's organizations but obviously not of the One Only Ones, or of the secret bead and handcraft society. The right to use these designs belonged to the woman's line, never to be sold or bestowed, but articles adorned with them could become cherished gifts.

Land was something one obviously could not own. It was held for tribal use and for posterity. Sale of land to the Sioux meant sale of the use. When Indians, from Plymouth Rock to Oregon, sold an area they thought of it as a temporary arrangement. When payment ceased, the land returned to the tribe, or so they believed as long as they could. To the Sioux, land, the earth, was revered as the mother force in the Great Powers from whom all things came. Plainly nothing could ever be done to diminish this land, nothing to make it less for all those whose moccasins walked upon it, and for all those whose tracks were still to come. Whisky and avarice and starvation changed the minds of some of the chiefs, but their hope of this inalienable right to their earth never really died in the Sioux until the Ghost Dance failed, the medicine dancing that was to bring back the buffalo and all the Indian country. The hope, the dream vanished in the roar of the Hotchkiss guns at Wounded Knee, South Dakota, that winter morning in 1890.

Without a written creed or an organized priesthood the religion of any people adapts itself to new regions, new situations, new ways of life rather quickly. Some Indians, like the Pawnees, carried their sacred place, their center of the earth, with them to the Plains, as the white man brought his altar with its cross and the symbols of the blood and the body of Christ into the farthest wilderness. The Plains Sioux, however, had left the concrete symbols of their religion far behind, and carried along only a few remnants of an agrarian worship, such as the fertility rites discernible in the sun dance and bits of the old corn dances. So intellectualized had their religion become for the more selfless leaders that they were sometimes called the Unitarians of the American Indian.

The realization of death came early and naturally to the young Sioux. There was no demonology left among these people, no evil beings or spirits to be appeased or circumvented. Or blamed. If things did not go well it was not due to supernatural spite or anger or temptation but because the individual or the people and their leaders were out of tune with the Great Powers. To discover what must be done someone had to purify him-

self of the demands of the flesh, of the selfish, either by fasting
on a high place in heat or cold, hoping for guidance in a dreaming, or through the mortification of the arrogant flesh in the
sun dance. The hope was for a sharper discernment, a clearer
understanding of what must be done, a heightened sensitivity to
the Indian's universe, his Great Powers, a closer identification
and atunement.

The ceremonial high point of the Sioux year was the sun
dance, a modified combination of several old, old ceremonials
and adapted to Plains life. It was usually performed in late
June or early July, to bring plenty of buffalo for the summer
hunt and to fulfill the vows offered during some great emergency the past year, perhaps for protection from cholera, small-
pox, measles or tuberculosis, all very fatal to the Indians because they had none of the white man's inherited tolerance for
them. Some years dancers had vowed "a red blanket spread on
the ground" meaning blood spilled, actual or symbolic, for escape from a great drouth, from some approaching danger like a
vast prairie fire, an overwhelming army, the power of the white
man to take the Black Hills and, the few years the dance was allowed on the agencies, against starvation because the rations
that were to pay for the land sold did not come.

The sun dance varied, depending upon the dreaming and
the medicine of the leader and the vows to be fulfilled, the tests
to be endured for future favor and enlightenment, but there was
a basic pattern. The preparation usually covered eight days
with interludes of ceremonials and dancing. The site was selected and a scout sent out to find a proper cottonwood tree for
the sun-dance pole. The sun lodge, a wide, ring-shaped arbor
without sides, was erected, the top covered with boughs, pine if
possible, to shade the drummers, the numerous dance helpers
and the spectators. Then a large group, with a leader, the vir-
gins, the mothers with babies whose ears were to be pierced, and
many others went out to bring in the pole. The tree was cut
down with a stone ax in the old way, cleaned of branches to a
foot or two above the forked top, trimmed off there and
dragged in to the center of the arbor. Fetishes and banners were
fastened to the top, including fertility images of a man and a

buffalo, tied on usually by a *heyoka,* a Contrary, and the pole lifted erect with old rawhide ropes.

When the decorated pole was in place the drumming and singing rose for the preliminary dancing and dedication. Finally the ordeal around the pole began. Each man endured his avowed mortification as well as he could. Some dragged buffalo skulls by thongs tied to skewers thrust through the back. Others took the rawhide thongs through the breast, the ends fastened to the top of the sun-dance pole, the dancers to circle and leap and jerk until the skewers broke the flesh, free. Some danced the sun-gazing ritual, never taking the eye from the sun, as Sitting Bull did in that desperate time of 1876, during the last great sun dance of the Plains, the Teton Sioux together. He finally fell into a trance and, revived, told of dreaming that many soldiers came tumbling into the Sioux camp. A few days later Custer and his men rode along the ridge of the Little Big Horn and fell there.

The explanations of the ritualistic elements of the sun dance differ, but to the old buffalo hunters uninfluenced by Christian symbolism and the missionary's Bible stories of pagans, demons and evil spirits, the ceremonial was based on the idea that all things come forth in travail. It was so with the buffalo cow producing the yellow calf, the earth breaking as the grass burst forth, the clouds splitting for the rain. Even the tree bled as the bow was cut and the stone as the arrowhead was shaped from its heart.

In such travail the vows were fulfilled for calamities avoided, and visions like that of Sitting Bull, of things to come, were born.

When the last of these stubborn and determined Sioux were finally driven to the reservations every effort was made to break up their ability to protest, all their will to resist. That meant that the tribal organizations and what gave them their unity and power—the Sioux religion which permeated every act of the Indians—had to be destroyed. Most of the ceremonials, all those that could be detected, were stopped, including the sun dance, which had gathered not only the band but the whole tribe in an annual unifying religious ceremonial. It was easy to secure public sentiment for the suppression, not only through the exaggerated reports of the self-torture in the dancing but the whispers of sexual exhibitionism in the little fertility figures tied to the top of the sun-dance pole. So, despite the Constitution's guarantee of religious freedom for all in the United States, the sun dance was outlawed for the Oglala Sioux in 1881 and not restored until 1930, "without torture" and in connection with what the old-time westerners called a pop-stand rodeo.

Several of us interested in the Sioux were there to watch the head dancer, seventy-eight, lean and gaunt as any of the buffalo-hunting followers of Crazy Horse out on the Powder River. Dusty in his paint and flapping breechcloth, the old dancer made his slow little jumping, slipping steps, always turned to face the broiling sun as the drummers pounded the green calfskin, the voices of singers rising and gone, to rise again. The dancer was supposed to maintain his movement each day from sun to sunset, but on the final afternoon he was beginning to move in a curious trance-like flow, almost without steps. Suddenly he stopped, cried out in a thin, high falsetto, gesturing to his bare breast, crying to the sky and the sun-dance pole and all around.

"He wants the thongs," a uniformed Indian policeman told us, as voices from the headmen replied to the dancer, patient at first, then angrily and with a denying tone, firm. It could not be allowed.

"Not allowed!" an old woman near us exclaimed, the words plainly unfamiliar upon her tongue but their meaning sudden and dark.

For a moment the lean old dancer hung as from a string that did not exist. Then he crumpled down into the dust. A murmur of horror swept the crowd, the eagle-wing fans still. Then there was silence, a naked stillness, the dull drumming and the song vanished, dead.

There was a scrabble of people getting to their feet and four men running out to carry the old dancer away to the sweat lodge, a low wickiup with water to throw on hot stones. An Omaha dancer came out posturing in the buffalo bull's fighting step, to paw the dust and shake his bustle of feathers that

switched the old bull tail hanging from the center. He was followed by others, dancing their special steps, but many faces kept
turning toward the sweat lodge and the men creeping in and
back out. After a while word spread that the old dancer was
alive, sleeping, his four-day ordeal cut short, finished. But there
would be bronco busting at the rodeo corrals, beginning immediately. The riding was good, and it seemed that almost no
one remembered, or even knew, that at the sun-dance pole an
old man's moment of hope and belief had come and gone.

The Sioux had two hundred years of contact with white
men who carried the cross with them in one guise or another
and on top of that, eighty-five years on reservations where
churches, Catholic and Protestant, were pushed, with political
favor for those who joined and a little coffee and perhaps
doughnuts for all in the hungriest times. Still the Indians didn't
take Satan and hell-fire very seriously, or the concept of an
avenging God. The idea of fear was too alien to their philoso-
phy, to their ideal of personal discipline and their whole idea of
the good life and the eventual death that comes to all, bitterly
resisted or embraced with grace. There was no fear of the dead
among the Sioux. The body of a warrior who fell in enemy
country was rescued immediately if possible, or by a later party
with the skin sack painted red for the honorable return. Often
relatives and friends went to sit at a death scaffold, later at the
grave, as they would have gone to the fireside of the departed
one. Children saw the sickness, the dying and the burial, and
sometimes went along to visit the place of the bones, to listen
to the stories of what had been done, and the duties and re-
sponsibilities left for those behind. Sometimes there was a song
or two, or some grave little dance steps.

The Indians have added much of their own religious con-
cepts to their notion of Christian beliefs and symbols, and, with
the peyote trances out of the Southwest, have formed the Native
American Church, which, judged good or bad, is their own.
But even those who joined the churches of the white man have
clung to some of their basic beliefs, which were broad enough to
encompass practically any formalized creed. One Sunday morn-

ing, while camped along an agency trail, I went out for wash water from the creek. As I stooped to dip it up, I heard low Indian singing and the swish of water below me. A naked young Sioux, glistening wet, knelt among the gray-green willows of the bank washing a blue shirt. I saw him lift it up out of the water toward the sky and then dip it to the earth and all around, as the pipe and food are offered. I slipped away, and a couple of hours later the young man came riding by, wearing the clean blue shirt. He raised his hand in greeting, palm out, in the old, old gesture of friendship—the left hand because it is nearer the heart and has shed no man's blood. He was on his way to mass at the Mission but it could have been to the little Episcopal church on a knoll, with the sermon and the Book of Common Prayer in Sioux, or any of half-a-dozen other churches, wherever his grandparents or his great-grandparents joined when they came in from the buffalo ranges. He was going in a shirt offered in the old way to the Powers of the world, in recognition of his brotherhood in them.

Among the Indians, as among any people, the depth and profundity of religion varied, and varies. There were always some who never rose above attempts to obtain help for selfish, personal ends, but it seems that the average Sioux tried to accept responsibility for what happened to him and his band, his tribe, mystically as well as in visible actuality. When misfortune struck there was no devil to blame. The individual or the group was out of tune with the Indians' universe. Farseeing men went to fast and wait for the vision of what must be done to regain the harmony with all things encompassed by the Great Powers.

"In them all things are one: the rock, the cloud, the tree, the buffalo, the man," Bad Arm used to say, ending with the sign, for the All—the flat right hand moving in a horizontal circle, high as the heart.

MISCELLANY

THE LOST SITTING BULL

HISTORY is the memory of the race and, like the individual's memory, it plays odd tricks. Not the least of these was the almost total disappearance, within eighty years, of one of the nation's real friends, and the transfer of his achievements and rewards to another, where they served as the final evidence of a treacherous nature.

For over ninety years the name of Sitting Bull has been well known, first as a leader of the warlike Sioux and then as the principal Indian attraction with Buffalo Bill Cody's Wild West Show. Over America and Europe he was a picturesque figure in a feather headdress selling his photograph to small boys. Sometimes he even put the painful scrawl that was his name in the white man's language upon pieces of paper.

Yet in the summer of 1876, after the shocking news of General Custer's annihilation by a lot of supposedly naked, whooping, bloodthirsty savages, an army officer said ruefully, "It must be true that Sitting Bull is a West Point graduate."

Whether this salved the army's wounds or not, the military pursuit of the Indians after the Custer fight was energetic, and with the buffalo very scarce, Sitting Bull decided to lead his

starving Hunkpapa Sioux out of their hunting grounds of the
Yellowstone and the Upper Missouri country north into Canada. Soon a newspaper man was circulating a spurious interview with the Hunkpapa leader, claiming that Sitting Bull was
an alumnus of St. John's College. Others produced other
schools, and listed the Bull as a student of French history particularly enamored of Napoleon. Some called him a linguist,
and finally R. D. Clarke came up with the real coup. In a
pamphlet called "The Works of Sitting Bull," he presented the
old buffalo-hunting Sioux as a writer of Sapphic verse in Latin.

But there were angry charges too, claiming that all the
years Sitting Bull was fighting the government, costing the nation millions of dollars and hundreds of lives, he was listed on
the rolls of an Indian agency, drawing the regular annuities
and rations, and, worse, ammunition for war. Accounts of such
reliable and unsensational papers as the New York *Tribune*
proved that Sitting Bull had visited Washington as a friend of
the whites several times and, the spring of 1875, received a
handsomely engraved repeating rifle from the President of the
United States. Yet a year later he was in the fight that left Custer and his men dead on the ridge overlooking the timber-lined
Little Big Horn. Six months after the battle the presentation
rifle was back in white-man hands, picked up outside of General
Miles cantonment on the Yellowstone, the brass mounting still
bright as gold to the Indians, the inscription untarnished:

> *Sitting Bull, from The President
> for Bravery & True Friendship*

There was no denying the rifle; millions had seen the story.
Many, including army officers, reported they had seen Sitting
Bull study the campaigns of Napoleon and knew that he liked
to look through any newspapers he managed to save from his
trips to the Overland Trail stations or the army posts, and that
he carried them along even while out fighting the whites from
the Smoky Hill of Kansas to the Bozeman Trail of upper Wyoming. Further, it was easy to prove that his name stood on the
agency rolls from the settling of the Bozeman war in 1868 until

long after the death of Custer. Here was the treachery of the redskin, plain to see.

Or it would have been treachery if this man on the agency rolls, this recipient of the gift rifle, had been the leader of the Hunkpapas. But he wasn't. This man was of the Oglala division of the Sioux, whose hunting grounds were from the Powder River into Kansas, and he was not only called Sitting Bull, but Sitting Bull the Good.

The two men were born about ten years apart, the Hunkpapa in 1831, the Oglala around 1841, when the traders' whisky was whipping the villages into such violence that his own grandfather, the head chief of the Cut-Off band of the Oglalas, was shot down in a drunken brawl by Red Cloud, who was already a great warrior then, and later was named the government's chief of all the Oglala Sioux.

Early in his youth the southern Sitting Bull,* called Drum Packer then, had found the white man full of curious and interesting ways. When the transcontinental telegraph line went through along the Overland Trail in 1861, Oscar Collister came to operate the station at Deer Creek, up above Fort Laramie. Because the Indian agent located there, and several traders, Deer Creek became a center of much pleasant loafing during those peaceful years before the war of 1864. The Oglalas grew very fond of the little white man who often let them try his talking wires. One of the most eager was young Drum Packer, whose name as warrior against Indian enemies was already Sitting Bull. In his letters Collister wrote of teaching him to use the tap-tap machine, and to speak and read English. This must have been a very elementary knowledge, and yet fairly striking in the company of young Sitting Bull's contemporaries. Travelers and army men, including Lieut. Caspar Collins, often mentioned the Sitting Bull of the Platte, amused by this son of the fighting Sioux, with his broad, bland baby-face bent over a book. Often it was Napoleon's *Campaigns,* borrowed from the post library at Fort Laramie for him.

---

* Often interpreted as Slow Bull, perhaps a term of ease and familiarity. When the old buffalo-hunting Indians spoke of either Sitting Bull by one name it was usually Slow, and in any amusing situation always Slow Bull.

When this Sitting Bull was away with his village he sent in by Bissonnette, the village trader married into the tribe, for the newspapers, perhaps writing his order with a lead bullet on a strip torn from a margin: "Want the black and white papers," and signed with the outline of a man's head, a buffalo on his haunches, a sitting bull, floating above it—his Indian picture signature. In an interview published in the *Annals of Wyoming* almost seventy years later, Collister still recalled this, but now in his old age he, or perhaps his interviewer, mixed up the two Sitting Bulls and made one man of the two. But back in the early sixties Collister's letters from the upper Platte show that he knew the man squatting at the fire in the telegraph station the winter of 1862-1863, braids falling over the maps in the *Campaigns,* was the head soldier of Little Wound's Cut-Off Oglalas. This band was a serious, individualistic lot who used to hold the southeast fringe of Sioux country, roughly across the middle of Nebraska, north and south, against the Pawnees, raiding their earthen villages, matching their own few guns and stone-age weapons against the best mounts and arms that the white man could furnish the Pawnees, his early trade allies.

In the meantime the Hunkpapa Sitting Bull was pretty busy in his own country. His father had died in battle and was left on a scaffold up on Cedar Creek, a tributary of the Cannonball, in the present North Dakota. Little Crow, fleeing west from Minnesota the fall of 1862 after the New Ulm uprising, found Sitting Bull around up there, a good three hundred fifty, four hundred travois miles from Collister at Deer Creek Station.

According to the Sioux accounts, the friendship of the southern Sitting Bull, the Oglala, for the whites lasted to the so-called Indian War of 1864, in which the Sioux raids closed the Overland Trail, and which ended in the massacre of the friendly Cheyennes at Sand Creek in Colorado that fall. Sitting Bull was visiting up in the Powder River camps at the time and, packing his medicine bag and shield, he rode down with the warriors under Crazy Horse in answer to the Cheyenne war pipe sent out in a call for help. On the way they stopped to look over the winter prairie around the Blue Water, where eight years earlier Crazy Horse had come upon the smoking camp of Little Thunder after General Harney had struck it. Women and children were scattered all around, torn by cannon shells, their clothing still smoldering, some not yet dead. Several of Sitting Bull's Oglala relatives had been visiting in the camp then, and died there, and yet he had remained a peace man. Now the two men talked of the sorrow of that day, and of this recent attack that had come to the Cheyennes. Always it was the friendlies who were struck, the peace-lovers staying in near the troops as the Great Father asked.

Now at last the remedy seemed plain even to the peace man Sitting Bull, the long-time white-man-lover. They must all fight, everybody be ready.

For the next four years, until his uncle, Little Wound, signed the treaty of 1868 that was to withdraw all the whites and their forts from the Indian country so long as grass shall grow and water flow, only Indian accounts can tell of Sitting Bull, the Oglala, for no white man saw much of him except his flying bullets. And none could know these, for bullets do not carry a man's mark as his arrows did, but they killed just the same.

The first killing was around Julesburg, Colorado, January 1865. From there the great camp of Sioux, Cheyenne, and Arapahos, out to avenge the Sand Creek massacre, moved north toward the Powder River, destroying ranches and Overland Trail stations, burning a strip a hundred miles wide clean of every white man. With the women and children, the pony herds, and all the goods and the warriors of the Indians usually remaining south of the Platte—they marched north through deepest winter, spreading death and fire and alarm all the way.

The following summer the Oglala Sitting Bull was with the three thousand warriors who attacked the Platte Bridge near the present Casper, Wyoming, named for Lieut. Caspar Collins, who had written so enthusiastically about his visits to the camps of the Oglalas, and of his friend Sitting Bull who liked to study the maps of Napoleon. Chance put the young officer at the Bridge station that one day. The attacking Oglalas recognized him in the fight and cried, "Go back, friend! Go back!" parting to let him through. But he had a wild horse that bolted on into

the Cheyenne warriors over the hill, and they knew only that
he was one of the hated blue coats who had killed their women
and children. When Sitting Bull and the others found out about
this, their hearts were so bad over their friend that they had to
kill ten more whites.

The rest of the summer of 1865 the Oglalas and their allies harried the Overland Trail from eastern Nebraska to South
Pass. Only large, troop-escorted wagon trains willing and able to
fight their way through were allowed to try it.

Up in the Hunkpapa country there was action too. The
summer of 1864 General Sully had struck at some of the Minnesota Sioux near Killdeer Mountain, far up in what is now
North Dakota. Sitting Bull, camped nearby, was drawn into the
fight but with small loss to the Hunkpapas. Angered by this and
other, larger grievances, Sitting Bull timed his attack on Fort
Rice with the Platte Bridge fight the summer of 1865, and
then chased the soldiers still marching around north of the
Black Hills, and attacked the gold seekers headed for Idaho.
The Oglalas found miners too, heading up through Wyoming,
on the Bozeman Trail, and then the 4,000 troops of the Powder
River Expedition spreading northward from the Overland Trail
to punish the Indians for their attacks in the Platte country.
But the best the soldiers could do was fight off the warriors they
had come to attack, until finally they were glad to start back to
Fort Laramie, barefoot, eating their starving horses as they fled
before the taunting Indians.

The next year brought new forts like Buford far up the
Missouri, where Sitting Bull the Hunkpapa kept up a casual
sort of siege. Three new posts strung northward through Wyoming started the Bozeman Trail War, and now Sitting Bull the
Oglala found himself drawn up across the Platte to follow Red
Cloud, the man who had killed his grandfather, back in the
bad, drunken times of whisky wagons in every camp. Now Red
Cloud was the man to follow in a very strong fight against the
enemy soldiers pushing into the treaty-guaranteed Sioux country. Under the leadership of Red Cloud, the powerful young
warrior force developed by the fighting of the last two years har-
assed the Bozeman Trail and kept Fort Phil Kearny under siege

until on December 21, 1866, they wiped out Fetterman and all his men.

By 1868 the fight against the encroaching soldiers was won, the Bozeman forts were dismantled, and a new treaty signed. It was a victory over the white man, and Sitting Bull, the Oglala, saw its glories, but he also saw that the buffalo was vanishing. Soon everybody must live on reservations, on the little islands in the rising sea of whites. To prepare for this some of the strong fighting men must go there right from the start to watch, to protect the women and children. So Sitting Bull, the Oglala, decided to go to an agency even though the head chief was Red Cloud. By 1870, although only twenty-nine years old, he had become so influential with both the white man and the Indians that he was selected as one of the twenty Oglalas to represent them well in Washington. His dignity and his face, still broad and almost as bland as a baby's, surprised everybody who heard his name, particularly the newspapermen. But the government was not confused. They knew about the Hunkpapa Sitting Bull too. He had grown vastly in power, as a medicine man, a diviner, a dreamer, as well as a leader in war and in the council of the Hunkpapas. He had turned down the gift of tobacco sent to coax him to Washington. He would hear no talk about settling on a reservation.

Although the Hunkpapas were busy thrusting the Crows back from the shrinking buffalo ranges the spring and summer of 1872, there was another problem. Troops were escorting the Northern Pacific railroad survey up the Yellowstone, right through the Indian country against all the Indian treaties. They hit the country of Sitting Bull, the Hunkpapa, first and he sent for help. Crazy Horse took his hostile Oglalas up, joining in the attack on Colonel Baker near the mouth of Arrow Creek on August 14. The soldiers got a good look at the Hunkpapa leader, recognizing his limp as he walked out between the battle lines and settled himself with a few of the more courageous followers to smoke a pipe, with bullets spurting up the dust all around. In the meantime the other Sitting Bull was in the midst of Red Cloud's fight against the proposed move of his agency from the Platte up to White River. April 14, 1872, the

Oglala agent, Daniels, reported anger and threats of war from the excited Indians. But Sitting Bull arose, quietly pointed out that they had already agreed to go and now they wanted the guns and ammunition they had been promised—which they got. October 25 Daniels made another report on his Sitting Bull. A couple of Indians had been found dead along the Platte, perhaps killed by whites or breeds. Immediately warriors came streaming in upon the agency, armed, painted, whooping, singing war songs.

"Our hearts are bad!" they cried. "It will take white blood to make them good!"

The white men barricaded themselves inside the stockade, thirty men against five hundred mounted warriors, while in the camps the skin lodges began to fall, the women and children hurrying into the sandhills out of range of any flying bullets, while the warriors circled the stockade, firing into the air, lifting arrows to fall inside. Haranguers on the roofs of the buildings roared for burning and for slaughter.

But fifteen young friendlies, guns pointed outward, planted themselves at the stockade gates. Leading them was Sitting Bull, high up now in the Head Band society—warrior sons of noted Oglala chieftains. Through the calm and influence of these men the attack was held off until General Smith's troops arrived from Laramie the next morning. Then the agent made a cracker and molasses feast.

Things were no quieter a year later after the agency was moved to White River in northwest Nebraska, far from an army post, up under the breaks of Pine Ridge that covered the approach from the hostile camps up north. The new agent, Saville, complained to Washington that the Crazy Horse hostiles were slipping in, although getting them to surrender was a major part of his job. Arrogantly, these wild Sioux pushed forward for a share in the annuities and demanded the right to trade for powder and guns, intimidating both the whites and the agency Indians. Many of the young men had been in the attack on Custer, August 1873, on the Yellowstone with Crazy Horse and the Hunkpapa Sitting Bull. They talked big, partic-

ularly some Cheyennes who had lost their families to Custer
down on the Washita.

"This time, if the cannons had not come hurrying up, he
would have been the one wiped out!"

So they bragged, and raced their good horses taken from
the whites. The new stockade had no gates, and often before going out on raids along the settlements of the Platte they rode
around the inside, four abreast, painted, singing war songs,
shooting into the windows while the whites cowered on the
floor. Saville finally got carpenters to finish the stockade gates,
but a northern Sioux whose brother had been killed came in
with his heart bad. At night he dragged loose lumber up to the
wall, climbed over, and shot Frank Appleton, the acting agent.

He got away, but by morning thousands of warriors rode
whooping around the stockade, fearing for their people in the
camps scattered out over the valley, showing their readiness to
fight any vengeance. The chiefs came in, admitting they could
do nothing with their young men. So the half dozen whites,
even those intermarried with the Indians, hid in the cupola at
one corner of the stockade, built up high to look out over the
White River plain from Crow Butte to the bluffs standing along
the north. They had one gun among them, the Winchester the
butcher used to kill beef for the old and helpless at issue time.
With a keg of water, and sacks of flour for barricading, they
stayed up in the cupola four days, the Indians milling around
below like a herd of Longhorns smelling blood. While the chiefs
counciled and Agent Saville was held as hostage, the whites
thought about the bull train that was overdue and with the
usual kegs of whisky surely hidden under the goods. If the warriors got to that it would be a massacre.

But outside Sitting Bull the Oglala was urging peace upon
the young men. If they burned the agency, soldiers would certainly come to shoot the women and children. Even those who
got away would have no lodges, or robes or meat and with winter upon them. He kept talking, hour after hour, and as the Indians cooled he planted his followers around the agency supplies and cupola while a squaw man living out from the agency

whipped his pony for Fort Laramie and the soldiers, with no
assurance that he would get through.

Finally there were mirror signals and new excitement
among the warriors. The bull train or the military?

It was the military—both horse and walking soldiers and
a train of army supplies moving dark on the Laramie trail. Immediately the Indians broke into factions, some wanting to
burn the agency and go north, others hurrying the women and
children into the breaks before the soldiers arrived and found
there was a dead white man to be avenged. The rest charged
the friendlies who had held them off until it was too late. But
Sitting Bull's following stood fast and it turned out that General Smith was not anxious for bloodshed. Once more presents
were made and a feast, with some of the wildest of the hostiles slipping away north afterward. Not Sitting Bull. He went
to sleep. When he awoke he found that the soldiers had started
a post there, called Camp Robinson, and knew they would
never go away again.

The next summer brought more provocation for trouble.
Custer marched into the Black Hills, where, by the treaty of
1868, no white man was ever to go. But the Northern Pacific
railroad was in financial difficulties and locating the gold
known to be in the Hills would promote investment. Custer
obliged; he reported gold at the grass roots, and made a starvation march back to the Missouri through country burned black
by the northern Sitting Bull's Hunkpapas and their allies. The
newspapers carried the stories of Custer and the Hunkpapa
leader and nobody bothered to point out that there was another man of the name who was saving the Red Cloud beef
herd from the wild Indians so there would be meat for the
agency hungry. Nor was there any action on the Indian complaints about issue pants and blankets that proved to be poor as
dark blotting paper in water, the sugar half sand, the flour
coarse and moldy and often double-sacked, so the outer ones
could be removed and the flour stamped and counted a second
time. Cattle, too, were double-tallied, cattle that were mostly

hoofs and horns to these Indians who had been fed on the finest fat young buffalo cows.

Understandably, the agent's life as Little Father of the Oglalas wasn't too peaceful. Even the friendlies were arrogant and demanding day or night, as one can be with a father. Along in October he announced that the chiefs and the agency employees should all have a rest on Sundays. To let the Indians know which was the day, he would raise a pole and run up a flag. So the agent, a political appointee innocent of any understanding of his Indians, brought on an incident that is still disputed among the Sioux. The one point of agreement was the expressed gratitude of both the military and the Indian Bureau to Sitting Bull, now called The Good.

It seems that the first objection to the flagpole came from the soured band of old Conquering Bear, who had been set up as chief over all the Sioux by the government back in 1851, and then killed in the Grattan fight of 1854 over a Mormon cow. When some long pine poles were dragged in from the canyons back of the agency, these Indians stopped their usual horse racing and pushed into the stockade. With their war clubs they chopped the poles to pieces.

"We will not have a flag on our agency! A flag means war!"

As usual, Red Cloud and his headmen were around, this time sitting on a pile of lumber inside the stockade. By now Old Red had six years experience as an ally of the white man. He filled his pipe, saying neither yes or no—waiting.

But the little agent recalled his nephew shot not long ago. He had the stockade gates slammed and sent a runner to the new Camp Robinson. That meant soldiers coming. The Indians, both friendly and hostile, came charging in from all directions, kicking up dust, roaring that soldiers must not come to their agency. Just then a pitiful little handful of troopers appeared, with angry, painted warriors racing along both sides, whooping, waving war clubs, shooting off their guns, while between them and the soldiers rode Sitting Bull and Young Man Afraid of His Horse and their friendlies, first one and then the other charging out against the wild Indians, pushing them back, Sitting Bull swinging his three-bladed knife long as a scythe against them as the troopers' hurried advance became a flight to the comparative safety of the stockade. The gates banged behind them but Lieutenant Crawford ordered them opened. Dismounting his men he faced the howling warriors. It was a brave thing, and stopped the Indians a moment. But the soldiers were mostly green eastern recruits, and so excited that Crawford had to whip them into something like a line with the flat of his sword. The whooping warriors crowded harder, but Sitting Bull and Young Man Afraid and another brave man called Three Bears stood against them—three against almost a thousand now.

"Burn! Burn the whites out!" the surging mass chanted, a few roaring back, "Burn! And kill the white-man-lovers!"

Now it looked like a real battle, and a few sons of the agency chiefs saw how it could end, with only Sitting Bull and the two others making the stand. They joined on their side, fighting anywhere they stood. One of them clubbed young Conquering Bear, son of the dead chief, from his horse. Instantly two Red Cloud followers were off and, laying a bow across the Bear's throat, stood on the two ends.

"You are all troublemakers!" one of them said to their struggling victim. "If your father had given up the Indian who killed the Mormon cow long ago, there would never have been a war with the whites. No soldiers here among us at all!"

But as the man on the ground stopped his struggling and began to turn black as a hanged one, the word of it spread back through the wild mass, and a dark, dangerous silence followed it. The Cut-Offs and Red Cloud men separated from the crowd of warriors and moved together, guns cocked ready for the first blood as the man on the ground seemed to die. And now even some of the wild northern Indians backed their horses out of the way of this brother-war.

Then Sitting Bull came pushing his horse through. He knocked the men choking Conquering Bear aside, and, turning upon the silent stand of warriors, he swung his great three-bladed war club before him.

"Think what you do, my friends! Would you shed your brother's blood here today? You are all small-braves—fighting each other in your own village, on your own agency!" he roared.

"Hah! Hear the small-brave talk!" a hostile of Red Cloud's family challenged. "He is the one who was too weak to wash out the blood of his grandfather when he was left dead on the ground by our man in there smoking. Would you stop before such a grandson as this Sitting Bull?"

So now it was finally coming out—a blood avenging between the Cut-Offs and Red Cloud's band—long, much too long deferred.

But this must not be, and Sitting Bull roared out against it, his warning lost in the *"Hoka hey!"* of the Red Cloud warriors, who charged him from all sides, their horses thrusting against his, their clubs striking at him. Then it came, the first bullet for him. It went past his braid, but before the man could reload Sitting Bull had knocked him into the dust. Then he sat back on his horse, his arms down, quiet in the fury upon him, and now the warriors faltered, drawing their plunging horses back before the set stoniness of the broad face that the whites thought looked bland as a baby's.

But one warrior was undaunted. He rode his horse straight up to Sitting Bull. "You are flesh like the rest and bullets will go through you too!" he shouted as he brought his rifle down against the scarred, dust-caked breast.

Sitting Bull sat motionless, his big club still unraised. "Yes, I am flesh," he said, "and bullets have gone through me— Pawnee bullets and from the Crows and the whites up around the Piney Fort, but you are not the man to put one there—" and as the Indian hesitated a moment, finger on trigger, one of the Head Band warriors grabbed him from behind and jerked him from the horse, the rifle booming into the sky.

Without glancing down upon the man, Sitting Bull pushed his horse out through the mass of Indians and the dust to a little rise. Then a Red Cloud man rode out to stop his horse alongside The Good's. Next two Cut-Off's followed, and many others, even some of the wild ones from the Crazy Horse camps, for it seemed that even a good friend of the whites could still be a brave man.

Slowly the alignments of agency bands broke, began to move around, mixing in with the hostiles, who seemed to be drifting away, the poor handful of soldiers in the stockade gate almost forgotten in what had so nearly happened.

With signs to his followers, Sitting Bull rode down to make a double line for the soldiers to ride out between. They went swiftly and afraid between the two silent walls of Indians who watched with their guns across their horses. When the troops were gone the warriors wiped the paint from their faces and hurried into line for the inevitable feast. Later forty fine blankets were distributed to the chiefs.

The trouble was reported to Washington by both Agent Saville and the military. The report from Camp Robinson, Nebraska, briefed to the essentials, said:

At the agent's call for help Lieutenant Crawford and 22 men started to the agency with the available men of the 3rd Cavalry. . . . At his arrival he informed me by courier that 200 Indians, mounted and armed, approached. Through efforts of Sitting Bull and other Oglalas, the Minneconjous were prevented from attack. . . .

The agent knew erection of the flagstaff would cause trouble . . . and should have waited until I had a stronger force (two companies from Spotted Tail, etc.). . . . Indians sent runners to all camps, thinking, of course, they were to be attacked. They were determined to fight. Had the Lieutenant's party been massacred, the agent and the person who held up two companies at Sheridan [Camp Sheridan, at Spotted Tail's agency 40 miles away, M.S.] would have been responsible. . . .

Sitting Bull and his band saved the agency and should be rewarded. . . . Red Cloud was passive inside the stockade during the troubles. Either he has no control of the Indians or he was afraid to do anything.

Although the troublesome warriors were underestimated in number, and dismissed as Minneconjous instead of mostly Oglala followers of Crazy Horse and disgruntled agency young men, ten days later it was admitted that there were three thousand wild Indians camped out on White River when Professor Marsh of Yale requested guides and protection for his scientific expedition into the Badlands. The wild Indians called him a gold thief, but the professor was good at listening to Red Cloud's complaints against his agent, so he got permission to go in if Sitting Bull the Good and an Indian escort went along. But the expedition came with a company of infantry to protect the wagons. Immediately a thousand angry warriors streamed in from the hills and with rifles and Colt revolvers cocked they surrounded the party. Once more women and children ran, lodges fell, and the agent ordered Marsh to get his infantry up to the fort before he provoked a massacre. The little column went, followed by whooping, shooting Indians all the way. Marsh made the usual feast but doubled it, and got appreciative pats on their stomachs from the Indians, and demands that he start back to the Platte tomorrow. So he made a night start for the Badlands, and, with the Sioux aversion to night fighting from the time when dew softened the bowstring, they let him go.

Once more the newspapers played up the story, denouncing the powerful Sitting Bull who made trouble all the way from the upper Missouri to the Platte River. And denouncing the government for feeding and arming this treacherous savage at taxpapers' expense. Both the military and Saville protested to Washington against such misinformation. An excerpt from the agent's letter of November 13, 1874, shows the tone of it.

Regarding quelling of disturbance at the agency—Sitting Bull is not the Uncpapa but an Oglala, the nephew of Little Wound, chief of the Kiosces, noted among the Indians for his courage and daring. During the late war he was a bitter enemy of the whites. Since the treaty he has been friendly and a warm friend

since I have been on the agency. He is head soldier of
the Head Bands, of which Young Man Afraid of His
Horse is chief. I have made him leader of the soldiers
whom I have armed with permission of the Department.

Once more, January 11, 1875, Saville wrote suggesting some
reward for those who helped in the flagpole incident. It would
help dispel the notion that only the bad the Indian does is reported, never the good, and that only the troublemakers are rewarded, adding:

A present in the name of the President would give satisfaction and prestige. The favorite present is a nice
gun.

The winter was a hard one for the friends of the white
man. The promised rations didn't come and the starving Indians moved in close to the agency to call attention to their
misery and finally up to Fort Robinson, leaving the stripped
bones of their butchered ponies under the eyes of the commander. Sitting Bull and his police tried their best by coopera-
tion and by anger to get the rations for the people but none
came. The buffalo had disappeared, even all the small game,
with so many hungry Indians around. Cold Indians, too, with
only one thin blanket for every three people, and wood very
scarce, the buffalo chips gone even if the ground weren't covered with snow.

In the north the hostiles were cold too this snowblind winter, but they managed to send some robes down to their relatives at Red Cloud, and fought the gold seekers willing to risk
freezing to death. With spring the gold rush to the Black Hills
was like snow water roaring in the gullies, and there was
news in the papers that the Great Father wanted the chiefs to
come to Washington to sell the Hills.

"One does not sell the earth upon which the people walk,"
Crazy Horse told the messengers come to draw him to Red
Cloud and another of the white papers that he would never

sign. Up north Sitting Bull the Hunkpapa was as strong in his refusal.

But the Oglala Sitting Bull went to Washington as the right-hand man to Red Cloud, who insisted he was only going to tell the Great Father about the thieving whites who starved his people. At Omaha they stopped and were feasted and given fine clothes and had their pictures taken. In Washington they found their agent still being investigated through the kindly intercession of Professor Marsh. Nothing came of that, although there was plenty proof of graft and thievery. Only nobody seemed to be doing it.

Nothing came of the Black Hills sale either. The southern Sitting Bull sat quietly with the Oglala delegation at Washington and kept out of the squabbling of Red Cloud and Spotted Tail, both between themselves and with the whites. After futile weeks the Commissioner of Indian Affairs got the whole unhappy delegation together and, according to the New York *Tribune*, June 7, 1875, said he was sorry nothing had been done. He scolded the old chiefs for it, and then turned to the younger men:

> Now, I want to say a word to Sitting Bull. I have heard from your agent and from the military officers at the agency of the great service you have rendered the government. You have proved yourself to be a very brave man—a friend of your own people and to the whites. Your good conduct has been reported to the President, and I am instructed to give you a token of his regard.

This turned out to be a fine rifle in a leather case, the *Tribune* reported, with a brass mounting that gleamed so the Indians called it gold, and engraved to Sitting Bull.

It was a very busy spring and summer for the Hunkpapas. Enough miners were getting killed up there so there was some fine victory dancing among the northern Sioux. Among the whites there were loud and urgent demands that the miners be given military protection in the Black Hills instead of being summarily expelled by General Crook's troops. A commission was sent out to buy the Black Hills, prepared, it was rumored, to go as high as seven million dollars, if necessary. Such figures brought a swarm of hungry contractors like a plague of Mormon crickets moving up the trail to Red Cloud Agency. The Hunkpapa Sitting Bull refused to come to the conference, but a lot of Crazy Horse's hostile Oglalas went down to watch Red Cloud and Spotted Tail and their jealous maneuverings and to warn them of their duty and the bullets that would enforce it. There was enough galloping, whooping, rifle fire, and prairie burning in the night to scare away the white women who came to the conference for a little amused sightseeing. At the Lone Tree council ground it was the same. While the circle of chiefs under the spreading cottonwood delayed and delayed, the little group of commissioners—senators, generals, a missionary, and so on—waited under the canvas flies that shielded them from the sun. At first the handful of soldiers close behind them seemed good protection, but gradually they realized that the soldiers too were walled in by the Indians, who stood eight, ten deep all around, mostly wild, painted warriors, their guns cocked. Beyond, a dozen haranguers for war rode up and down, shouting, singing. "It is a good day to die! A very good day to die!"

All that was needed now was one wild shot that hit—

On a little rise Sitting Bull sat his horse quietly, his hand ready on the bright breech of his gift rifle, his face still bland and emotionless. For a long while it seemed that none would ever dare rise to speak in this council because the first word might bring a bullet, many, many bullets. Then Young Man Afraid got up from the circle of chiefs and stood, his blanket drawn about him, a bold, steady target for all to see. When no one fired, he gave a signal and Sitting Bull ordered his warriors to clear the grounds. Now the whites held their breath, and the Indians too, the chiefs squatting on the ground motionless as stone, knowing it could be the end of every one of them, with both the Indian and the trooper guns turned their way. No hostile moved to leave. Swaggering and threatening, they waited. Here and there a shot was fired, but still into the air.

On his knoll Sitting Bull waited without one motion, the

September sun warm on his dusty braids. Without shifting an eye he saw the sickness of the white-man faces, the soldier guns nervous, the warriors seeing this too, and pushing in, hot for the start.

Once more he gave the harsh command. "Back! Back, my friends!" saying it angrily, his lip curling in the deep scorn of the Sioux.

This time the hostiles drew back, one, then another, more, and through their thinning the commission was rushed into the ambulances and hurried off to the agency stockade. To both sides of them the slopes were dark with watching Indians who knew that once more the Black Hills had been saved.

"Wholesale Massacre of Commission Barely Averted!" the newspapers screamed out across the nation.

The year 1876 was the high point in the career of the Hunkpapa Sitting Bull, but it was the tragic year for the one called The Good. While his Oglala relatives with Crazy Horse helped whip Crook on the Rosebud and then, a week later, wiped out Custer, there was a commensurate tightening at the agency. The usual buffalo hunt was canceled, and when the Cheyennes went out anyway, they were whipped back to the starvation of the agency, the women who remembered Sand Creek scuttling in terror before the soldiers.

By September another commission came to buy the Black Hills. This time there was no such foolishness as an open conference. It was held in the agency stockade, with the wild Indians shut out. The treaty, already complete, was read to the chiefs. They must give up all their hunting grounds of the Powder and the Tongue and the Yellowstone, move to little agencies among the whites of the lower Missouri or go south to the starving people of Indian Territory. The chiefs protested, and were told they would be kept in the stockade until the pen was touched, and there would be no rations for the women and children until it was done.

Stunned, the headmen sat silent in their blankets, Red Cloud surely recalling that only eight years ago the U. S. government had backed down and dismantled a whole string of forts at his command.

But one man was not silent here. That was Sitting Bull the Good. With the butt of a revolver sticking from his belt, the gift rifle in one hand, his great war club in the other, he harangued the commission and the chiefs. This was not treaty-making but trickery—with the chiefs locked up and the women helpless! It was foolish to talk of selling the Hills with so few people here, most of them away north, where there was still meat.

When Red Cloud taunted him with his friendship for the whites, Sitting Bull ordered the gates thrown open and not a word from the whites was spoken to stop him. Whipping the chiefs out, he roared, "Get out! Go north! Maybe there a man can still live in honor for a little while!"

With his war bag packed Sitting Bull the Good started north for the camps of Crazy Horse. He went openly and nobody challenged his departure. Safe from disturbance now, the conference reconvened in the agency stockade and the chiefs had to sign away the gold-bearing Hills and their hunting ground forever.

Up north Sitting Bull's heart fell down when he saw the poorness of the children of the hostiles, the scarcity of winter meat and of lodges and robes, with soldiers following them across the snow like wolves tracking the blood of a wounded buffalo. He went up to see the Hunkpapas too, and heard the messengers from the northern agencies try to coax those Indians in there. He heard the other Sitting Bull tell of his council with General Miles, saying that he wanted peace for his people but that he could not lay down his gun while the soldiers were in his country. So Miles had turned the council into a battle. One Indian was killed and the rest had to scatter because the women and children were along and ammunition was very scarce.

Hopelessly Sitting Bull the Good returned to Red Cloud. Everything was done. The military asked him to go right back with a message to Crazy Horse. He went. It was not that he believed the whites any more. While he was north Red Cloud and Red Leaf, long-time government chiefs, had been surrounded in the night, their guns and ponies taken so even the winter wood had to be carried on the backs of the women. Once more the Sioux were back to the dog travois they used before the coming of the horse, but now without the buffalo, or even the freedom to move to wooded shelter.

He went north carrying the word of General Crook: Come to Red Cloud, get food and blankets and peace. But that was two hundred miles over winter Wyoming, and into the power of the crooked tongue, as even he had to admit now. He was told that General Miles, settled on the mouth of the Tongue River, was offering them the same, right here in their own country. The Missouri Indians who went in there two moons ago were well fed and warm.

So Crazy Horse decided to go talk to him. Sitting Bull the Good, the friend of the whites, was sent ahead, carrying a lance with the white flag the general had sent for their coming. Beside him rode three others, all unarmed, and behind them four more, bringing some horses stolen from the post herds by the wild young men. A ways back several older men sat smoking, one holding the gift rifle of Sitting Bull until his return, while on a little knoll Crazy Horse and his headmen waited to see how it would be, and far back the women waited too, and hoped.

The story of that day is told in General Nelson A. Miles' report, dated December 17, 1876 (AGO Records, Military Division of the Missouri, Sioux War, 1877, National Archives), of which the following are briefed excerpts:

Unfortunate affair at this place yesterday. Five Minneconjou chiefs came in bearing two white flags, followed by 20 or 30 other Indians and were passing by the Crow camp. The five in advance were surrounded by Crows, 12, and instantly killed. The act was an unprovoked cowardly murder, the Crows approached them in a friendly manner, said "How!" shook hands with them and when they were within their power and partly behind a large woodpile, killed them in most brutal manner. At the first shot the officers and men rushed out and tried to save the Minneconjous, but could not reach them in time. The Crows were aware of the enormity of the crime as they saw the Minneconjous had a flag of truce and had been warned the day before against committing any act of violence against messengers or other parties coming in for friendly purposes. They tried to hide the flag and taking advantage of the momentary excitement, while efforts were being made to open communication and bring back others who had fled to the bluffs, the guilty Crows jumped their ponies and fled to their agency in Montana. . . . These five chiefs and the followers were within a few hundred yards of the parade ground, where they were deliberately placing themselves into hands of the government and within the camp of 400 government troops. These, with heads of others, would have given us leaders of the Minneconjous, Sans Arcs, and possibly the Oglala tribes, representing fully 600 lodges and at least 1000 fighting men of the hostiles and completed and secured beyond doubt the fruits of our efforts. The Crows were immediately disarmed, 12 of their horses taken from them and with other considerations, together with letters explaining the whole affair, sent to the people and friends of those killed, as an assurance that no white man had any part in the affair and had no heart for such brutal and cowardly acts.

A note attached to a letter of February 1, 1877 from General Crook to General Sheridan reports that the Indian messengers returning to Cheyenne Agency said Sitting Bull the Good from Red Cloud was among those killed in the attack on the hostile flag of truce. Four fell where the Crows jumped them and the rest ran back, the Crows following and killing one about two miles from the post.

When their emissaries fell, the waiting chiefs had to get their women and children away. The old man who was caring for Sitting Bull's rifle ran and was overtaken by the Crows. In the fighting the unloaded weapon slipped from his hands. It was surrendered to Miles in the Crow disarming and was added to the Miles collection. Automatically, by its inscription, it became the former property of the Hunkpapa, although he had never been much nearer Washington than the east bank of the Missouri.

If there had been no Crow attack that December day, General Miles would have had all the hostile leaders except those with the Hunkpapa Sitting Bull. It would have ended most of the winter campaign that lasted to May. With a good word from Crazy Horse even the Hunkpapa Sitting Bull might have come in, instead of finally retreating to Canada.

Sitting Bull had been reported killed in the Custer battle and then turned up fighting, strong as ever. One more rumor of his death was just another shot into the empty air. So Sitting Bull the Good disappeared from the knowledge of most white men. But not his achievements, his name on the agency rolls, his trips to Washington or his gift from the President. They became divergent and contradictory elements in the character of the great leader of the Hunkpapas, and compelling evidence of great treachery, treachery that became the ready cant of every lover of Wild West shows. Presented as the honest and upright man that the Hunkpapa Sitting Bull was, he might very well never have died from a white man's gun in the hands of an Indian either. It was fear of treacherous intentions that sent the Indian police to root him out into the gray dawn of morning, naked from the sleeping robes, and to shoot him down. It was December too, the fifteenth instead of the sixteenth, and 1890—fourteen years after Sitting Bull the Good died up in the country of the Yellowstone.

⊂≥ THE HOMESTEAD IN PERSPECTIVE

THE HOMESTEAD ACT was the hope of the poor man. Many who had wanted a piece of government land felt that preempting, which required an eventual cash payment of $1.25 or more an acre, was too risky for the penniless. If the preemptor failed to raise the money at the proper time, in addition to building a home in the wilderness and making a living for a family, he lost the land and with it all his improvements, his work, and his home. The Homestead Act offered any bona fide land seeker 160 acres from the public domain with no cash outlay beyond the $14 filing fee and the improvements he would have to make to live on the place the required five years. His house, barn, sheds and corrals, his well, the tilled acreage and the fencing, all counted toward the final patent to the land, and most of these improvements could be made by the homesteader's own hands, his and the family's.

It was this offer of free land that drew my father, Old Jules Sandoz, west to a homestead in the unorganized region that was to become Sheridan County, Nebraska, and he stressed "free land" in all the letters he wrote to the European and American newspapers for the working man, letters that drew the hundreds of settlers he located.

The home seeker, as late as the end of the Kinkaid Homestead days of my childhood, came by every possible means, even afoot. I was born too late to see the Czechoslovakian couple who crossed much of Nebraska pushing a wheelbarrow loaded with all their belongings, including, it was said, the wedding feather tick. But we saw many land seekers walk in, some coming much farther than the seventeen miles from the railroad. There were dusty men, worn and discouraged until they got a good wash-up at the Niobrara River near our house or at our well, followed by one of mother's hearty suppers and a big dose of Old Jules' enthusiasm and faith in the country. Some came by livery rig or the mail wagon, or were picked up by a settler returning home from town. Many of the more serious land seekers left their families back east until they were located. Often these drove in by wagon in the old way although the wire fences of settlers, and, in the free-land regions, the cattlemen, prevented the accustomed movement up along the streams, as Old Jules himself had come, following the Niobrara to Mirage Flats.

We children had the usual curiosity about outsiders but we were even more thoroughly disciplined than most homesteader children, who were taught to keep out of the way and never push into grown-up affairs. But we tried to hear the answer to Old Jules usual western query: "What name you traveling under?"

This question from a rough, bearded man with a strong foreign accent and a gun on his arm was not reassuring to strangers. But perhaps a potential settler should realize from the start that homesteading was not for the timid, and as soon as a man could say "I'm looking for me a piece of government land—" he was among friends. He and any family he had were welcome to eat at our table and sleep in our beds even if we children were moved to the floor. This was naturally all free beyond the twenty-five dollar locating and surveying fee Old Jules charged whenever the settler managed to get the money. Often the family stayed with us until their house was up, the wife perhaps criticizing father's profane and bawdy tongue and complaining contemptuously about mother's bread from unbleached macaroni wheat that we grew and hauled to the water mill on Pine Creek.

For us children the important home seekers were the boomers, the covered wagon families. Evenings we watched them come down into the Niobrara valley, rumble over the plank bridge, and climb the steep sandy pitch to the bench on which our house stood. There, on a flat camping-ground, the panting horses were allowed to stop, and barefoot children spilled out of the wagon, front and back, to run, galloping and bucking like calves let out of a pen. We stared from among the cherry trees, or in the summer, from the asparagus patch where the greenery stood over our heads. We saw the tugs dropped, the harness stripped off and piled against the wagon tongue, while the woman ordered the children to this and that task as the fire began to smoke in the little pile of stones always there for campers.

Finally the man might come to draw a bucket of the clear water from our well, water so cold it hurt the teeth on hot days.

By the time we were old enough to notice, father had no trouble waiting until after supper to talk land to such men.

"Boomers!" he would say, in contempt. "Probably been to Oregon and back, living off the country, picking up anything that's loose. Hey, Mari, go hide all the hammers and bring in my rifle——" meaning the 30-30 that usually hung on the antlers outside the door.

"And shut up the chickens——" mother would add.

Old Jules was usually right about the boomers of the 1906-12 period. The man would come in to talk land but even if he showed any enthusiasm for homesteading, the family might be pulling out at dawn, seldom with anything of consequence that belonged to us. That stack of guns in a corner of our kitchen-living room, and father's evident facility with firearms, discouraged more than petty thefts of, say, a pair of pliers or a slab of bacon from the smokehouse.

"Sneaky thieves!" mother would snort. "If they were so

hungry I would have given them more than that, so long as we could spare it."

A few stayed to follow father's buckskin team into the sand-hills, to live in the covered wagon until a dugout or a soddy could be prepared on the new homestead. Some of these left when the drouth and hot winds of August struck, along with others who had walked in or came by hired rig. The winters seemed particularly hard to the latter-day boomers, and often the first fall blizzard sent them rolling toward Texas or Arkansas. Some stuck it out. Several of these Kinkaid-day boomers are growing fine blooded stock in Nebraska, the older members spending the winters in Florida or California and damning the government.

We tend to forget that the homesteaders were not a type, not as alike as biscuits cut out with a baking-powder can. They varied as much as their origins and their reasons for coming west. There were Daughters and Sons of the Revolution located next to the communal communities of the Mennonites, say, or the Hutterians. An illiterate from some other frontier might be neighboring with a Greek and Hebrew scholar from a colony of Russian Jews in the Dakotas. A nervous-fingered murderer who fled west under a new name might join fences with a non-violent River Baptist or a vegetarian who wouldn't kill a rabbit eating up his first sprouts of lettuce, no matter how hungry the settler might be.

Yet there was apparently a certain repetition of characters in the homestead communities. Those who thought that Old Jules Sandoz was incredible or at least unique should go through the many thousands of letters I received from home-steaders and descendants of homesteaders. Apparently, men with some Old Julesian traits lived in every pioneer com-munity—even as far away as Australia and New Zealand—men with the vision of the community builder, the stubbornness to stick against every defeat, the grim ruthlessness required to hold both themselves and their neighbors to the unwelcoming virgin land.

There was considerable difference between the homestead-ers who came into western Nebraska in the 1884-90 period and the Kinkaiders of 1906-12, that is, after the cattleman fences were removed from the government land. The homesteaders of the earlier period were generally young, many under the required twenty-one years, but with a family or a flexible conscience. In the height of the Kinkaid Homestead days many were in their forties and some much older—usually office workers or teachers and so on—retired people or those who had lost their jobs in the retrenchment of 1906-08. There were many women among these, not only among the fraudulent entries by the cattlemen (often only names of old-soldier widows) but among the bona fide homesteaders. These women were classified roughly into two groups by the other settlers. Those with genteel ways, graying hair, downy faces and perhaps good books to loan to a settler's reading-hungry daughter, were called Boston schoolteachers, no matter who or where from. The others, called Chicago widows, weren't young either, or pretty, but their talk, their dress, and their ways were gayer, more colorful, more careless; their books, if any, were paperback novels, with such titles as *Wife in Name Only,* or *Up from the Depths.* Several had a volume of nonfiction called *From Ballroom to Hell,* with every step of the way well illustrated and described. Among the tips offered was a solution for a recurring problem: To fill out your corset cover, roll up two stockings and pin into place, but be sure the stockings are clean, to avoid an offending odor.

It is true that in the largely male population of our homestead regions more of the Chicago widows got married than the Boston school ma'am type.

There was a saying among the settlers that the first spring of a new homesteader told whether the man or the woman was the boss. If the house was put up first, plainly the woman ran things; if a corn patch was broken out before any building, the cowboys told each other that this homesteader would be hard to drive off. But there were other factors to be considered. An April settler was wise to throw up a claim shack of some kind and leave the sod breaking for May, after the grass was started well enough so it would be killed by the plowing. Nor were the women, bossy or not, always easy to drive out. Some clung to the homestead even after their husbands were shot down by ranch hirelings. Nebraska's State Senator Cole grew up in the sandhills because his mother stayed with her two young sons after their father was shot off his mower.

Old Jules' first claim dwelling was half dugout, half sod, but the home of his family was a frame house in which the water froze in the teakettle in January. We envied our neighbors with good sod houses, the deep window seats full of Christmas cactus, century plants, and geraniums blooming all winter, the fine shadowiness of the interior cool and grateful in the summer, while our house was hot as an iron bucket in the sun. Old Jules permitted no cooling blinds or curtains at the windows. He wanted to see anyone coming up. Evenings he always sat back out of line of the lighted windows.

Although I never lived in a sod house I went to school in one and taught school in two others, both pretty decrepit at the time, with mouse holes in the walls; one with a friendly bullsnake living there. Sometimes the snake was fooled by the glowing stove on a chilly fall day and came wandering out and down the aisle during school hours. A snickering among the boys always warned me, and the snake too. Licking out his black forked tongue speculatively, the autumn-logy snake turned slowly around and moved back to his hole in the wall.

The three immediate needs of the new settler were shelter, food, and water. Of the three, only the food that he must grow had a tyrannical season. As locater Old Jules never showed a home seeker a place without a piece of corn land. At a potential site he would push his hat back, estimate the arable acreage, and sink his spade into an average spot. Turning up a long sod, he examined the depth and the darkness of the top soil and shook out the rooting of the grass. If he was satisfied, he looked around at the weeds, not just on spots enriched by some animal carcass long ago, but in general. Where sunflowers grew strong and tall, corn would do well.

But even the best of sod had to be turned and planted at the proper time. With two fairly good draft horses, preferably

three or four against the tough rooting, and a sod plow, the settler could break the prairie himself. Or he could hire it done,
usually by exchange of work with some of his neighbors. I like
to remember the look on the faces of some of these new homesteaders as they tilled the first bit of earth they ever owned. Like
any toddler, when I was two, three years old I couldn't be kept
from following in the furrow of any plowing done near the
house. Later it seemed to me there was something like a spirit-
ual excitement about a man guiding a breaker bottom through
virgin earth, with the snap and crackle of the tough roots as
they were cut, the sod rolling smooth and flat from the plow, a
gull or two following for the worms, and blackbirds chatter-
ing around.

Sometimes corn, beans, or potatoes were dropped in the furrow behind the sod plow and covered by the next round but
more often the corn was planted later by a man, a woman, or
an energetic boy or girl. With an apron or a bag tied on for the
seed, and a spade in the hand, the planter started. At every full
man's step or two steps for the shorter-legged, the spade was
thrust down into the sod, worked sideways to widen the slit,
two kernels of corn dropped in, the spade swung out and the
foot brought down on the cut to seal it. All day, up and down
the sod ribbons, the rhythmic swing of step and thrust was maintained. To be sure, the spade arm was mighty work-sore the
next morning, but every homesteader's child learned that the
remedy for that was more work.

Millions of acres were planted this way, sometimes with
beans and pumpkin seeds mixed with the corn for a stretch.
Good breaking grew few weeds except a scattering of big sunflowers, so the sod field was little care. With the luck of an
early August rain, turnip and rutabaga seed could be broadcast
between a stretch of rows for the winter root pit. Up in South
Dakota, some homesteaders tried flax instead of corn, the seed
harrowed into the sod just before a rain, and were rewarded by
an expanse as blue as fallen sky in blooming time.

The second spring the sod was backset, and ready for small
grain, perhaps oats or rye but more often the newer varieties of
wheat broadcast on the fresh plowing from a bag slung under

one arm, much like the figure of the Sower on the Nebraska capitol. The seed was covered by a harrow or drag. If there was no harrow, a heavily branched tree, a hackberry, perhaps, would be dragged over the ground by the old mares or patient oxen. Mechanical seeders drawn by fast-paced horses or mules helped spread bonanza wheat farming from the Red River down to Oklahoma and deep into Montana and Alberta. But the new homesteader still broadcast his small grain by hand.

The settler too late for the land along the streams was in urgent need of water from the day of his arrival. True, there might be buffalo wallows and other ponds filled by the spring rains for the stock a while, but many settlers hauled at least the household water ten, twelve miles, and farther, until a well could be put down, or had to be, to quiet the womenfolks. Where the water table was not too deep the first well was usually dug—cheap but dangerous for the novice. Every community had its accidents and tragedies. Uncurbed wells caved in on the digger. People, adults and children, fell into the uncovered holes and were perhaps rescued by a desperate effort of everyone within fifty miles around, or were left buried there, with a flower or a tree planted to mark the grave.

The well in our home yard was the usual dug one, curbed to the bottom, with a windlass and a bucket that had been a black powder can, larger than the usual pail, the fifty-pound powder size, I think, and came painted a water-proof blue outside. All of us were very careful around wells, perhaps because we had a constant example before us. Old Jules was crippled his first summer on his claim on Mirage Flats. He had finished his new well and was being drawn up by his helpers. As he neared the top the two practical jokers yanked the rope to scare him. The rope, frayed by all the strain of lifting the soil from the sixty-five foot hole, broke. The digger was dropped to the bottom and crippled for the rest of his life. Only the extraordinary luck of getting to Dr. Walter Reed, of later yellow-fever fame, at the frontier post, Fort Robinson, kept him alive at all.

Our well on the river had a solid ladder inside the casing, the kind of ladder that could have saved Old Jules all those

crippled years if he had nailed one into the curbing of his
first well and climbed out instead of standing in the dirt bucket
to be drawn up. Whenever a foolish hen jumped up on the water bench of our well and let the wind blow her in, it was Old
Jules who clambered ponderously down the deep hole after
her. Practically any other emergency, except something like
sewing up a badly cut leg, he let his wife or his children handle
—ordered them to handle—but he was determined there would
not be another well accident in his household.

In the deep-soiled sandhills, most homesteaders put down
their wells with a sand bucket—a valve-tipped short piece of
pipe on a rope to be jerked up and down inside the larger well
piping that had an open sand point at the bottom. Water was
poured into the pipe, to turn the soil into mud under the plunging sand bucket and be picked up by the valve in the end. Full,
it was drawn out, emptied and the process repeated. Occasionally, the larger pipe was given a twist with a wrench until its
own weight forced it down as fast as the earth below was soaked
and lifted out in the sand bucket. When a good water table
was reached the end of the sand point was plugged, a cylinder
and pumprod put in, and attached to a pump, homemade or
bought from a mail-order catalogue, and the homesteader had
water.

"Nothing's prettier'n a girl pumpin' water in the wind,"
the cowboys used to say, obviously of homesteader daughters,
for no others were out pumping.

As long as there were buffaloes, settlers could go out to the
herd ranges for meat and even a few hides to sell for that scarc-
est of pioneer commodities, cash in the palm. The early settlers
learned to preserve a summer buffalo or two in the Indian way,
cutting the meat into flakes thin as the edge of a woman's hand
to dry quickly in the hot winds, with all the juices preserved.
Well-dried, the meat kept for months and was good boiled with
a touch of prairie onion or garlic. With vegetables, the dried
buffalo or deer or elk made good boiled dinners or meat pies,
and was chopped into cornmeal mush by the Pennsylvanians
for scrapple until there was pork.

Much could be gleaned for the table before the garden even started. Old Jules brought water cress seed west and scattered it wherever there was a swift current and in the lake regions where the earth-warmed water seeped out all winter, and kept an open spot for cress and mallard ducks. Dandelions start early and as soon as they came up brownish red, we cut them out with a knife for salad, very good with hard-boiled eggs, the dressing made with vinegar from wild currants, plums, or grapes and the vinegar-mother we borrowed from a neighbor who had brought it in a bottle by wagon from Kentucky. Later there was lambsquarter, boiled and creamed and perhaps on baking days spread into a *dunna,* which looked like a green-topped pizza. Meat the homesteaders could provide—antelope and deer, and after these were gone, grouse, quail, and cottontails, with ducks and geese spring and fall. Old Jules was an excellent trapper and hunter as well as gardener and horticulturist, with his wife and the children for the weeding and the harvest. Consequently we seldom lacked anything in food except the two items that cost money—sugar and coffee. Roasted rye made a cheap and poor coffee substitute. Other homesteaders grew cane and cooked the sap into hard and soft sorghum but our sweetening was often nothing but dried fruits eaten from the palm or baked into buns and rolls. Once a whole winter was sweetened by a barrel of extra dark blackstrap molasses father got somehow as a bargain. It made fine pungent cookies.

Mother was a good pig raiser and we usually had wonderful sausage looped over broomsticks in the smoke house with the hams and bacon, the good sweet lard in the cellar in crocks. In our younger days butchering was a trial. It meant father had to be disturbed from his plans, his thinking, to shoot the fat hog. The washboiler was put on the stove, with buckets and the teakettle filled for extra scalding water. A barrel had to be set tilted into the ground with an old door laid on low blocks up against the open barrelhead. When everything was ready, the hog up close and everybody out to keep it there, Old Jules had to be called, mother shouting to him, "That one there! Shoot quick!"

But by then the hog might be gone, to be fetched back after

a chase through the trees. When father got a shot he put the bullet cleanly between the eyes but he was often experimenting with the amount of powder that would kill without penetrating into the good meat. Sometimes the hog was not even stunned but ran squealing for the brush, and had to be shot again. Sometimes it fell soundlessly and mother thrust the sticking knife into father's hand. With disgust all over his face, he drove the knife in the general direction of the jugular vein and when the dark blood welled out, stepped back while mother ran in to roll the animal to make the blood flow faster. When grandmother was still alive she usually hurried out with a pan for the makings of her blood pudding but none of the rest of the family would even taste it.

Now the hog was dragged up on the old door, ready for the scalding. Everybody ran for the boiling water, the washboiler, the buckets.

"Look out! Look out!" father kept shouting most of the time as he limped around. When the barrel was steaming with the hot water, he and mother shoved the dead pig down into it head first, because that was the hardest to scald well, and worked the carcass back and forth by the hind feet, to get every spot wet, while mother yanked off handsful of the loosening bristles, shaking the heat from her fingers. Then the hog was drawn out upon the door, turned and the hind half thrust into the stinking hot water, and pulled out upon the door again. Now everybody fell to scraping, clutching butcher knives by the back or working with ragged-edge tin cans, the bristles rolling off in wet clumps and windrows.

No butchered animal looks finer than a well-scalded and scraped hog—pink and plump and appetizing. That evening there was fresh liver for supper, and the frothing brain cooked in a frying pan. I liked pork tenderloin with the animal heat and sweetness still in it. I fried this for myself, and never tasted a finer dish. Meat still animal-warm was credited with helping to cure many sufferers from bleeding stomachs sent west to a government claim by their doctors. Whole communities of stomach patients settled on the Plains, and usually died of other complaints, including old age.

Butchering for most homesteaders, particularly the lone ones, was a matter for neighborly help, as were many larger undertakings, particularly threshing. Most of the threshing outfits that finally reached the homesteader were small horse-powered machines with the owner probably feeding the separator himself to keep greenhorns from choking it, tearing it up. Usually three, four hands, including the horse-power driver, came with the outfit. The rest of the sixteen, eighteen man crew was drawn from the settlers, exchanging work. Often neighbor women came to help with the cooking. Reputations were made or broken by the meals put out for the threshers, and many a plain daughter owed a good marriage match to the wild plum pie or the chicken and dumplings of her mother at threshing time.

The homesteader got most of his outside items through mail-order catalogues, including, sometimes, his wife, if one could call the matrimonial papers, the heart-and-hand publications, catalogues. They did describe the offerings rather fully but with, perhaps, a little less honesty than Montgomery Ward or Sears Roebuck. Unmarried women were always scarce in new regions. Many bachelor settlers had a sweetheart back east or in the Old Country, or someone who began to look a little like a sweetheart from the distance of a government claim that got more and more lonesome as the holes in the socks got bigger. Some of these girls never came. Others found themselves in an unexpectedly good bargaining position and began to make all kinds of demands in that period of feminine uprising. They wanted the husband to promise abstinence from profanity, liquor, and tobacco and perhaps even commanded allegiance to the rising cause of woman suffrage. Giving up the cud of tobacco in the cheek was often very difficult. A desperate neighbor of ours chewed grass, bitter willow and cottonwood leaves, coffee grounds, and finally sent away for a tobacco cure. It made him sick, so sick, at least in appearance, that his new wife begged him to take up chewing again. Others backslid on the sly, sneaking a chew of Battle Axe or Horseshoe in the face of certain anger and tears.

But many bachelors had no sweetheart to come out, and some of these started to carry the heart-and-hand papers around until the pictures of the possible brides were worn off the page. In those days the usual purpose really was marriage, not luring the lonely out of their pitiful little savings or even their lives. "We married everything that got off the railroad," old homesteaders, including my father, used to say.

Usually the settler was expected to send the prospective wife a stagecoach or railroad ticket. Perhaps, even though he had mortgaged his team to get the ticket, the woman sold it and never came and there was nothing to be done unless the U. S. mails were involved. Most of the women did arrive and many of these unions, bound by mutual need and dependence, founded excellent families. Of course, there was no way to compel a mail-order wife to stay when she saw the husband's place. Usually she had grown up in a settled region, perhaps with Victorian sheltering, and was shocked by her new home, isolated, at the best a frame or log shack with cracks for the blizzard winds, or only a soddy or dugout into some bank, with a dirt floor and the possibility of wandering stock falling through the roof.

The long distance to the stagecoach or the railroad, with walking not good, kept many a woman to her bargain. There are, however, stories of desperate measures used to hold the wife—ropes or chains or locked leg hobbles, but the more common and efficacious expedient was early pregnancy. That brought the customary gift for the first child—a sewing machine, and many a man, including my own father, scratched mightily for the money.

The women, particularly the young ones, brought some gaiety to the homestead regions, with visitings, berryings, pie socials, square dances, play parties, literaries at the schools, and shivarees for the newlyweds. The women organized Sunday Schools, and sewing bees. When calamity or sickness struck, the women went to help, and if there was death they bathed and dressed the corpse, coming with dishes of this and that so the bereaved need not trouble to cook and were spared the easing routine. Doctors were usually far away and scarce and expen-

sive. Old Jules, with his partial training in medicine, had a shelf
of the usual remedies and for years he was called out to care
for the difficult deliveries. Several times middle-aged people
have come to me to say that Old Jules brought them into the
world, perhaps back in the 1880's or 1890's.

There were problems besides sickness and death, besides
the lack of cash and credit that dogs every new community, besides the isolation and drouth and dust storms. Fires swept over
the prairies any time during practically ten months a year, although the worst were usually in the fall, with the grass standing
high and rich in oily seed. The prairie fires could be set by fall
lightning, by the carelessness of greenhorns in the country, by
sparks from the railroads and by deliberate malice.

"Burning a man out" could mean destroying his grass,
crops, hay, even his house and himself. Once started, the heat of
the fire created a high wind that could sweep it over a hundred
miles of prairie in an incredibly short time. Settlers soon
learned to watch the horizon for the pearling rise of smoke from
prairie grass. At the first sign of this, everyone hurried to fight
the flames with water barrels, gunny sacks, hoes, and particularly plows to turn furrows for the backfiring. Even more important was the awareness of the danger ahead of time, early
enough so fireguards were plowed around the homestead, at
least around the buildings. In addition everyone was told the
old Indian advice: "Come fire, go for bare ground, sand or
gravel or to big water. Make a backfire against small creek or
bare spot, to burn only into wind, and stay where ashes are.
Best is to go on a place with no grass, and do not run."

Old Jules' Kinkaid in the sandhills bordered on the Osborne valley, which had a prairie-fire story. An earlier settler
and his wife and two small boys had lived in the Osborne—a
wet hay flat with miles of rushes and dense canebrakes, and a
small open lake in the center that dried up in the summers.
Early one fall a prairie fire came sweeping in toward the place.
The settler and his wife hurried out to help fight the flames,
commanding the two boys to stay in the house. It was sod, with
a sod roof, and surrounded by a wide fireguard. Here they were
safe. But when the smoke thickened and the fire came roaring

over the hill toward the house the boys ran in terror to the swamp, clambering through the great piles of dead rushes and canes for the lake bed. The fire caught them.

After that the settler and his wife moved away but the story of the boys remained as a warning to all of us. When my brother James and I were sent down to hold the Kinkaid for a few months alone, we often went to the Osborne swamp to hunt ducks but never without searching the horizon for prairie-fire smoke. There were mushrooms growing where the sod house of the early settler had been, good mushrooms, fine fried with young ducks or prairie chicken.

The most dreaded storm of the upper homestead region was and still is the blizzard. The first one to kill many people was the Buffalo Hunter's Storm of the 1870's, although the School Children's Blizzard of 1888 is sadly remembered, and even the one of 1949. Most of the people who died in blizzards died through some foolishness, some stupidity, and a few years later would have known better. There are always signs before the worst storms: unseasonal warmth, calm, and stillness, as on January 12, 1888, and old timers were ready with warnings of what to do if caught in a blizzard. "If lost in the sand hills, any blowout will give the directions. The wind cuts the hollows from the northwest and moves the sand out southeastward. If so confused that directions are useless or you are too far from shelter, dig in anywhere to keep dry, with a fire if possible, but dry, even if it's only under a bank somewhere, into the dry sand of a blowout. Don't get yourself wet and *don't* wear yourself out. Practically anyone with a little sense and a little luck can outlast a blizzard."

Not all the danger is in the storm itself. The homestead region had few trees and fewer rocks and a May blizzard left an unbelievable glare of unbroken whiteness in the high spring sun, enough to make cows snowblind, and people, if the eyes were not protected. Of all the dangers of homestead life, our family escaped all but two, Old Jules' well accident and my snowblindness in a May blizzard that cost me all useful sight in one eye.

Much of what I have been saying comes out of my childhood but could have come out of the childhood of practically anyone brought up on a homestead. Those first years on a government claim were a trial, a hardship for the parents, particularly the women, but the men too. Usually only one in four entrymen remained to patent the claim; in the more difficult regions and times only one in ten, or even fifteen. A large percentage of those into any new region had been misfits in their home community, economic, social, or emotional misfits, both the men and the women. Some of these, unsettled by the hardships and the isolation, ended in institutions or suicide if they did not drift on or flee back to relatives or in-laws. Those who stayed might be faced by drouth, grasshoppers, and ten-cent corn, sometimes followed by the banker's top buggy come to attach the mortgaged team or the children's milk cow. The men gathered at the sales and at political meetings, with many women, too, speaking for reforms, for a better shake for the sparsely settled, sparsely represented regions.

None of these things could be kept from the children. They saw the gambles of life and the size of the stakes. They shared in the privation and the hard work. All of us knew children who put in twelve-, fourteen-hour days from March to November. We knew seven-, eight-year-old boys who drove four-horse teams to the harrow, who shocked grain behind the binder all day in heat and dust and rattlesnakes, who cultivated, hoed and weeded corn, and finally husked it out before they could go to school in November. And even then there were the chores morning and evening, the stock to feed, the cows to milk by lantern light. If there had been tests for muscular fitness as compared to European children then, we would have held our own.

Often there was no difference in the work done by the boys and the girls, except that the eldest daughter of a sizable family was often a serious little mother by the time she was six, perhaps baking up a 49 pound sack of flour every week by the time she was ten. Such children learned about life before they had built up any illusions and romanticisms to be clung to later, at the expense of maturity. Almost from their first steps, the homesteader's children had to meet new situations, make decisions, develop a self-discipline if they were to survive. They learned dependence upon one's neighbors, and discovered the interrelationships of earth and sky and animal and man. They could see, in their simpler society, how national and international events conditioned every day of their existence. They learned to rescue themselves in adulthood as they had once scrabbled under the fence when the heel flies drove the milk cows crazy. What they didn't have they tried to make for themselves, earned money to buy, or did without. Perhaps somewhere there are individuals from homestead childhoods who grab for fellowships and grants, for scholarships and awards, for special influence and privilege but I don't know of any. The self-reliance, often the fierce independence, of a homestead upbringing seems to stay with them. They may wander far from their roots, for they are children of the uprooted, but somehow their hearts are still back there with the old government claim.

⊂⊃ *SNAKES*

My LITTLE old German-Swiss grandmother believed in hoop snakes, cow suckers, sting tails and snakes who, in moments of danger, swallowed their young, to be released later unharmed. She also believed that witches sometimes turned themselves into dangerous serpents. She believed all this as firmly as she believed in the little red Testament always in the pocket of her petticoat. Hadn't her own second cousin been chased down a long hill by a snake, tail in mouth, bounding along like a hoop from a hog's head? The poor man had only escaped by reaching water just in time. Yes, it was so, and the frustrated snake, apparently a drylander, was left behind, unrolled, and lashing the bank in anger with the long tail.

My early reluctance to give up any caterpillars or tomato worms I found annoyed Grandmother but her real concern for me had begun the day she found me asleep under a tree with my bottle tight in my fist and a little sandviper coiled up on my chest, also asleep. She shooed the timid snake into the grass and carried me to the house as fast as her full skirts permitted.

Mother was not greatly disturbed, it seems, but Grandmother was even more worried when I proved to be unbitten.

"No good will come of her! It is against the law of God for a girl child to be friendly with a serpent. The woman must crush the serpent's head, and he shall sting her heel for death. It is the law."

"Oh, the little snake probably smelled the milk she left in the bottle," my scientific-minded father said, tolerantly. "Anyway, the snake is the classical sign of the healer. Maybe the little Mari is to become a doctor."

Scornfully silent the old woman hurried me away to a shady spot under a cottonwood. There she read from the little Testament over me. It seems I finished my interrupted nap.

As I grew older I brought home other queer things—tiny puff balls, for instance, perhaps because Grandmother called them snake eggs. I put them under a setting hen hoping to hatch out young blue racers as a neighbor boy did wild ducks. I planted horse hair in bottles of water and set them in sunlit windows but the bottles always disappeared before the hair could possibly have turned into snakes. I wore the rattles of diamond backs pinned to my sunbonnet as cowboys sometimes did in their hat bands to ward off heat stroke and headaches. I hung any dead snake I found on the nearest barbed wire fence, underside up, to bring rain. Grandmother said it would, and in our region we needed rain most of the time. I can't recall that it helped.

We were taught that snakes keep mice and moles from the fields and the orchard and so we didn't kill many away from the house. Now and then we found one crippled by a plow, a mower or a wagon wheel.

"Kill him," Father always ordered. "Don't let him suffer." Old Jules was crippled for life by a crushed ankle and could not bear to see any maimed creature live on.

Once I found a little sparrow perched on a Russian thistle, wings spread wide, its bill open with a thin cry, waiting for the swaying head and glassy eyes of a coiled blue racer. I drove the reluctant snake away and took the bird home until it could fly again. I never told Grandmother how I caught the sparrow.

"Keep away from the rattlers; the others won't hurt you," Father always told us. We knew that if we were bitten the two pinpricks must be cut wide open to bleed hard and be sucked if possible. Then a tourniquet must be applied and we must walk home, not run or get excited. At home we were to apply crystals from the bottle of potassium permanganate on the high shelf of poisons to the open wound. The chief precaution was the sharp knife always in our pockets, for the crisscross of swift cuts, wide and open.

Until I was eleven I had seen only one rattlesnake to remember, although my brothers killed many in their roamings over the bluffs of the Niobrara with their twenty-two-caliber rifles. The one I saw resented my cutting off his retreat. The angry *br-r-r* of the stubby tail, the swift strike of the arrow-shaped head at my probing stick surprised me so that I jumped back, my bare feet suddenly most naked, even though I knew the snake could not strike more than about a third of his length— no more than the top coil and his alert head. Plainly the rattler was no relative of the meeker bullsnakes I liked to watch move in such deliberate grace and beauty. With the rattler still coiled I called loudly for my father. He brought the shotgun and blew the snake's head off. Then he explained to us that even the rattler usually slipped away quietly and only strikes man when aroused, or is shedding, his lidless eyes, never very sharp, totally blinded by the dead skin separating from the eyeballs.

"Keep away from rattlers. Only try to kill them if you have a long stick or a hoe or a gun."

Father was, among other things, a locater of settlers on government land. He was always disappearing into the sandhills off to the east, usually with the home seeker on the wagon seat beside him to drive the half-wild runaway buckskin Indian ponies. If he went alone and saw a flock of wild ducks or followed the flight of a grouse he generally forgot the team entirely. Sometimes the wagon and the surveying tools were scattered for a mile over the prairie, the ponies down in a tangle of harness or even in some draw, the wagon upset on top of them. Yet somehow the wily ponies always got out unhurt, no matter how little was left of the wagon and the compass.

Usually my brothers went with Father, holding the team

at gates and for little hunts while I stayed home to watch whoever was the baby at the time. The summer I was eleven I was
permitted to go along into the sandhills for the first time. I was
to drive the buckskins and incidentally see our new homestead,
twenty-five miles away, where an occasional gray wolf still
roamed and where every prairie dog town was full of rattlesnakes. I watched along the rutted trail, when there was one,
but I saw only one snake and it escaped down a dog hole before
Father could raise his pumpgun. But the sight of the perky rattle vanishing into the ground started him telling stories of the
early days. There was the one about the rotted limestone bluff
down the Niobrara—the wintering place of the rattlers. When
the spring sun warmed the broken slope one could shoot the
rattlesnakes all day there. He added the story of the man
named Polk who lay down on the bluff-top one warm March
day and looking over the edge shot snakes in the crevices of
the crumbling stone below him until his ammunition ran out.
When he started up he put his hand on a rattler that had
crawled out of a hole beside him.

All day Father and I bumped over cowtrails and bunchgrass deeper into the sandhills. As the valleys grew broader, the
land harder, more fertile, there were more claim shacks, dug-
outs, and soddies. We stayed all night at Cousin Pete's and the
next morning we went several miles farther on, over more hills.
About nine o'clock we reached the little one-room pine board
shack Father said was ours.

"Hold the ponies," he ordered. "I just want to see nobody's broken in and took my tools."

He got out and vanished around the shack to where he had
hidden the hammer with which he nailed the door against
snoopers. Before I had the nervous buckskins quieted, Father
was running toward the wagon, his mouth to the back of his
hand, his face gray-white above his beard.

"Bit by a rattler—watching for cottontails under the
house!" he said, spitting clear saliva. "Git my knife!"

I opened his pocket knife. He hacked at the puffy swelling
rising like dough in a hot oven about the two pin pricks that

wouldn't bleed. But the swelling was spongy as a rag and throwing the knife from him, Father grabbed his pumpgun from the wagon bed, slapped his palm down on the hind wheel and laid the muzzle against the swelling.

"Hold the horses!" he shouted, and clamping the gun between his body and the wagon bed, he pulled the trigger.

At the shot the buckskins plunged forward. Bracing my feet against the dash I sawed at the lines until the team slowed and swung back to Father, stumbling across the bunchgrass, his gun in his good hand and shaking great clots of black blood from the back of the other. I ripped his shirt sleeve and made a tourniquet below the shoulder. Then he climbed heavily into the back of the wagon and lay down.

"Drive for Pete's place and drive like hell!"

Too frightened to ask the direction, I swung the long willow whip over the buckskins, giving them their heads. They shot forward. My sunbonnet flew off; the board seat went next. Behind me Father bounced like a heavy bed roll in the wagon.

Foam from the ponies' mouths hit cold against my cheek. We tore down a long hill without brakes and across a vacant valley. No animal, no house, no road in sight. Another valley, more hills and still no road.

Then I saw the windmill and Pete running out to stop what he considered just another of the buckskin runaways. We got Father into the house and to a cot. Then Pete rode the hills to a homesteader for whisky. There had been a quick consultation about who might have some; it was decided that the most religious man around would probably keep a bottle stashed away, perhaps because he didn't have the thirst.

I stood inside the door and looked at Father's swelling arm, his puffed, purpled hand and the black-crusted wound over most of the back of it. He was quiet, his face pale and still as plaster above the heavy beard, his breath wheezing. I twisted my hands into my dress and remembered that a sheepherder who was bitten by a rattlesnake never awoke from his whisky stupor. And this was September, considered the worst month in the year.

By the time Pete was back with about an inch of brown

liquid in a tall bottle, the arm was blackening to the shoulder and the swelling spreading to the chest. Father gulped the whisky with difficulty. "It's not enough," he said and sank back hopelessly. "Get me home. I want to die at home."

I ran to the buckskins but my legs were like dead water. I didn't know the way; the gates were hard; the ponies would surely run away at one stop or another, throwing Father out on the prairie to die in the grass. Suddenly I pushed my face between the spokes of a wheel and cried as no member of our family was ever supposed to cry.

By now Pete hitched his wild team to his top buggy, helped Father in and swung around to lift me to sit in the buggy bed at Father's feet. The horses sprang forward. After four or five miles of sand they slowed, their lathered sides heaving. Once Father spoke. "Swelling's spreading into the lungs," he panted thickly. Pete whipped his team with the line ends but they soon dropped back into their plodding, the sand following the wheels, spilling back.

We stopped at shacks and soddies, found no whisky, no potassium permanganate. Everywhere we found only frightened faces. Women who clutched their children to them in the sudden realization of what might face them any day. Some of the flying sand settled over Father's dark and swollen arm. He began to roll a little and I stood up between him and the buggy top, steadying myself with a hand on the back of the seat, holding his heavy body slumped against my shoulder until I ached to move just a little, ever so little.

In sight of the blue bend of the Niobrara River, Pete whipped the gaunt team into one last spurt of speed. Mother came running out of the house.

"Get the doctor!" Pete shouted, but of course our telephone was out of order, and the only horses around were Pete's, both down in the harness. It was up to me to go. I started to a neighbor a mile away, to try his telephone. Dropping into the dog trot previous emergencies had taught me I could hold for a mile I finally reached the man's door, and fell to the step gasping out something.

Toward midnight I was awakened by my brothers, shouting in my ear. Father was all right, the doctor said. But he would have been dead hours ago from the potent September venom if he hadn't shot it off.

"—And we saw the doctor's red automobile!"

I was sorry that Grandmother wasn't with us. She might have liked this snake incident; for once I was against the serpent.

Later we moved to the sandhills to live. The first summer we killed over a dozen rattlers close around the house—with little more fuss than if they had been bullsnakes.

⊂⊃ COYOTES AND EAGLES

So LONG as the great buffalo herds moved over the Plains, scavengers like the coyote lived largely on the remains of the kill by the big prairie wolves and the meat hunts of the Indians. When the hide men came with their guns to destroy the millions of buffaloes, taking no more than the skins and perhaps the tongues, the coyote became enormously fat and lazy. Then suddenly there were only the stretches of bleaching bones to gnaw; almost any sustenance for the gaunted bellies had to come from rabbits, grouse and other small creatures that had to be captured, creatures provided with some protective speed and guile. Next the settler arrived, to set up his home on the public domain, bringing his stupid domestic poultry and sheep, even pigs, young colts and calves. With such easy prey the coyote often became a killer. Not content with the hen or duck or turkey he could carry away, he often dropped his first catch and plunged into the scattering flock with the fierceness of a sheep-killing dog, pursuing the squawking or gabbling fowl, grabbing one here, another there, breaking the neck or cutting the throat in a flurry of feathers, leaving the dead behind him on the grass and through the brush.

Old Jules Sandoz kept his Winchester handy on the antlers outside the door for any coyote and eagle that dared come within rifle shot of the house. A favorite skulking place of both, but particularly the coyote, was at the bottom of the orchard, where a deep canyon opened from the hard upland prairie into the Niobrara River valley, with a sort of small-game trail that crossed through a patch of clearing so ancient it was used for ceremonials by the prehistoric Indians who often camped near by. There were always fresh coyote tracks in the little open place, and one morning a string of the family turkeys lay dead where they had tried to flee from a coyote. He had caught them, snapped off one young head after another. On the nine dead only one was carried away, the rest killed and then left untouched.

It was too early in the fall for prime hides, but Old Jules knew that the killer coyote would be back and so he decided to spread poison in the clearing. Usually he prepared the baits in the house. All the children, down to the smallest toddler, were to understand some of the purpose and the danger in the high drug shelf in the gunshop leanto of the house—boxes, vials and bottles, many marked with skull and cross bones. So the children were led to understand poison as they learned the danger in guns by daily familiarity with those set in the quarter circle behind the kitchen door and always loaded—taught to understand the boom they made, and the death they brought. (The first time that a baby crawled toward the gun corner he was dragged back and spanked hard, hard enough to remain a sharp memory in the young mind, much as the mare kicks her new colt that misbehaves, or a cat—wild or domestic—slaps her kittens while still blind to teach them early the things they must never forget.)

To poison the turkey-killing coyote Old Jules used the method he had perfected in his early years in northwest Nebraska and distributed to wolfers and settlers over the western country:

Strychnine, alkaloid, *not sulphate* (Mallinckrodt, St. Louis, preferred)

Snowbirds, about half a dozen, freshly killed
Poison dose: size of wheat kernel on tip of knife blade.

The white strychnine crystals were crushed in the bottle with a match or other small stick, to be carefully burned afterward. Then he made a deep, narrow incision in the breast of the snowbird and inserted the dose carefully with the pocket `nife blade, thrusting it deep down, taking care to leave no speck of the white powder on the feathers or the edges of the slit to betray the poison by the bittter taste. The opening was then pressed down hard with the thumb to close it securely. The baits, four to six, were to be arranged in a small circle as snowbirds customarily feed, this time on the barish spot where the turkeys had been attacked. At the clearing the approach was on the sod. It would have been better if there had been some hard surface spots to walk on—gravel or stone. (If it was impossible to hide the man-tracks in soft earth or snow, the sign was brushed away with a willow branch or perhaps scraps of old weathered cowhide nailed to the end of a stick.)

Every morning Old Jules or some of the family went down close enough to count the baits. If any were missing a radius of a hundred to three hundred yards was searched for the dead coyote, farther if the bait was frozen. The poisoned snowbirds were good for several weeks in warmish weather and up to two, three months in freezing cold. At the end of the prime fur period all the remaining baits were to be collected and burned to pure ashes with any remaining coyote carcasses, or at least the visceral parts. A better method, if the ground was thawed, was deep burial.

Snowbirds, as natural prey for coyotes, had several advantages over the usual chunks of meat. The poison, which will spread its bitterness through the flesh during a thaw, will not be tasted through the feathers and will make the bait more difficult to vomit at the first effect of the poison. A very important factor was the outdoor dog's common aversion to snowbirds, protecting the usual hunting or farm dog.

Sometimes instead of poison Old Jules set one of his two

Swiss bear traps in the little clearing for the eagles that haunted the old game crossing as well as for the coyotes. The place was too near the house, where stock—a pig, calf, colt—or a human foot might trip the pan of a regular steel trap and be injured. The great old bear traps were made by family members back in eighteenth-century Switzerland. The jaws, powerful enough to break a horse's leg, were safe for stock and even wandering children because there was no pan to release the powerful jaws. The bait had to be pulled away with a stout, determined jerk.

The traps were set at home with a long-handled lever that required a strong arm to force the jaws open, and then secured against accidental tripping by a small peg, usually wooden, thrust through matching holes in the gear of jaws and spring. A strong cord tied to the release had been threaded through a pipe extending to the center of the open jaws. A bait, usually a freshly killed cottontail rabbit or a grouse, was tied close. With the safety peg withdrawn at the clearing the trap was fitted into a shallow hole and well covered so no sight or smell of iron or man could betray it. As with most traps the hiding, the camouflage, was important. The spring and jaws were sprinkled with a layer of fine dry leaves topped by sand or earth, very dry, to avoid freezing. A hungry coyote approaching would spring forward, grasp the bait and pull, the giant jaws snapping his throat, usually killing him on the spot.

Eagles, golden heads, of course, generally fell upon the baited trap from the sky, and so were caught by the legs. The eagle pounded his great wings, perhaps with a six-foot spread, against the air trying to lift the heavy trap five or even ten feet, but never much higher. If the golden heads, nesting in the wild bluffs up the river, were flying, the trap was inspected several times a day. It might be gone, but never very far, the eagle probably hidden in the buckbrush to rise once more in his desperate effort to escape as the trapper approached.

Cash was always scarce with Old Jules and usually his Indian friends or the Indian trappers were happy to pay him five dollars in money or Indian goods for each golden-head eagle. The wings became the dignified fans of the prominent men in the tribal councils, the two fluffy breath feathers under the tail were the ones that made up the proper war bonnets, and were needed to restore the fading regalia of the great hunting days.

A BIBLIOGRAPHY OF THE
WRITINGS OF MARI SANDOZ

Three stories in *Prairie Schooner:* Jan. 1927; Winter 1928; Winter 1929

"The Kinkaider Comes and Goes," NF, *No. Amer. Review,* Apr., May 1930; repr. *Hostiles and Friendlies*

"Sandhill Sundays," NF, *Folksay* 1931; repr. *Midcentury;* repr. *Roundup: A Nebraska Reader*

"Pieces to a Quilt," SS, *No. Amer. Review,* May 1933; repr. *The Writer,* Oct. 1935; repr. *Hostiles and Friendlies*

"Musky," NF, *Nature,* Nov. 1933; repr. *Hostiles and Friendlies;* also in *This Is Nature; Trails of Adventure; Everyman's Ark*

Old Jules, 1935; BOMC Nov. 1935; 20th Anniversary Ed. 1955; 25th Anniversary Ed. 1960; paperback repr. 1962

"I Wrote a Book," NF, *Nebraska Alumnus,* Nov. 1935; repr. *The Writer,* Feb. 1936

"The New Frontier Woman," NF, *Country Gentleman,* Sept. 1936; repr. *Roundup:* repr. *Hostiles and Friendlies*

"Mist and the Tall White Tower," SS, *Story* Magazine, Sept. 1936; repr. *Hostiles and Friendlies*

"White Meteor," SS, *Ladies Home Journal,* Jan. 1937

"Stay Home, Young Writer," paper, Writers' Guild; repr. *Quill,* 1937

"River Polak," SS, *Atlantic Monthly,* Sept. 1937; repr. *Hostiles and Friendlies*

Slogum House, Novel, 1937; paperback repr. 1952

"The Devil's Lane," SS, *Ladies' Home Journal,* Apr. 1938; repr. *Hostiles and Friendlies*

"The Far Looker," tale, *The Sight-giver,* Feb. 1939; repr. *Hostiles and Friendlies*

"Bone Joe and the Smokin' Woman," novelette, *Scribner's,* Mar. 1939; repr. *Hostiles and Friendlies*

"Girl in the Humbert," SS, *Sat. Eve. Post,* Mar. 4, 1939; repr. *Out West;* also in *Brave and the Fair; Winter Thunder and Other Stories*

Capital City, Novel, 1939

Crazy Horse, 1942; reissued 1955; paperback repr. 1963

"Peachstone Basket," SS, Prairie Schooner, Fall 1943; repr. *Prairie Schooner Caravan;* also in *American Writing; Hostiles and Friendlies*

"Sit Your Saddle Solid," SS, *Sat. Eve. Post,* Feb. 10, 1945; repr. *Palomino and Other Horses*

"The Spike-Eared Dog," SS, *Sat. Eve. Post,* Aug. 11, 1945; repr. *Search for the Hidden Places;* repr. *Winter Thunder and Other Stories*

The Tom-Walker, Novel, 1947

"Martha of the Yellow Braids," NF, *Prairie Schooner,* Summer 1947; repr. *Hostiles and Friendlies;* repr. *Winter Thunder and Other Stories*

"There Were Two Sitting Bulls," NF, *Blue Book,* Nov. 1949; repr. (uncut version, title "The Lost Sitting Bull") *Hostiles and Friendlies;* also in *Old Jules Country*

"The Lost School Bus," novelette, *Sat. Eve. Post,* May 19, 1951; repr. *Post Stories, 1951;* issued as book (title *Winter Thunder*) 1954

"What the Sioux Taught Me," NF, *Empire,* Feb. 24, 1952; repr. *Reader's Digest,* May 1952; repr. ("The Son") *Hostiles and Friendlies*

Cheyenne Autumn, 1953; reissued 1961; paperback repr. 1964

"The Indian Looks at His Future," NF, *Family Weekly,* Apr. 1954

The Buffalo Hunters, 1954; paperback repr. (British) 1964

Winter Thunder, book repr. of "The Lost School Bus," 1954; paperback repr., *The Lost School Bus and Other Stories*

"The Search for the Bones of Crazy Horse," NF, N. Y. Westerners' *Brand Book,* 1954; repr. *Hostiles and Friendlies*

"The Look of the West," NF, Denver Westerners' *Brand Book,* 1955; repr. *Hostiles and Friendlies*

"Some Oddities of the American Indians," NF, Denver Westerners' *Brand Book,* 1955; repr. *Hostiles and Friendlies*

Miss Morissa, Doctor of the Gold Trail, Novel, 1955; reissued 1960

"Nebraska," NF, Holiday, May 1956; repr. *American Panorama*

"The Neighbor," NF, *Prairie Schooner,* Winter 1956; *repr. Hostiles and Friendlies;* repr. *Winter Thunder and Other Stories*

The Horsecatcher, Short Novel, 1957; repr. Reader's Digest Condensed Book Club

The Cattlemen, 1958

"Tyrant of the Plains" (section of The Cattlemen), NF, *Sat. Eve. Post,* June 7, 1958

"The Smart Man," SS, *Prairie Schooner,* Spring 1959; repr. *Hostiles and Friendlies*

Hostiles and Friendlies (collection of short writings), 1959

Son of the Gamblin' Man, Novel, 1960

"Look of the Last Frontier," NF, *American Heritage,* June 1961

These Were the Sioux, 1961

Love Song to the Plains, 1961

"Fly Speck Billie's Cave" and "The Buffalo Spring Cave," tales, in *Legends and Tales of the Old West,* 1962

"Outpost in New York," NF, *Prairie Schooner,* Summer 1963

"The Homestead in Perspective," NF, *Land Use Policy and Problems in the United States,* 1963; repr. *Old Jules Country*

The Story Catcher, Short Novel, 1963

The Beaver Men, 1964

"Evening Song" (Cheyenne chant) and "Snakes" and "Coyotes and Eagles" (NF) in *Old Jules Country,* 1965

Old Jules Country (selection of nonfiction writings), 1965